the cinema of RAÚL RUIZ

DIRECTORS' CUTS

Other select titles in the Directors' Cuts series:

the cinema of MICHAEL MANN: *vice and vindication*
JONATHAN RAYNER

the cinema of AKI KAURISMÄKI: *authorship, bohemia, nostalgia, nation*
ANDREW NESTINGEN

the cinema of RICHARD LINKLATER: *walk, don't run*
ROB STONE

the cinema of BÉLA TARR: *the circle closes*
ANDRÁS BÁLINT KOVÁCS

the cinema of STEVEN SODERBERGH: *indie sex, corporate lies, and digital videotape*
ANDREW DE WAARD & R. COLIN TATE

the cinema of TERRY GILLIAM: *it's a mad world*
edited by JEFF BIRKENSTEIN, ANNA FROULA & KAREN RANDELL

the cinema of TAKESHI KITANO: *flowering blood*
SEAN REDMOND

the cinema of THE DARDENNE BROTHERS: *responsible realism*
PHILIP MOSLEY

the cinema of MICHAEL HANEKE: *europe utopia*
edited by BEN McCANN & DAVID SORFA

the cinema of SALLY POTTER: *a politics of love*
SOPHIE MAYER

the cinema of JOHN SAYLES: *a lone star*
MARK BOULD

the cinema of DAVID CRONENBERG: *from baron of blood to cultural hero*
ERNEST MATHIJS

the cinema of JAN SVANKMAJER: *dark alchemy*
edited by PETER HAMES

the cinema of NEIL JORDAN: *dark carnival*
CAROLE ZUCKER

the cinema of LARS VON TRIER: *authenticity and artifice*
CAROLINE BAINBRIDGE

the cinema of WERNER HERZOG: *aesthetic ecstasy and truth*
BRAD PRAGER

the cinema of TERRENCE MALICK: *poetic visions of america (second edition)*
edited by HANNAH PATTERSON

the cinema of ANG LEE: *the other side of the screen*
WHITNEY CROTHERS DILLEY

the cinema of STEVEN SPIELBERG: *empire of light*
NIGEL MORRIS

the cinema of TODD HAYNES: *all that heaven allows*
edited by JAMES MORRISON

the cinema of ROMAN POLANSKI: *dark spaces of the world*
edited by JOHN ORR & ELZBIETA OSTROWSKA

the cinema of JOHN CARPENTER: *the technique of terror*
edited by IAN CONRICH & DAVID WOODS

the cinema of MIKE LEIGH: *a sense of the real*
GARRY WATSON

the cinema of NANNI MORETTI: *dreams and diaries*
EWA MAZIERSKA & LAURA RASCAROLI

the cinema of DAVID LYNCH: *american dreams, nightmare visions*
edited by ERICA SHEEN & ANNETTE DAVISON

the cinema of KRZYSZTOF KIESLOWSKI: *variations on destiny and chance*
MAREK HALTOF

the cinema of GEORGE A. ROMERO: *knight of the living dead*
TONY WILLIAMS

the cinema of KATHRYN BIGELOW: *hollywood transgressor*
edited by DEBORAH JERMYN & SEAN REDMOND

the cinema of WIM WENDERS *the celluloid highway*
ALEXANDER GRAF

the cinema of
RAÚL RUIZ

impossible cartographies

Michael Goddard

 WALLFLOWER PRESS LONDON & NEW YORK

A Wallflower Press Book
Published by
Columbia University Press
Publishers Since 1893
New York • Chichester, West Sussex

Copyright © Michael Goddard 2013
All rights reserved.
Wallflower Press® is a registered trademark of Columbia University Press

A complete CIP record is available from the Library of Congress

ISBN 978-0-231-16730-7 (cloth)
ISBN 978-0-231-16731-4 (pbk.)
ISBN 978-0-231-85050-6 (e-book)

Series design by Rob Bowden Design

Cover image of Raúl Ruiz courtesy of the Kobal Collection

CONTENTS

Acknowledgements   ix

Introduction: A New Cartographer?   1

1   Ruiz's Cinema in the 1960s and 1970s
    PART 1: Beyond Socialist Realism: Ruiz's Cinema in Chile   9
    PART 2: From the 'Dialectics' of Exile to the *Tableau Vivant*   31

2   The Cinema of Piracy, the Sea and Spectral Voyages: Ruiz's Neo-Baroque Cinema of the 1980s   61

3   Cartographies of Complexity: Ruiz's 'French' Cinema Since the Mid-1990s   103

Conclusion: Ruizian Cartography from Chile to the Cosmos via the Littoral, or *The Film to Come*   167

Appendix: Raúl Ruiz Interview (Paris, November, 2009)   171

Select Filmography   185
Bibliography   193
Index   199

for Adriana Amaral, my impossible muse, who has led me, like the protagonist of *Mysteries of Lisbon*, to Brazilian shores

ACKNOWLEDGEMENTS

Over the long period of researching and writing this book, there are numerous individuals and institutions who have been a great deal of help. Research was conducted at the British Film Institute (BFI), London, the Bibliothèque Nationale de France (BNF), Paris, the Bibliothèque du Film (BiFi), Paris and the Cinématek in Brussels. Some of this research was supported by the William Hope award for Archival Research at the University of Salford. Several individuals also helped me to locate rare and hard to find Ruiz films including Alison Smith and Marco Grosoli. Useful advice was also received from Laleen Jayamanne and Adrian Martin. Special thanks are also due to Garin Dowd and Alejandra Rodriguez-Remedi. Not only did they participate with me in the very helpful Ruiz panel at the *Film and Philosophy* conference in Dundee in 2009 but also helped my project in more practical ways; Alejandra through assisting me in getting in touch with and interviewing Raúl Ruiz and Garin through reading and insightfully commenting on a chapter draft. Both of them also generously shared their writing and thoughts on Ruiz's cinema, making me feel we were part of small Ruizian micro-society. At Salford, Ania Kowalczyk also read and commented on a draft chapter and conversations with Benjamin Halligan were always a productive sounding board. The Ruizian annotated filmography compiled by Adrian Martin in *Rouge* 2, and the Website *Le Cinéma de Raoul Ruiz,* maintained by Pierre-Alexandre Nicaise were more than just useful resources, rather veritable guides in the labyrinth of Ruiz's work that frequently aided me in the orientation of this book. Thanks are also due to the Network for European Cinema and Media Studies (NECS) at whose conference in Lisbon in 2012 I was able to organise a panel on Ruiz with Garin Dowd and Felicity Colman. Special thanks were due to Raúl Ruiz himself, who gave such a generous interview, and to both he and Valeria Sarmiento for inviting me into their home to conduct it. It goes without saying that I continue to be amazed by and appreciative of Ruiz's energy and creativity that continued up to, and arguably beyond, the much too early end of his life, and which gave me so much fascinating cinema to engage with.

This book has the strange and sad paradox of beginning life and being largely completed as a work engaging with a living cinematic auteur, and being published as being about one who has recently died. While changing tenses where necessary for sense, I have tried to maintain the sense of Ruiz's cinema as a living and contemporary one, that is at the same time untimely and spectral, even while Ruiz was still with us; then again, following the indetermination between life and death in many of his films, and the concept of 'cryptesthesia' he describes so vividly in the the interview that concludes this book, to a great extent he remains with us, pushing us to go further in both creative practices and their theorisation.

INTRODUCTION: A NEW CARTOGRAPHER?

Raúl Ruiz presented something of an enigma in relation to contemporary cinema, seeming at once like an unfashionable *auteur* filmmaker out of sync with the more commercially oriented present, while at the same time open to all kinds of projects that cross media (film, writing, video installation) as well as film forms (features, short films, 'art' documentaries, filmed theatre and films dealing with folklore). This book will argue that rather than simply being an anachronistic, 'European' auteur, Ruiz used this role as a way of conducting research into cinematic images and their combinations that is highly resonant with the emergence of the new media sphere that we are inhabiting today. As such, Ruiz's highly heterogeneous work can best be understood as a type of cartography, a mapping of emergent perceptions, images and spaces. Since this cartography is not a representation of already existing spaces or cinematic forms but is rather oriented towards the new, it could be described as a cartography of the virtual; however, since Ruiz's work makes a point of departing from the normative rules of cinematic construction as a first principle, this book will outline Ruiz's cartography of images as a cartography of the impossible. While most of Ruiz's work has been conducted as 'film', these films have tended to problematise traditional cinematic forms such as the conflict driven narrative and experimented with new ways of combining images in line with Ruiz's formula; for 250 shots, 250 films.

The first problem that has to be confronted in relation to Ruiz's oeuvre is its sheer prolificness. Taking into consideration only films, Ruiz made over one hundred, many of which are very hard if not impossible to get hold of and are only screened at periodic retrospectives such as those held at Bobigny in 2001 or at the Rotterdam Film Festival, 2004. It is sometimes difficult to believe that this large or even monstrous output, while demonstrating a remarkable consistency, can be the product of a single filmmaker. Ruiz's films are, of course marked by collaborations with a wide range of others from gifted cinematographers like Sacha Vierny and Henri Alekan, to writers such as Pascal Bonitzer and Gilbert Adair to artistic figures such as Pierre Klossowski or Jean Miotte, to performance groups such as the New York collective, The Kitchen. Apart from the question of collaboration, it is also possible to detect several different Ruizs across his work giving rise to distinct phases of cinematic and other productions. The clearest break in Ruiz's career was that between his work produced in Chile up until 1973 during the Allende era, and that produced subsequently when Ruiz was based in France. Even his first name underwent a transformation, so that he was known in France as Raoul rather than Raúl. For Ruiz this was not, however, an obvious change in his work from political to art cinema, for example, as some critics have seen it. In fact it is possible to see many of Ruiz's later aesthetic strategies and preoccupations already in his work in Chile and conversely, many of his films made in France have a political dimension, sometimes directly or indirectly related to Latin American politics. However it is certainly true that whereas Ruiz's Chilean films were produced in relation to a collectivity, the films made afterwards express the relative distance and relative isolation of exile, despite the many productive collaborations referred to above.

This might be the clearest break in Ruiz's career but it is by no means the only one; while it is impossible to pinpoint any absolute break between the two periods there are definitely considerable differences between Ruiz's more experimental works of the 1980s, frequently associated with the sea and made in a variety of European locations and the cycle of seemingly more conventional films that began in the 1990s with *Trois vies et une seule mort* (*Three Lives and Only One Death*, 1996), featuring big stars such as Catherine Deneuve, Marcello Mastroianni and John Malkovich, and which appear to be much closer to the aesthetics of the French art film. To insist too much on a break would be to occlude the considerable continuities between films made in these periods as well as to ignore a number of exceptions, films which do not quite fit into the period in which they were produced. Despite these problems, however, it is still valuable to consider Ruiz's work as constituting a number of phases, characterised by different ways of working, styles of *mise-en-scène* and aesthetic strategies. This is, therefore, the way this book will be organised with chapters corresponding roughly to the successive periods of Ruiz's work since the late 1960s. Before going into the organisation of the present study, however, it is worth first examining one of Ruiz's many short films, *Zig-Zag* (1980), a film that encapsulates many of the aesthetic themes and procedures that cross Ruiz's work as a whole.

Zig-Zag *(1980), or Cinematic Cartography*

Ruiz's short film *Zig-Zag*, entitled in French *Le Jeu de L'Oie: La Cartographie* (1980) can be considered as an allegory that condenses and emblematises not only themes from Ruiz's work as a whole but also key dimensions of his filmmaking practice. Especially apparent in this film is the idea of film as a form of impossible cartography. While the cartographic exploration of impossible spaces is evident throughout Ruiz's work, it is particularly clearly demonstrated in this film. The first striking thing about this film is its title, whose multiple forms show the difficulty of reducing it to a simple or single conventional phrase. In the film itself it appears as a first title of *Zig-Zag*, followed by a second one of *Le jeu de l'oie (une fiction didactique à propos de la cartographie)* (*Snakes and Ladders (a didactic fiction about cartography)*). *Zig-Zag* shows a man H, played by the French film critic and collaborator with Ruiz on many projects, Pascal Bonitzer, who we are told during the credit sequence has woken up at the wheel of his car, on a deserted road, without any wounds or other indications of an accident. He encounters two men playing a kind of board game and who seem to be expecting him, while at the same time showing a complete indifference to his predicament or need to be at a certain rendezvous. It soon becomes clear that the game they are playing is an unusual one in that the players themselves must move through space according to the successive dice throws. It soon appears that the main character is caught up in the game himself, which he describes as a nightmare of the worst kind; a didactic nightmare. What follows is a series of rendezvous with the same other players, in which the seemingly random movements of H are revealed to be the moves of an ever-shifting game. We are given a clue as to these transformations by a montage of different games that then shows a map of Europe and then several other maps, indicating that in a sense the board games were really a red herring and the true focus of the game and the film is cartography itself, or more precisely the unstable relations between cartography and the territory of which it is supposed to be a representation. In the film, this gets played out by means of a series of levels, from the neighbourhood, to Paris, to Europe to the earth and ultimately the cosmos, which the protagonist navigates by a variety of means from walking to travelling by car, train and plane.

As the film progresses more and more cartographic images appear, until, at the end, it becomes apparent that this film is in part a pretext for presenting an exhibition of maps which the final credits indicate is taking place at the Pompidou Centre: *Cartes et figures de la terre* (*Maps and Figures of the Earth*, 1980). Rather than simply present this exhibition though, the film incorporates cartography gradually into its highly idiosyncratic narrative structure in which a game is played out on a variety of levels, that is suggestive of a limbo space between life and death and in which cartography itself is both interrogated and pushed to the cosmic level of an impossible cartography. The film not only engages with actual maps but also with cartographic theories, articulated by a second, female narrator and which become increasingly delirious. Near the beginning, for example, we are presented with a tripartite proposition that the discrepancy between the map and the territory is because the territory has departed from the original map, that the territory is yet to conform to the superior logic of the map and thirdly that the city destroyed by some cataclysm is being recreated according to the map, thus combining the previous two options. These speculations lead quickly into Borgesian ones about the perfect map, which would have to be on a scale of one to one with the territory, or else would be the superimposition or else subtraction of all existing maps. There is also exploration of the domain of false maps of non-existent or imaginary territories, such as the non-existent mountain ranges seventeenth-century cartographers added to their maps to give them more harmonious boundaries. All of this cartographic delirium is related in the film to a series of interwoven dreams or nightmares, further emphasising the delirium of the cartographic project. For example, when H is on a real plane traversing an apparently real territory, he falls asleep and sees

Flying above the labyrinth in *Zig-Zag*

himself with his interlocutor on a ludicrous model plane traversing a series of maps from different cultural origins and historical periods (presumably from the exhibition), so that he journeys as much in time as in space.

While there are many fascinating aspects to this short film, what it reveals as an emblem of Ruiz's filmmaking practice is a strong critique of representation coupled with an association between cinema, dreams and cartographic exploration. This might seem strange, given that maps are usually seen as particularly bound to representational logic but as the film shows, their multiplicity calls this logic into question. Similarly the film itself departs from the usual narrative models, whether those of fiction or non-fiction cinema. In the place of a character caught up in any kind of narrative conflict, we have a dreamer negotiating a series of levels both cartographic and oneiric via a series of encounters and according to the logic of a highly enigmatic and shifting game. In this way, instead of a straight-forward exposition of the materials of the exhibition, they are also caught up in the game-like logic of this didactic nightmare, rendering them far more enigmatic and enticing than any more conventional presentation. However, what is really interesting in the film is the association of cinema with this project of cartography, as the mapping of a series of spaces on different levels, rather than as merely using space as a backdrop for a story. In the film it is not only cartographic images but cinematic ones that are explored from banal explorations of a Parisian neighbourhood, to aerial photography to truly cosmic images. Early on in the film there is an image that is repeated of a hand projected onto the sky that then rolls dice that presumably determine the course of the unfolding game. This not only literalises the philosophical problem of god playing dice with the universe but is explicitly rendered as a cinematic projection, the cosmic hand flickering as if produced by the cinematic apparatus itself. The implication is that cinema is not only a form of cartography, or the exploration of space, before it is the ground for any kind of narrative but that it is a cosmic, impossible cartography, not merely representing what exists but like the various forms of false cartography mentioned in the film, what is no longer or is yet to be, or even what has never existed and can perhaps never exist except as an image. Cinema is therefore not the cartography of a real territory but of the impossible or virtual and is an especially simulacral practice. Nevertheless, in order to locate Ruiz's own cinematic practice of impossible cartography on a recognisable map, it is necessary to situate it in relation to the styles with which it has most often been associated, namely Magical Realism, Surrealism and the baroque.

Surrealism, Magical Realism and the Baroque

The relations between Ruiz's aesthetics and Surrealism, Magical Realism and the baroque are complicated both by the considerable overlap between these three styles and Ruiz's pragmatic treatment of them all as visual or narrative rhetorics to be used or discarded according to the requirements of a particular project, without fully subscribing to any of them. It is further complicated by Ruiz's invention of new stylistic terms such as 'chaste realism' or 'negative anthropology' to account for his own work. Nevertheless it is worth re-examining these more conventional aesthetic tendencies, if only to get a clearer idea of how Ruiz is most often critically situated.

While some critics have related Ruiz's work to the Latin American literary genre of Magical Realism, others have seen it rather as a continuation of Surrealism. While images and modes of filmmaking corresponding to both these aesthetic styles are certainly present in Ruiz's works, Ruiz's own statements and indeed his films themselves demonstrate clearly that these styles are more a source of images or systems of images that he makes use of, in the same way that he makes use of images and narratives from popular culture such as the melodramatic *feuilleton*. In fact, Ruiz has said that what interests him in Surrealism are its kitsch shock effects rather than its idealist utopian aspirations, and he has also referred to Magical Realism in terms of kitsch. Furthermore Ruiz's use of these stylistic tendencies is highly variable throughout his work both in terms of general periods and specific projects, which make use of these and other visual regimes in one project, only to parody them or simply abandon them in another.

This complex layering of different styles in Ruiz's work is a clear expression of his diasporic experience in that it combines and superimposes styles and sources associated with Latin America with European styles, creating a hybrid and complex form of cinema that defies categorisation. A more complex understanding of this cinema can be reached via the idea of the baroque or neo-baroque as Christine Buci-Glucksmann suggests in her essay 'The Baroque Eye of the Camera' (Buci-Glucksmann 2004: 31–44). The Baroque is a particularly slippery category in the history of art that frustrates attempts to contain it whether in a specific historical period, or geographical location, and in Latin America it continued to play an important role well beyond the period of colonisation (according to Ruiz the Spanish colonisation of South America was itself a baroque act) and arguably up until the work of modern writers like Borges and the whole style of Magical Realism. As Buci-Glucksmann has also shown in her work on Walter Benjamin there is a direct link between the baroque and European modernity and modernism (and one might be tempted to say even postmodernism), passing through figures like Baudelaire and Benjamin himself. In this optic, Surrealism itself, at least in some of its variants can be understood as a particular instance or return of the baroque in relation to modernity.[1]

What characterises the baroque most of all is an emphasis on the fragment over the whole and a resulting complexity in which there are multiple levels coexisting within the same work, which are not reducible to an overall scheme or perspective. This is the great distinction made by Benjamin between the baroque and romanticism; whereas romanticism presents fragments as symbols of a totalisable whole or essence, even if this whole is absent, in the baroque there are only allegories, which are enigmatic signs leading only to other signs and therefore ultimately to a non-totalisable infinity of irreconcilable points of view. The use of this kind of system is most clearly evident in Ruiz's *L'hypothèse du tableau volé* (*Hypothesis of the Stolen Painting*, 1978), which he qualified as a baroque system, as opposed to the gothic system of the conventional detective film (Ruiz 1992: 2). However much knowledge we might bring to bear in interpreting the signs we are presented with, we will never get to the core of the mystery, as this core is itself only another enigma and besides there is always a 'missing painting' or an irremediable gap in our knowledge that prevents the system of interpretation from ever reaching the unitary totalisation of a solution. However, more than just a baroque cinema, an attribution that could be applied to a number of other modern directors such as Fellini, Buci-Glucksmann refers to Ruiz's cinema as a second degree baroque cinema, or baroque of the baroque in the following terms:

> A baroque gaze that opens out, in which a film is always several films, in a sort of aborescent proliferating structure which respects no chronology, no dramatisation of the action, no Euclidean space: everything cited, everything mixed, passing (as in [Ruiz's] 1970s cinema) through all the regimes of the image and of the visual (liberated painting, stilled photo or postcard, theatre opened up to cinematic space, cinema theatricalised). As if in this gigantic combustion of forms, the cinema can only be a baroque palimpsest, a theatre of shadows and memory. ... Ruiz's cinema would be a sort of second degree baroque – a baroque of the baroque. (Buci-Glucksmann 2004: 33).

One could argue that this second degree baroque is a specifically postmodern form of the baroque, a neo-baroque aesthetics also evident in writers such as Jorge Luis Borges and Witold Gombrowicz, in which the complexities of baroque systems are explicitly played with and pushed to the point of their dissolution into chaos, which is indeed precisely what takes place at the end of several of Ruiz's films such as *Hypothesis of the Stolen Painting*. For this reason, while this book will certainly explore the magical realist, surreal, baroque and neo-baroque dimensions of Ruiz's work it will avoid reducing his work as a whole to any of these aesthetic systems, instead seeing it as a complex cartography of gestures, styles, genres, places and above all cinematic images.

Organisation of the Book

As an attempt to construct some type of order in the labyrinth of Ruiz's extensive and complex filmography, this book will follow Ruiz's work more or less chronologically identifying four major periods of its elaboration. The first begins in Chile in the period leading up to and during the Allende socialist government. In this phase, Ruiz's work was pursued in the context of the new Latin American cinema, although Ruiz's films were already highly distinctive both formally and politically. In the place of magical or social realism, Ruiz's films of this period can be seen as a micropolitical cartography of social gestures and behaviours, in relation to but critical of surrounding political and cinematic movements. After the Pinochet coup, Ruiz like most of those working in Chilean cinema was forced into exile, a condition that was treated in his first major film project, *Diálogos de exiliados* (*Dialogues of Exiles,* 1974). However, Ruiz soon embarked on an exploration of different styles, genres and formats, producing both films of varying lengths and experimental television work. This enabled an experimentation with visual and narrative rhetorics, increasingly distant from and critical of normative conceptions of political cinema. In the second chapter, the book will deal with one of Ruiz's most expansive periods, the 1980s during which Ruiz returned emphatically to producing feature films, developing a distinctive style drawing on Magical Realism, Surrealism and the baroque and dealing with a cluster of themes around the sea, piracy and childhood. Ruiz's practice took on an incredible diversity in this period and was extended both in terms of geography, especially with the production of several films in Portugal but also in an expressive heterogeneity of cinematic images. Finally from the mid-1990s to his most recent films prior to his death, Ruiz's cinema has presented cartographies of complexity which, despite more conventional appearances (in some cases), are no less subversive than their predecessors of the 1970s and 1980s. In these films, cartography no longer refers primarily to gestures, styles, or places but different forms of multiplicity, whether in terms of subjective identity, narrative events, nationality or cinematic images themselves. While these successive cartographies in Ruiz's work are overlapping rather than absolutely distinct, their identification will allow for the forging of a path through the Ruizian cinematic labyrinth which, however artificial, is nevertheless a necessary precaution for its effective navigation.

Note

1   See Christine Buci-Glucksmann (1994), *Baroque Reason: The Aesthetics of Modernity.* London: Sage.

CHAPTER ONE

Ruiz's Cinema in the 1960s and 1970s

PART 1: BEYOND SOCIALIST REALISM: RUIZ'S CINEMA IN CHILE

Introduction

As the introduction to this book already suggested there was a profound transformation of Ruiz's cinema over the course of the 1970s. In fact, the shift from Raúl Ruiz as a Chilean director associated with the collective social experiment of Allende's Chile to 'Raoul Ruiz' as a European cinematic auteur based in Paris is generally considered the most profound break in Ruiz's career. While it would be ludicrous to contest the radical nature of this break, it is worth examining in more detail what exactly its effects were on Ruiz's cinematic practice by examining some of Ruiz's Chilean films, before a consideration, in the second part of this chapter, of the first films Ruiz made in France leading up to his 'collaborations' with the French writer Pierre Klossowski. This examination will aim to bring out the challenges Ruiz's work presents to aesthetic and political stereotypes in both his Chilean and French work, suggesting continuities between the two periods while acknowledging their considerable differences. In particular, there will be a focus on the relations between politics and aesthetics in Ruiz's work throughout the 1970s, demonstrating that any strict demarcation between a political or militant Chilean cinema and an aestheticist European art cinema in Ruiz's work is a highly unstable distinction. Since many of Ruiz's Chilean films are not widely available, only the pre-Allende film *Tres tristes tigres* (*Three Sad Tigers*, 1968) and the Allende period *La colonia penal* (*The Penal Colony*, 1970) will be analysed in detail. However, in order to situate the analysis of these films, some context will be given of Ruiz's film-making practice in the context of Chile prior to and during the Popular Unity period. This chapter section will then examine Ruiz's Chilean work leading up to the Pinochet coup and Ruiz's forced exile along with most other Chilean filmmakers, in particular showing the intertwining of aesthetics and politics in Ruiz's early work that would continue to be a key feature of his work in exile.

Impressions of Chilean Political History

Chile, like other Latin American countries has a complex history of colonialism, 'Hispanic capitalism', nationalism, social struggles and political conflicts.[1] However, relative to the political violence in many other Latin American countries, Chile was a relatively stable parliamentary democracy, at least from the 1920s, leading to its description as the England of South America. Nevertheless, despite appearances, the political and economic structure of the Chilean state inevitably resulted in social conflicts. Chilean independence was at first characterised by instability and both economic and political power were principally wielded by the oligarchic families who owned most of the land. The development of mining industries, especially of copper, played a crucial role in the development of the Chilean economy and led to changes in the country's social structure. This was not only in the emergence of new industrial elites but also the emergence of an industrial and unionised working class that became very politically active in the late nineteenth century. Technological changes in the mining industries led to its concentration in a few and foreign hands, mainly the United States, which in turn was a crucial factor in future political struggles throughout the twentieth century. Meanwhile politically, the first major challenge to the powers of the oligarchy, namely the Balmaceda presidency of the late nineteenth century, resulted in a bloody civil war and the reinstatement of the power of the oligarchy, while at the same time establishing a parliamentary system albeit one characterised by political instability (Skidmore and Smith 1997: 122). There was also considerable labour unrest at the beginning of the twentieth century, with numerous strikes and protests, mostly emerging out of the industrial mining sector. After a period of relative stability there was an increase in labour mobilisation in the 1920s ultimately leading to military intervention into the Allesandri presidency in 1924 and the adoption of legalised unions and welfare state policies in order to channel the demands of the working classes. However, as these measures failed to curb union activities, they were followed by a harsh crackdown and the installation of the General Ibanez dictatorship in 1927 (Skidmore and Smith 1997: 125).

The late 1930s saw a shift towards the left with the ascendancy of the Popular Front coalition, which in many ways was the model for the future Popular Unity party of the 1960s. A broad alliance of anti-fascist forces ranging from communists to democrats, the Popular Front was able to dominate Chilean politics until the late 1940s. Following the collapse of the Popular Front due to a combination of internal tensions, conflict with the conservative dominated congress and anti-communist pressure from the US, Chilean parliamentary politics became highly polarised, competitive but nevertheless stable in the sense of free of the political violence taking place elsewhere in Latin America. However, the Chilean voters were strongly divided between the conservatives, representing the interests of the landowners, the centre represented by the Radical Party and the newly emergent Christian Democrats and the Socialist-

Communist alliance (FRAP) that regrouped the legacy of the Popular Front and which was regaining support under the leadership of Salvador Allende. The *dramatis personae* of Allende, Allesandri the conservative/liberal candidate and the Christian Democrat Edouardo Frei would dominate Chilean presidential politics throughout the 1960s.

In 1958, Allessandri had a narrow victory over Allende, which prompted in the next election an alliance of the Conservatives with the Christian Democrats despite misgivings over their reformist agenda. The absence of a right-wing candidate, coupled with a smear campaign against Allende who was represented as taking orders from Moscow led to a clear majority for Frei, although support for Allende had actually increased to 39%. Frei's government walked a tightrope between highly polarised social forces. This was especially apparent in relation to the hotly debated issue of the copper industries. Rejecting both the total nationalisation advocated by the left and the business as usual approach of the right that would continue to disadvantage Chilean interests, Frei initiated a partial ownership of these industries by the state, whose benefits were less spectacular than anticipated. Agrarian reforms were also initiated that involved a limited expropriation of land from oligarchic landowners, with full compensation, in favour of the rural peasantry. Both these measures were seen as middle of the road compromises and had limited success but internationally, Frei's government was seen as a model of a reformist, centrist politics that was supported by foreign governments, especially the US, as well as the World Bank. However, by the end of the 1960s things were not looking so rosy for the Christian Democrats; their attempts at creating processes of popular participation in the form of cooperatives and grass-roots organisations had not been able to head off the more advanced initiatives of the left in this domain and furthermore the Conservatives, having backed the Christian Democrats out of sheer opportunism, now believed they could win the presidency outright and thereby put an end to a reformist process that they had never been comfortable with. This resulted in the three-way contest that elected Salvador Allende over Allesandri despite US support for the latter. The Christian Democrat candidate, whose reformist policies were only a more moderate version of Allende's, received just 28% of the vote. Allende was only able to assume office after making a number of constitutional promises to the Christian Democrats, while elements of the right immediately involved themselves in unsuccessful CIA-backed military plans to block Allende's presidency. It was in this highly charged and anomalous political context, culminating in Allende's 'democratic path to radical socialism', that the new Chilean cinema including that of Ruiz began to develop.

Beginnings of the New Chilean Cinema

The new Chilean cinema had its origins in the 1950s in the cinema club founded at the Universidad de Santiago de Chile in that decade (King 1990: 169). A key figure in this context was the documentary filmmaker Sergio Bravo who was the first director of the Centre for Experimental Cinema that sought to extend the activities of the cinema club into production. There was a strong documentary and ethnographic orientation to this initiative with the idea of finding a cinematic language capable of portraying the lives of the different peoples of Chile, with a particular interest in the lives and customs of its rural indigenous inhabitants. This initiative was part of a larger popular transformation of Chilean culture that rejected colonial, European definitions of Chilean culture and sought to revive forgotten indigenous traditions. This tendency was therefore closely aligned with the pressures for political reform and was in opposition to the political stagnation that had characterised Chilean politics under the Allesandri and Ibanez administrations. A key demonstration of this combination of new forms of culture with progressive politics was in the Chilean new song movement that built on the activities of the musician, amateur ethnologist and educator Violetta Parra. By the late 1960s there were numerous groups such as Quilapayún whose songs combined popular, indigenous music traditions with an advocacy of social change. These groups would perform both at small clubs and massive political demonstrations and were a key feature of the election rallies of the late 1960s. Later, some of these groups would tour the world and were a central feature of international Chilean solidarity events after the Pinochet coup. At the same time there was a revival of Chilean theatre with many avant-garde groups forming that would later provide performers for the films of the New Chilean Cinema. There was also the massively important figure of the communist poet Pablo Neruda who stood in the 1970 elections as the official communist party candidate despite the support of many communists for Allende's Popular Unity Party, while at the other extreme there was the counter-cultural 'anti-poet' Nicanor Parra, Violetta Parra's brother (King 1990: 171).

Just as the Christian Democrats had attempted mild political reforms, they also initiated similar cultural policies, including in relation to cinema. A council was created to support Chilean cinema but as in the case of the copper industries or agrarian reforms this was done conservatively without threatening the hegemony of foreign controlled distribution and exhibition interests. Nevertheless there was some limited support of local production through supportive protectionist measures aimed mainly at producers. Despite the timidity of these gestures, a new Chilean cinema did begin to emerge with five key features produced in 1968 and 1969 including Ruiz's *Three Sad Tigers*. Other key directors of this cinema were Miguel Littín who made *El chacal de nahueltoro* (*The Jackal of Nahueltoro*, 1969) and Helvio Soto who directed *Caliche sangriento* (*Bloody Nitrate*, 1969). Aldo Francia and Carlos Elsesser also directed their first features. To give an idea of the scarcity of resources for filmmakers in this period it is enough to point out that Ruiz, Littín, Elsesser and Francia made their films consecutively using the same camera (ibid.).

Francia had already organised a meeting of Latin American filmmakers in 1967 at the Viña del Mar Film Festival, the most important film festival in Chile. Filmmakers from seven Latin American countries were present and films from nine countries were screened there in an event that emphasised the commonality of Latin American cinemas and rejected national isolationism: 'There can be no Chilean view of Latin American cinema for the simple reason that we do not see here cinema from Latin America [...] Latin American cinema is one of debate, a cinema of struggle' (Francia cited in King 1990: 71). This initial meeting proposed an ambitious project of Latin American co-operation which, even if it was not able to be fully realised, encouraged the development of new cinemas throughout the continent. Of course, these movements also drew on developments that had already taken place in European cinemas, particularly Italian neorealism and the *politique des auteurs* that had first been articulated by the key filmmakers of the French New Wave. However, filmmakers in Latin America were keenly aware of their colonial histories, leading to cinema movements that were more politicised and internationalist than their European counterparts. This tendency was expressed most forcefully in the Argentinian filmmakers Fernando Solanas and Octavio Gettino's manifesto for a Third Cinema which was one of the first theoretical expressions of postcolonial cinema (Solanas and Gettino 1997: 33–57). While it is beyond the scope of this book to deal with Latin American new cinema movements in general, it is important to underline that the emergence of new film directors in Chile took place in this context of international co-operation and shared cultural and political goals. As Ruiz himself put it: 'Suddenly we found ourselves with a cinema which in a very obvious and natural way, without any inferiority complex, was being made with very few resources [...] and with a freedom that earlier Latin American and European cinema did not have. It is in this sense that the festivals [at Viña del Mar] were very important to us' (Ruiz cited in King 1990: 72). The Chilean films produced at the end of the 1960s may have been less politically militant than Solanas's *La hora de los hornos* (*The Hour of the Furnaces*, 1968), or less aesthetically exuberant than Glauber Rocha's *Deus e o diabo na terra do sol* (*Black God, White Devil*, 1964), but they shared with both the desire to invent a cinematic language adequate to the expression of Latin American social and political realities and therefore constituted an immediately political, postcolonial cinema, in advance of any corresponding political transformation of Chilean society.

This political aspect of the new Chilean cinema is confirmed by an examination of the first films that it produced. Francia's *Valparaíso mi amor* (*Valparaíso my Love*, 1969) continued the legacy of Italian neorealism in its depiction of children as the victims of underdevelopment and social inequality, while at the same time echoing the poetic realism of French pre-war cinema in its lyrical depiction of the port of Valparaíso. Soto's *Bloody Nitrate* painted a broader historical picture of the nineteeth-century war with Bolivia and Peru from an anti-imperialist perspective. The victor of this conflict in Soto's film was British commercial interests in alliance with the Chilean oligarchy, an imperialism that would be continued in the form of US domination over Chilean mineral industries. Michael Chanan has noted that there is a particularly cinematic resonance of the subject of this film since Chilean nitrate was a key chemical ingredient for early film-stock (Chanan 1976: 7). So the colonial history of Chile depicted in the film, that resulted in British domination of the nitrate industry has a direct, material impact on the history of cinema itself. More inventive cinematically and more politically radical was Littín's *Jackal of Nahueltoro*. While referring to events taking place under the previous government of Allesandri, the film clearly targeted the failures of the Christian Democrats to address the plight of the rural landless poor. The story, based on a real incident in which a poor farmer, José, murdered a landless woman and her five children in an act of drunken violence, Littín's film was multi-layered and based on extensive research into the social conditions surrounding the case. The different elements that make up the film range from documentary reconstructions of the facts and interviews of the case, to the fictionalisation of the protagonist's miserable childhood as part of the rural poor. The second part of the film shows José's progress in prison as he learns to read and write and adopts civilised values but also becomes aware of the social conflicts surrounding his own crime but all under a death sentence dictated by vengeful institutions. According to John King, in this film 'Littín mercilessly exposes the ideological state institutions of the law, the penal code, education and religion which distort José's growing consciousness and then support his execution' (King 1990: 173). As the last and most popular of these pre-Allende Chilean films, *Jackal* played an important role in Popular Unity mobilisation for the 1970 election. In retrospect, some critics have also seen the film as allegorical of the Allende period that it preceded: 'the experience of the entire Chilean masses, their struggle to express themselves and take charge of their destiny, might appear to us now as a struggle inevitably condemned to a brutal termination' (Chanan 1976: 3).

Ruiz's film *Three Sad Tigers* contrasts with all these examples in its adoption of a much more experimental style, both in its cinematography and in its story, which shares a lot with the more radical works of the French New Wave by Godard or Rivette. It also conveys a different conception of politics. Rather than a political subject matter, the film concerns a banal series of incidents occurring in the lives of quite ordinary lower-middle class characters. The politics of the film lies elsewhere, in the attempt to create a new relationship between the camera and the people that appear before it and to develop a cinematic language adequate to contemporary Chilean life. In this regard it constitutes a critical ethnography of contemporary Chile that forcefully brings out the atmosphere of casual compromise that was endemic to the Frei period by showing how it is expressed in everyday gestures, actions and lives. As such it is arguably more political than the other Chilean films of this time, since rather than dramatising political events, it holds a mirror up to contemporary Chilean everyday existence and is therefore an exemplar of a political way of making films rather than a cinema with a political content. This film will be returned to later in this section.

Allende, Allende: Chilean Cinema and the 'Democratic Path to Socialism'

According to Michael Chanan in his introduction to his book on Chilean cinema, which was compiled shortly after the Pinochet coup, 'it is possible to trace almost the entire history of Popular Unity through the new Chilean cinema that was born in the early 1960s and went into exile on 11 September, 1973' (Chanan 1976: 2). However, few of the cinematic examples Chanan refers to were made during the Allende period itself but rather shortly before or afterwards. To take the example of Ruiz, while *Three Sad Tigers* and Ruiz's post-Allende cinematic work circulate as different exemplars of artistic cinema, most of the films he made during the Allende period have barely been seen outside of their initial release in Chile and several of them have been described as cinematically undistinguished works. The only film of this period that has had any international circulation is *The Penal Colony* and even this film has circulated only in a mutilated form and usually provokes a perplexed reaction even among viewers sympathetic to Ruiz's cinema. To understand the reasons for this, it is necessary to look at the political, economic and cultural conditions of film-making during the Allende period and especially the ways that filmmakers including Ruiz viewed their own work at this time in socially engaged or militant rather than purely aesthetic terms.

When Allende came to power in 1970, the tasks of implementing radical economic and political reforms were hampered not only by hostile opposition from the right but also by the internal tensions at the heart of the Popular Unity movement itself, which was composed of no less than six parliamentary parties as well as the support of the extra-parliamentary MIR (Revolutionary Left Movement) an urban guerilla movement that supported the Popular Unity government but was also difficult to control. In particular, there were conflicts between the communists who saw the Allende victory as the first step towards full proletarian revolution and the socialists whose political intentions were more moderate. According to some commentators the Allende government, 'instead of trying to resolve these differences, [...] circumvented them, expecting, [...] that they would be superseded by the political struggle' (Faundez 1988: 280–281). This led in practice to deadlocks and contradictory policies, as well as to the internal perception that the government was either too timid or too revolutionary and the external one that it was both 'ruthless and aimless' (1988: 281). In these circumstances, it was very difficult to formulate coherent strategies and yet the government did have initial successes, for example, in nationalising the copper industry, some banks and expropriating land (King 1990: 174). There were high hopes also regarding Chilean cinema, as evidenced in the Miguel Littín drafted manifesto that greeted the Allende victory and which stated that Chilean cinema would be 'national, popular and revolutionary' (ibid.).[2] Key points in this manifesto outlined the role of Chilean filmmakers during the Allende period and included statements such as 'before being filmmakers we are men engaged with the political and social phenomenon of our people, and in their great task: the construction of socialism [...] Chilean cinema, because of an historical imperative, must be a revolutionary art' (Chanan 1976: 83–84).

Turning this revolutionary rhetoric into reality was, however, not so simple, even with Littín as the new director of Chile Films. First of all, distribution was controlled by a small group of companies, many of them US-owned, whose profits were entirely based on screening US films. After the announcement by Henry Kissinger that retaliatory measures would be taken against a country that had been 'silly' enough to elect a Marxist government and the statement attributed both to AT&T and Richard Nixon that the US would aim to 'make the Chilean economy scream,'[3] it was not surprising that Chilean cinema too would be affected by the informal economic boycott, which was the retaliation for nationalising US companies operating in Chile. As part of this boycott, which was accompanied by an increased funding of opposition newspapers, all US film imports were suspended from June 1971. While the government tried to counter these moves through the importation of films from Cuba, Hungary and Czechoslovakia, this helped fuel accusations they were only showing communist propaganda and some independent cinemas refused to show the official government newsreel. By 1973, Chile Films only controlled thirteen theatres and ran four mobile units and while it benefited in a sense from the boycott in a 25% share of distribution, this did not necessarily translate into popular support.

Littín's initial enthusiasm and innovative ideas for Chile Films immediately ran into several major obstacles. Not least of these was that one of the constitutional promises of the Allende regime was to guarantee the jobs of bureaucrats who were largely hostile to the new government and therefore tended to obstruct rather than implement many of Littín's proposals. Tiring of both this bureaucratic opposition and inter party conflicts, Littín retired from his post after only ten months (King 1990: 175). His suggestion to set up film workshops dealing with the various areas of film production were undermined by this party political struggle over resources, with tangible results only occurring in the area of documentary. Not a single feature film, funded by Chile Films, was completed during the Allende period, although some films were made independently, including by Ruiz, that benefited from the facilities of Chile Films. However, the cinematic activity during the Allende period cannot be judged according to its final products, as several Chilean filmmakers at the time pointed out. Instead it needs to be understood in terms of the political antagonisms which were not just taking place outside Chile Films but within it; the situation that Chilean films found itself in was a volatile and revolutionary one that may well have produced results similar to the high points of Soviet or Cuban cinema had it been given time to develop. To expect these results to be immediately apparent would be like expecting the full development of the cinema of Eisenstein, Pudovkin and Vertov by 1920. As Helvio Soto put it, the lack of feature films was because:

> At one point it was the Socialist Party which controlled Chile Films [...] but it wasn't a question of definitive power. That's to say it wasn't the state which defined a general policy for communications, cinema, television ... two or three months later it was the Communist Party which took control of the cinema and which [...] made facilities available for its militants. The consequence of this situation was that nobody did anything. [...] People spent three years discussing projects that changed according to the balance of power within Chile Films. First they concentrated on this project, then on another, and finally they did nothing. (Soto cited in Chanan 1976: 41)

In other words, Chile Films as an institution embodied the volatility of the Chilean political situation more generally, meaning that in this period of dramatic nationalisations, it was those filmmakers who could work independently of the state including, ironically enough, Miguel Littín after he had left his position as head of Chile Films, who were actually able to produce work during the Allende period. The most prolific of these independent filmmakers was in fact Ruiz, who completed at least seven films of varying lengths during the three years of the Allende period, developing a range of flexible strategies for film production that would also prove to be useful after his departure for France. In a much quoted interview, Ruiz in fact proposed making films in three inter-connected ways during the Allende period. This consisted firstly in an engaged cinema, (which was about making the means of production accessible to the workers), secondly, a cinema which sustained government decisions and thirdly an expressive cinema properly speaking. Crucially, for Ruiz, all of these modes of cinema had to be closely linked so that the social and political transformations taking place in Chilean society could not only find cinematic representation but actually come to influence the artistic expression of Chilean cinema, without reducing the latter to the kitsch codes of socialist realism of which Ruiz was undoubtedly the harshest critic among Chilean filmmakers. We will come back shortly to Ruiz's complex position within the 'cinema of Allende' but first there will be a biographical sketch of Ruiz's career up to this point, in the hope of shedding light on Ruiz's unique place within Chilean cinema before, during and after the Allende era.

The Pre-history of Ruiz's Cinema

When it comes to dealing with Ruiz's origins, one is confronted with something much more resembling what some critics have referred to as a 'biographical legend' than a necessarily reliable history but a legend of which even the most delirious elements may well prove to be true.[4] It is telling that one of the few critics to attempt this, Charles Tesson, did it in the form of an associative game, thereby referencing Ruiz's *Zig-Zag*, entitling the exercise, 'A Didactic Nightmare (or the foolish attempt to establish a bio-filmography of Raoul Ruiz)' (Tesson 1983: 13–18). In other words he presents an associative, ludic cartography rather than a linear trajectory, which is in fact a general mimetic tendency in writings on Ruiz's cinema. However, in keeping with the perversely chronological structure of this book, the following will attempt to reconstruct Ruiz's biographical legend in a more or less linear fashion, notwithstanding that this might be a line full of deviations, gaps, fractures and bifurcations.

Ruiz was born in the town of Puerto Montt in the south of Chile in 1941 and then his family moved to Valparaíso. His father was a sea captain, who he described in an interview with Fabrice Revault d'Allones and Christine Buci-Glucksmann as having a displaced authoritarianism: 'Furious when we behaved well, and happy to see us do terrible things' (Buci-Glucksmann and Revault d'Allones 1987: 84). A type of personage that would populate his cinema but only in the 1980s. In the same interview he denied having anything but a banal childhood, 'like any-one else' (1987: 86) and one that was only obliquely related to his subsequent oneiric representations of childhood in his films. He was, however, exposed from an early age to a great deal of cinema, especially serials, and it made a big impression on him when actors like Vincent Price or Robert Taylor would die in one film only to be resurrected in the next, having been transformed from a cowboy into a lawyer or a Soviet spy (1987: 84). The family having relocated to Santiago de Chile, Ruiz took up studies of both law and theology, the latter which he referred to later as a joke but one that had to be taken to its logical conclusion. He also maintains that he managed to study both simultaneously: 'since law only occupied my mornings, I did theology at the end of the afternoons' (1987: 86). In fact, theology served as a good introduction to philosophies of logic and both logic and theology itself would reappear in several of Ruiz's films. Concurrently with these studies Ruiz apparently set himself the seemingly arbitrary task of writing one hundred plays which he completed in 1962 after six years.[5] Later he explained that some of these plays were only a few pages long but according to Charles

Tesson (1983: 14), most were around a hundred pages; some of these plays would form the basis of a few of Ruiz's later films.

It was around this time that Ruiz frequented the cine-club of the University of Santiago and was surprised to discover that there were people who took cinema seriously, for whom cinema was something structured and complex and who discussed and argued about films, for example, about the relevant merits of De Sica and Rosselini's use of point of view (Buci-Glucksmann and Revault d'Allones 1987: 87). But Ruiz was not content merely to discuss film and in 1963 he made his first, unfinished film *La Maleta (The Suitcase)* based on one of his plays (this film was presumed lost until rediscovered in Chile in 2008; Ruiz then completed the film, by adding a new soundtrack, in 2010). It shows a large man carrying a suitcase around town containing a much smaller man. When the carrier becomes tired, the two men exchange places (Tesson 1983: 14). As such it partakes of a similar atmosphere to early Roman Polanski shorts such as *Dwaj ludzie z szafa (Two Men and a Wardrobe,* 1958), although this is a case of resonance rather than any influence, a 'Polish' dimension of Ruiz's work that would resurface throughout his career.[6]

In 1964, Ruiz worked on another film of a similar length entitled *El regreso (The Return,* 1964), which was definitively not completed. Apparently this film, which was shot in Buenos Aires and featured the Chilean actor-director Lautaro Murúa who had relocated there, concerned a man trying to return from work and becoming lost in an urban labyrinth, resonating with Ruiz's later film, *The Territory* (1981). Around this time, Ruiz seems to have had some trans-continental adventures including such activities as ghost-writing Mexican TV serials, presenting a daily sports show on Chilean TV and attending film school in Santa Fé, Argentina, which he dropped out of after a year, according to an interview with Jonathan Rosenbaum, as a rejection of the idea that it was 'the duty of every human being in Latin America to make documentary films' (Ruiz cited in Rosenbaum 1995: 223). In 1967, Ruiz embarked upon a loose fictional adaptation of a Daphne du Maurier novel, again set in Buenos Aires, entitled *El Tango del Viudo/The Widower's Tango* and which was produced by the cine-club of Viña del Mar, the organisers of the first Latin American film festival. This film reverses the Du Maurier story, 'The Ghost and Mrs Muir,' in that it concerns a widower who is pursued throughout his house by the ghost of his departed wife. This widower becomes a fetishist and transvestite, trying on the clothes of his departed wife and ultimately becoming her physically, anticipating narrative motifs of gender subversion that would later appear in *Dog's Dialogue* (1977) and *Three Crowns of the Sailor* (1982). Apparently a full negative of this film still exists in Chile.

Already in these early, unreleased works questions of cartography and space were clearly paramount. Ruiz described the approach in these films as an interest in discovering anomalies in the everyday, thereby circumventing classical debates about reality versus the imaginary or realism versus the fantastic or even Surrealism. If anything they partake of what his friend and collaborator Waldo Rojas has referred to as 'Surreachilism' (Rojas 2004: 8). Ruiz relates this to the Cuban surrealist writer Alejo Carpentier's concept of 'fantastic realism' but also to a type of discontinuous or aleatory perception of the world, which he describes as polysemic and polyphonic

(Buci-Glucksmann and Revault d'Allones 1987: 90). In essence it is an approach to the world based on fragments of speech and gestures, and it is especially the latter that were of particular interest to Ruiz in the beginnings of his cinematic career. According to Ruiz, even Hollywood films are composed of these multiple polyphonic fragments and are only secondarily integrated into organic, narrative wholes, or at least that is the way he perceived these films in Chile. Later he would mount a frontal attack on the unifying tendencies of American and global cinema that he would refer to in terms of 'central conflict theory' (Ruiz 1995: 9–24), but for now the key element to maintain is the focus on the polyphony of everyday gestures and through these gestures the indiscernibility of reality and the fantastic. Yet in Ruiz's next period of filmmaking, the fantastic would take a back seat to an ethnographic or even entomological approach to Chilean and Latin American existence without, however, relinquishing the obsessive focus on gesture, now presented in a more materialist, even Brechtian, framework as a kind of 'social *gest*', the everyday habits and behaviours that reveal the unconscious social and political relations of a given society.[7] In Ruiz's words:

> I am first of all interested in the strangeness of comportments and then in the explosions of speech. [...] My characters don't know where to go but that doesn't mean that they remain perplexed or that they do nothing. The character goes towards a project, but he stops, goes back, leaves again animated by another project ... the change becomes more and more spectacular but each action smaller and smaller (Ruiz in Buci-Glucksmann and Revault d'Allones 1987: 91).

This citation gives a good introduction to the atmosphere of Ruiz's first released film, *Three Sad Tigers*, which was his real debut into the by now effervescent context of the New Latin American cinema.

Three Sad Tigers (1968)

'Tres Tristes Tigres' is a Spanish tongue-twister that was also the title of two works of Latin American literature in 1967, the Cuban writer Cabrera Infante's *Ulysses*-like novel and a play by the Chilean playwright Alejandro Sieveking set among a group of undistinguished lower-middle class characters in Santiago de Chile, over the course of a summer weekend. The confusions, however, do not stop there, as there was also an earlier 1961 Mexican comedy western with the same name, with which, even in Chile, Ruiz claims his adaptation of Sieveking's play was frequently confused.[8] To the viewer accustomed to Ruiz's later work, *Three Sad Tigers* is something of a surprise, being an anti-illusionist, almost neo-realist vision of a mostly nocturnal Santiago, in apparent proximity with the more ethnographic tendencies of the French New Wave. As a way into the aesthetics of the film it is worth citing again the reminiscences of Rojas, who described the environment, he, Ruiz and their friends inhabited in not dissimilar terms to the *mise-en-scène* of the film: 'The Santiago night – with its sordid mysteries, its streets with their flat, semi-hidden perspectives and almost aggressively dim lighting, its violence poorly contained and even less well hidden – somehow lifted the challenge of Santiago-by-day, grey and pale' (Rojas 2004: 8). According to Rojas, it was in forays into this 'secret' nocturnal city, well-fuelled by local cuisine and alcohol and in an effort to escape the growing tendency towards the emergent certainties of political rhetoric and socialist realism that the concept of 'chaste realism' was born, based on 'considering reality no longer as a received idea, nor as the supreme discovery, sublunary and imperturbable but as a system of dissimulations' (2004: 9). In other words reality was neither the pre-conceived reality of conventional systems such as the bourgeois order or Classical Hollywood, nor was it a pure goal to be aimed at as in doctrinaire socialism or the Bazinian reading of neorealism, but rather a veneer or mask behind which were no doubt further masks, an approach that would be only become increasingly pronounced in Ruiz's work over the 1970s. The chaste or austere aspect lay not in any minimalist style but in the refusal to take 'reality' for granted and instead the desire to probe its surfaces and provoke it to reveal its dissimulations which, as Rojas points out, was precisely the procedure of *Three Sad Tigers*. It is for this reason that Rojas insists on the well-served table and concludes that 'the subsequent stage of chaste realism was to definitively abandon the title of artist or intellectual in order to simply become professional drinkers' (ibid.). A comparison could be made between this chaste realism and the formulations of the *Dogme 95* Vow of Chastity but would reveal the latter to be not only more rigid but also much more superficial. This is especially since Ruiz's chaste realism had a much more artificial and less naïve idea about what constitutes reality and would certainly reject the idea that it can best be attained by following a set of pre-formulated rules such as the use of only available light, colour, location shooting and hand-held camera.

Nevertheless, *Three Sad Tigers* did seek to provoke reality precisely through its own set of technical constraints. The most important of these was the exclusive use of a 28mm lens which effectively meant that the camera was constantly 'in the faces' of the actors, irritating and provoking them and thereby operating as a protagonist in the film, filming its situations from within, rather than from the conventional external point of view. This had the effect of making the actors constantly aware of how they were being framed and continually passing out of the frame, leading to what Ruiz described as 'a constant state of aggression' (Ruiz cited in Chanan 1976: 28). A second intention of this investigation of relations between the performers and the camera, of this situation of mutual stimulation that also extended to relations with the other performers and with Ruiz himself, was the setting up of multiple centres of attention only some of which were actually visible. This technique, which Ruiz compares to 'bad' television programmes that fail to frame the right object of attention at the right time, creates a disquiet in the audience, who become uncertain of what they should be focusing on, coming to suspect that what is foregrounded in the image may be insignificant compared to what is not visible in the off-screen space, a formula that is also reflected on the level of story. Charles Tesson goes as far as to assert that the whole film is characterised by an inversion in which 'the landscape becomes a character in close-up, the story becomes a background landscape and the characters become pure décor' (Tesson 1983: 14).[9]

To reconstruct the narrative of the film in a less abstract way, it concerns a group of lower-middle class characters inhabiting the Santiago night, among them Tito the main character who, rather than bringing some important papers to a meeting with his boss, prefers to enjoy a good meal in a restaurant with his sister and a stranger they have encountered that night. During this dinner, there are multiple digressions on such topics as Chilean cuisine and a fight nearly breaks out with a neighbouring table of young men who are singing patriotic songs. Later in order not to be fired, Tito meets with his boss and 'offers' him his sister in exchange for keeping his job. This seemingly slight and melodramatic story is really just a pretext, however, for putting its protagonists under the microscope of the 28mm lens and observing their mannerisms, gestures, and speech, the way that they handle difficult situations and the violence that is constantly bubbling beneath the surface only to erupt unexpectedly. While there are some direct references in the film to the compromised political situation of the Frei period, the film is much more interested in the compromises expressed in the smallest of gestures; it foregrounds the mutual exploitation of close relationships such as siblings and friends and shows their alienated nature but is much more interested in how this happens, in what kind of décor. For example, in an early scene in which Tito is trying to impress a girl he takes her to a tasteless apartment, which turns out only to be 'borrowed' from his boss, when the landlady comes round for the rent.

The film is political, therefore, not in dealing with national themes, or presenting an explicitly political situation but for the way its very structure communicates a sense of people leading shallow, unsustainable lives, in spaces which are not theirs and on borrowed time. In this sense, the film has something in common with the early 1960s films of Antonioni such as *L'eclisse* (*The Eclipse*, 1962) despite using a radically different style more akin to that of Cassavetes' *Shadows* (1959), which was an acknowledged influence. As Ian Christie puts it the film's 'temporal ambiguity, seeking to represent the suspended tempo of Chilean life, looks forward to Ruiz's later more stylised and cerebral projects' (Christie 2004a). This film is also the only Ruiz film to have something in common with Godard's new wave cinema both in its ethnographic aspects and its refusal to give a clear perspective on the whole of the situation that would give the viewer the ability to orient themselves within it. However, rather than any stylised use of montage or static camera, Ruiz achieves similar alienation effects through this constantly probing and mobile camera, so that the very form of the film expresses the kind of everyday complicity experienced by the characters in the film. The camera is like a wanderer through different facets of Chilean reality such as restaurants and strip clubs, casual political arguments in cafés, car show-rooms and cheap apartments, generating an almost documentary feel for contemporary life, gestures and speech, while refraining from any explicit judgement of this reality. The one apparent exception to this is when Tito and his sister return home with their dining/drinking companion Luis and are confronted by an inspector in a bus station who points out that this man has the habit of throwing his money around and neglecting his wife and his work, a judgement that has little effect on the protagonist's behaviour. It is as if they are suddenly confronted by a piece of social reality and reject it immediately as they are reluctant to give up the illusions on which their untenable lives are based. As François Bovier has pointed out scenes like this function less as a form of political judgement than as a type of political cartography of Chile (2009: 64–66).

Another key element of this film is the particular treatment of language as another formal element to play with. The characters in the film are endlessly talking, usually about everything but what is important, ranging from recipes for Chilean dishes to recounting endless stories and jokes. The language they employ while full of local colloquialisms and dialect, is at the same time quite literary and very much in the style of the contemporary counter-cultural poet Nicamor Parra, who the film is dedicated to in the opening credits. Parra reacted against the doctrinaire Marxism of Chilean poets like Pablo Neruda by coming up with a paradoxical language including such expressions as in the following anti poem: 'Independently of the Catholic Church/I declare that I am an Independent Country/May the Central Committee forgive me' (Parra cited in King 1990). This poem, more than just being word play was clearly showing the continuation of structures of power even when they are given new names. Equivalent Parra-like deformations of dialogue in Ruiz's film include the following: 'Two characters are walking down the street and one asks, "aren't you from here?" "Me yes, but my family no", the other replies, "I yes, all my family are from Antofagasta"' (Ruiz cited in Chanan 1976: 36). For Ruiz, these anomalies of everyday speech are far more politically revealing than when the characters actually talk about politics, in that they show in miniature a social *gest*, 'a certain behavioural imbalance, a certain weakness of character and […] an alienated society' (1976: 36).

In the same interview Ruiz rejects the leftist reception of the film that ignored its formal innovations and saw it as merely the indictment of a marginal social group, and therefore a political film in the limited sense of a film dealing with a social question, in this case social criticism of the unproductive and compromised role in society of the urban class caught between the values and ways of life of the proletariat and the bourgeoisie. This criticism was seen as an insufficiently profound social criticism. Ruiz, however, asserts that the film was merely the attempt to find an adequate image for the contemporary condition of Chilean society, an aim that it did not fully succeed in and certainly did not aim to go beyond. Nevertheless, Ruiz's following remarks suggest a different politics operating in the film that he calls 'the culture of resistance'. For Ruiz, *Three Sad Tigers* was primarily an investigative film connected to a pre-supposed culture of resistance which Ruiz took to be 'the synthesis of techniques of rejection of a precise order' (1976: 30). In other words, he aligned his cinema with a range of social or perhaps anti-social techniques for rejecting civilised norms which might range from the refusal of education and civilised behaviour to alcoholism. For Ruiz, this non-conformist underbelly of Chilean society, a kind of social unconscious that reveals itself through obsessive behaviours, anomalous speech and incongruent perceptions was essential and he went so far as to maintain, even during the Allende period that 'if we don't know how this culture functions, it's impossible, to put it crudely, to "create" Chile' (ibid.). What Ruiz is talking about has an uncanny resemblance with the Polish writer Witold Gombrowicz's particular conception of 'subculture', not as the organised forms of expression of youth cultural consumption but precisely as the unformed, uncivilised and immature elements that are necessarily constituent of a given social formation. This culture of resistance, which by no means corresponds to any mature political programme or ends but are precisely the techniques by which the population deviate from imposed ends, is in fact the true subject, aesthetic procedure and goal of *Three Sad Tigers,* an aim that was perhaps never pursued so successfully in Ruiz's later Allende period films. As such it anticipates Ruiz's strong critique of the tendency that would become dominant in the Allende period to 'create' Chile by 'creating' its historical heroes as social realist monsters, rather than paying attention to this everyday culture of resistance, this submerged social unconscious that eludes ideological capture but can be glimpsed through everyday habits and gestures, which was exactly what Ruiz was attempting to do in his films of this period; later on it would become the basis for his particular appropriation of Benjamin's concept of the optical unconscious.

Although this film was only seen by around 30,000 people in Chile, it was nevertheless relatively successful and also received international acclaim at festivals such as Locarno where it won the Golden Leopard in 1969. It was also shown at the second Latin American film festival at Viña del Mar, as was Solanas and Gettino's militant documentary *The Hour of the Furnaces,* fresh from its controversial premier at the 1968 Pesaro Festival of New Cinema at which the reception of the film had exploded onto the streets of the small Adriatic resort. As the Uruguayan producer Walter Achugar put it, 'Fernando Solanas was carried out into the streets in a spontaneous demonstration of support. [...] there were many confrontations with the police' (cited in Pick 1993: 22). However, the authors of 'Towards a Third Cinema' received a much more divided reception at Viña del Mar, and the Chilean filmmakers selected Ruiz as a spokesman to 'argue against the political dogmatism of some interventions' (Pick 1993: 23). This was less a rejection of political cinema than of the positing of certain modes of both cinema and political action as necessary models to be implemented, a formula that Ruiz would later critique in the following terms: 'things would go better in other socialist experiences if one eliminated this horrible intermediary: "the militant artist," [...] who is neither a good artist nor a good militant' (Ruiz in Buci-Glucksmann and Revault d'Allones 1987: 93). The questions confronted at the second Viña del mar festival whose two extreme poles were *Hour of the Furnaces* and *Three Sad Tigers,* included the following; the development of cinema in a socialist state, filmmakers and the state in a dependent capitalist context, problems of scarcity in relation to production and the question of whether to engage with existing capitalist distribution systems or to construct alternative networks, question of the appropriate film language to express conditions of underdevelopment, question of national reality and the relations between filmmakers and 'the people' (King 1990: 69). These questions, which were already being confronted in Latin American contexts as different as Cuba, Brazil and Argentina, would become especially pressing in the political transformations in Chile unleashed by the election of the Allende government, described by Ruiz in retrospect as a social laboratory in which different forms of utopia were tested, 'three years of quite costly experiences' (Ruiz in Buci-Glucksmann and Revault d'Allones 1987: 92).

Ruiz in the Context of Socialist Realism

The development of Ruiz's cinema after *Three Sad Tigers* was profoundly affected by the political process that was a consequence of the election of the Allende Popular Unity government, to the extent that a certain 'new wave' Ruizian cinema, which might have followed on from *Three Sad Tigers*, had neither the opportunity, nor the resources, nor the inclination on the part of Ruiz to be further developed with the possible exception of one Allende period film, *Nadie dijo nada* (*Nobody Said Anything*, 1971). Even the one other completed pre-Allende short film, *Militarismo y Tortura* (*Militarism and Torture*, 1969), seemed to point ahead not only to the politicisation of the Allende period but to its aftermath, in its juxtaposition of military training and brutal torture, a combination that would also characterise Ruiz's later film, *The Penal Colony* (1970). Produced by the Catholic Film Institute of the University of Chile, the film was a collaboration with the Aleph theatre group. The film is based on the alternation of the two autonomous series dealing with torture and military training respectively that over the course of the film come to increasingly encounter and interfere with one another. The resonance with the *coup d'etat* that would take place four years later, which similarly articulated militarism with torture, hardly needs to be spelt out. What is perhaps more significant is the use of this structure of interfering series that would be repeated with variations in many of Ruiz's later films, the beginnings of a combinatory method of investigating the relations between images and complicating the linear conventions of narrative filmmaking. In fact, Ruiz said of the films of this period that he remembers the structures more than the content.

Accounting for Ruiz's filmmaking during the Allende period presents a number of difficulties, not least being the difficulties in actually obtaining the films themselves. Furthermore, even those films that are obtainable tend to circulate in poor quality and incomplete versions. But the difficulty is not only in getting to see these films but also in being able to understand them today, since in many cases they were explicitly intended as part of a complex political process, the 'costly experiment' of Popular Unity socialism referred to above and therefore resistant to conventional 'capitalist' forms of consumption based on spectacle and entertainment. A comparison could be made with the difference between the films of Godard before 1968 and those of the Dziga Vertov group, especially in the sense that several of the films Ruiz made at this time were also experiments in collective means of expression or at least steps in that direction; however, whereas Godard, Gorin and their collaborators were trying to imagine a post-capitalist society that was in reality limited to a militant counter-culture, if it existed at all, Ruiz's films were taking place in the context of national political process, and can be seen as the attempt to come up with a cultural or artistic equivalent to the material, economic and social transformations that were taking place in Chile in the antagonistic and sometimes contradictory manner already described. Therefore it makes no sense to compare the films from this period either to conventional Hollywood cinema or European art cinema but instead they should be contrasted with the other strategies adopted by both Chilean and other Latin American filmmakers whose work was addressed to comparable social and political conditions. In this regard, we have already seen Ruiz's rejection of both the obligation to make documentaries, the choice of several of his contemporaries such as Patricio Guzmán, director of *La Batalla de Chile* (*The Battle of Chile*, 1975/77/79), and his even stronger rejection of the third cinema mode of militant filmmaking as both bad militancy and bad cinema.

In terms of fiction, the dominant mode during the Allende period was a type of heroic Socialist Realism that had been already developed by filmmakers such as Soto and arguably even Littín, albeit in a more complex manner than his contemporaries. This form of Socialist Realism, however, has to be distinguished from its Soviet versions in which it was an official policy imposed on writers, artists and filmmakers, whose contravention might lead to the premature end of creative careers, imprisonment or exile. Even if the Allende government had wanted to impose some kind of state directives on its filmmakers, it was far too chaotic and too concerned with other matters to do so in any consistent way. So if there was a tendency towards Socialist Realism it was entirely generated by the filmmakers themselves, as was evident in the already cited manifesto. Of course, the films that were produced were certainly the subject of debate in publications of various political persuasions but, at least according to Ruiz's own account of this period, he never encountered any direct censorship from the government, however much his films might have called into question official policies such as land expropriation. In fact he stated that political disapproval of his films tended to come from other artists who were much more hard-line than the government itself:

> From the side of the government I had very few problems. According to them, to find an artist who was interested in politics was in itself a marvellous thing and one worth preserving. What's more, if this artist intervened to point out what wasn't going well, that one could do better, he was all the more appreciated. (Ruiz in Buci-Glucksmannn and Revault d'Allones 1987: 93)

For Ruiz, the tendency towards Socialist Realism was not due to government pressure but constituted a kind of artistic temptation, given the desire to support what the government was doing on the part of filmmakers which could lead ultimately to a sort of national mythmaking rather than a real engagement with the political process, especially given that key filmmakers including Ruiz and Littín were directly involved with the Popular Unity Party and Chile Films. Both Soto and Littín, for example, had made films about triumphant moments from Chilean history granting national or popular figures heroic status. Ruiz, while sharing the same 'programme' as his contemporaries, nevertheless considered it crucial to resist this temptation: 'The first temptation is to 'create' the men who created Chile; in short, to devote ourselves to the exaltation of our supposed national heroes, popular heroes, to foster the popularity of these heroes, making films about O'Higgins, Manuel Rodriguez and the other sacred monsters. Creation of this kind seems easy enough to me, but quite dangerous' (Ruiz in Chanan 1976: 30). Ruiz was equally suspicious of the fetishisation of indigenous Indian culture and its combination with socialism that had developed out of the popular song movement, which he referred to as the 'Quilapayún type of culture' (1976: 32) and saw as an equally dangerous sort of kitsch, ersatz socialist culture, the failed attempt to dress up 'progressive content' in old forms. All of these strategies assume a mimetic efficacy of cinema and other art-forms, their ability to hold up a mirror to society, which for Ruiz is a naïve approach to political cinema; if cinema is able to reflect society it is only, for Ruiz, in an inverted form, that necessarily distorts or falsifies its social context. In this situation, the only authentic way of making films is to do so in a way that acknowledges the imperfections of cinematic representation, one that foregrounds its distortions, which can use cinema to show what is usually hidden in 'normal' perception, in other words the 'optical unconscious' of a given social formation.

It is in this context that Ruiz preferred to a single strategy, the adoption of three inter-related modes of filmmaking; the abovementioned engaged, propagandist and expressive modes of cinema. The maintenance of an expressive dimension of cinema is crucial here as it attempts to forego the sacrifice of an artistic dimension in the favour of the utilitarian pressures involved in building a new society. Ruiz in this way accepted the civic obligation of the filmmaker not only to promote government policies but more importantly to make the means of cinematic production available to workers and peasants, for example through the setting up of film workshops in centres of artisanal and industrial production, to make films with workers, local story tellers and performers and not just about them. However, this did not entail giving up the expressive or investigative elements of his cinema but rather allowing it to be profoundly affected by the surrounding political and social environment: 'our aim was that the cinema, born from the workers' base and with the help of the working laboratory would excite such ferment that this would decidedly influence the films which actually had artistic objectives' (Ruiz in Chanan 1976: 32). The extent to which Ruiz's films of this period were the expression of these aims cannot be overemphasised.

Que Hacer? (*What is to be Done?*, 1970), which started out as a simple collaboration with the left-wing US documentary filmmaker Saul Landau, certainly seems to have been characterised by a collective process but apparently a highly conflictual one, whose results were not entirely satisfactory. According to Ruiz, the project began from the desire to expand on his 'more or less irreverent and irresponsible conversations' (1976: 38) with the American filmmaker, to portray the less heroic, everyday aspects of a revolutionary process before it became codified into a unified mythology. However, both filmmakers feared that this 'free adventure' was flying in the face of history and tended to question every aspect of it, in relation to the debates on culture unleashed by the Allende victory. According to Ruiz, their 'group became a parliament' and 'whoever came along and watched us shooting, directed a couple of scenes as well' (1976: 38). While Ruiz at the time he was interviewed had not seen the film, he understood it to be mostly worthless and certainly did not claim it as his own. A review in the New York Times in 1973, after the coup, described it as 'a deft blend of fiction and documentary [...] mordant, self-aware, wary of caricature' (Van Gelder 1973: 73), all qualities that show the imprint of Ruiz's filmmaking of this time, even if his actual involvement in the finished film was limited. Ruiz's reaction to the excess of political discussion that characterised this film was to make *The Penal Colony*, which undoubtedly was an example of expressive rather than collective filmmaking even if the film suggests a political reading. Ruiz himself described the film as being about the conditions of existence of Latin America, which is presented in terms of torture, militarism and economic dependence; as this film is the Allende period film that has had the widest circulation it will be engaged with in more detail shortly; apparently the film was funded by a friend's inheritance.

Ruiz's next film *Nobody Said Anything*, was equally at odds with the politics of the present, being a combination of a return to the milieu of *Three Sad Tigers*, coupled with an engagement with the problem of nationalism, which at this time was by no means a central political issue. The partial explanation for the anomaly of this film, which seems to be at once a throwback to Ruiz's pre-Allende chaste realism and to anticipate his subsequent development of a baroque style, is that it was co-funded by the Italian TV Network RAI as part of its 'Latin America as Seen by its Filmmakers' series that also funded films in other Latin American countries. Therefore it was aimed at an international audience rather than a domestic one familiar with the complexities of Allende-era politics. While this film features some of the same Santiagistas as *Three Sad Tigers*, both they and their surroundings seem considerably more dilapidated than two years previously. This time round, however, the drinkers roaming the streets of Santiago are writers who, according to Ruiz 'live in their own reality and imagine it is Chile' (Ruiz in Chanan 1976: 39). The story, loosely adapted from the story *Enoch Soames* (1919) by Max Beerbohm, concerns a writer who, through a pact with the devil, is able to travel into the future to discover from this perspective whether he will be remembered as a great writer. The film is the story of what is revealed to him. While there are certainly elements of a critique of the intelligentsia who remain disconnected from social realities, the film itself is disconnected from its political present and seems more an ambivalent farewell to Ruiz's pre-Allende artistic social world, now rendered anachronistic due to the political transformations that remain off-screen and conforming to Rojas's already cited predictions of the inevitably alcoholic outcome of chaste realism (2004: 9). According to Rosenbaum (1995: 224), Ruiz made this film so cheaply he was able to use the remaining funding for his next two major film projects.

The same year as this film, Ruiz also completed the didactic short, *Ahora te vamos a llamar hermano* (*Now We are Going to Call you Brother*, 1971). This film set the tone for productions to follow in that even when dealing with official government policies, in this case the granting of full civil and political rights to the indigenous Mapuche Indians, the first legal action of the Allende government, Ruiz took an ironic, problematising approach to political issues rather than a strictly propagandistic one. The procedure here, as in other didactic films, was to confront the ideals of official government policies, with the realities of their realisation, a gap that Ruiz typically presented through irony. In his words, 'irony is an important tool of political analysis ... [it] is necessary to refresh and clarify our perception of things' (Ruiz cited in King 1990: 177). Ruiz took this ironic approach even further in his next major film, *La expropriación* (*The Expropriation*, 1971), which again concerned a central government policy. Expropriation was the practice of taking land from the hands of wealthy land-owners and redistributing it to the peasants who worked on it and was both an official government practice and a key element of the extra-governmental practice of popular power, often backed up by groups such as MIR. In Ruiz's film, a paradoxical case of this practice is presented in which a wealthy land-owner, under the pressure of a government officer charged with implementing this new law of expropriation, agrees to give his land to the peasants; however, they perversely refuse to accept it. The rest of the film concerns the exacerbated government officer's attempts to reason with the peasants and convince them to follow their own interests. Ultimately the peasants threaten then kill the government officer. Again it shows the gap between official policy and actual reality, the ironic resistance of cultural habits to political change, even when these habits seem contradictory. In fact the film presents the resistance of the peasants to a political process imposed by the government officer, whose cultural habits, like those of Allende himself, are every bit as bourgeois as those of the land-owner. This questioning of official policy meant that this was the one film of Ruiz's that was subject to a form of censorship; while it was given a limited release on the pretext of its length, in reality its approach to the issue of expropriation was considered too incendiary to be shown to the general public, perhaps for fear of peasants taking its critique too literally and taking expropriation into their own hands, which did indeed happen in many cases after 1972. The film is also of interest in that it combined narrative complexity with elements of documentary reality so that when the peasants are denouncing the government officer, this is in fact the expression of real attitudes towards the new government.

The fullest development of this kind of film-making, however, came with the four hour film *El realismo socialista* (*Socialist Realism,* 1973) of which no complete version currently exists. Ruiz once again employed the parallel structure that had characterised *Militarism and Torture,* in this case to present the twin trajectories of a petit-bourgeois intellectual, who works as a publicist for the conservative opposition, who becomes increasingly militant, joining a party of the extreme left, and developing utopian and much reflected upon political projects. The other thread concerns a worker who becomes increasingly involved with the extreme right, an unpopular but timely subject to deal with considering the subsequent involvement and support of truck drivers and army personnel in the Pinochet coup. The worker participates in a collective factory occupation and then steals essential materials in order to start his own factory and so is expelled by his co-workers. The activist in his turn is rejected by the organisation he works for, for his support of the class enemy and fearing for his life, retains the services of a bodyguard, who turns out to be none other than the right-wing worker. Eventually the intellectual is driven to despair at the failure of his political projects, while the worker becomes involved in acts of sabotage and terrorism. Again Ruiz combined a complex fictional structure with elements of realism by using real militants, both workers and intellectuals and allowing them to improvise real debates that responded to key problems and experiences of the political transformations that were currently taking place. According to Tesson this provoked not only wild debates but physical fights among the two camps represented in the film (Tesson 1983: 16).

Incongruously, for such a politically charged context, Ruiz has referred to this film as a kind of game, but it is a serious type of game based on activating already existing social dynamics. The way the game worked was simply to provoke certain relations among the performers, which would then be amplified in the relations between the film and its viewers, given that all of the above elements were participants in the same intense political process. In Ruiz's words:

> We were living within a political reality that was so intense that in order to represent it, it was enough to bring three workers together, tell them that somebody intended to occupy a factory, that the Party thought they should prevent it, and the thing proceeded by itself. (Ruiz in Chanan 1976: 36).

In other words, as opposed to the Socialist Realism referred to in the title of the film, that would aim to heroically represent the unity of the revolution as a united struggle of workers and intellectuals, Ruiz was aiming more at incorporating the dissonances between different elements of the revolutionary process directly, in a sense without the mediation of representation, despite the framing of politics within an elaborate fictional structure. Again it is very much a case of the attempt to capture the political unconscious, the way politics is actually lived, rather than how it tends to be represented according to a unified, linear and propagandistic story. This is not to deny the clearly didactic function of this and other films Ruiz made at the time but rather to emphasise the way that this didacticism was pursued through a thorough search for an adequate cinematic form to present political reality as it unfolded rather than an official truth only existing in the optimistic dreams of government members. From Ruiz's point of view to be truly for the revolutionary process meant being willing to question its most central beliefs and practices, in order to support the reality of the political process and oppose any retreat into empty ideals, ideologies and utopias.

At the end of Ruiz's interview with Francesco Bolzoni included in Chanan's book, he summed up his position in the following terms that are worth quoting at length:

> If you have a minimum feeling for the people around you, and you see that they change, you are obliged to change what you show. If, moreover ... you are a militant in a Marxist party you are obliged to reflect upon certain events. You realise that the instruments of information, once concentrated in the hands of the right, will soon belong to the left. [...] It means that if nothing else, there will be a way of making cinema which allows greater participation, a cinema endowed with a greater possibility of analysis, more open to daily life, a cinema that truly tries to transform our reality. (Ruiz in Chanan 1976: 40)

This quote clearly delineates a militant cinematic project, to put it in terms that Godard articulated but was not able to pursue as radically as Ruiz, of making films politically rather than making political films, meaning a cinema in proximity to and incorporating a living political process rather than representing it through the exemplary political stereotypes of Socialist Realism. Once again this is a cinematic path that was cut short by political events themselves, this time the Pinochet coup of September, 1973, which had the effect of rendering Chilean cinema within Chile impossible and forcing it into exile.

The Penal Colony

Franz Kafka's story, 'In the Penal Colony' (1919/2007), is a uniquely prescient example of European literary modernism in its combination of militarism, colonialism and torture.[10] This type of combination was so much a part of Latin American reality that Ruiz has gone so far as to say that 'for us, Kafka is a Latin American writer' (Ruiz in Buci-Glucksmann and Revault d'Allones 1987: 85). As was typical for Ruiz both at this time and throughout his career with a few recent exceptions, adaptation in this case was much more a case of inspiration than representation, although the imaginary island that Ruiz invented certainly does have some of the atmosphere of the Penal Colony described by Kafka. Ruiz has stated that despite the apparent departure from the realist anti-illusionism of his other Allende period films, the penal colony does have a link to political realities in that it depicts the conditions of existence of Latin America in a metaphorical or allegorical form. At the beginning of the film we are given a brief history of the island, somewhere off the coast of Ecuador or Peru in which the action takes place; a former leper colony, it was later a penitentiary, before being consecutively a pilot community funded by the United Nations and then a free territory. However, all these historical layers seem to co-exist in the present constitution of the island which is now a form of socialist dictatorship. The key to the whole film, which in typical Ruizian fashion is withheld, at least from the only print currently circulating, is that the sole export of the island is the production of news stories about torture, hence associating the brutality that takes place on the island with its situation of economic dependency on the West. The entire island seems to be a militarised zone and its inhabitants speak a non-existent language composed of fragments of archaic Spanish and English. A journalist arrives on the island and is entertained by the dictator himself, who insists on singing to her and soon gets to witness the anticipated scenes of torture. However, due to her reports being unfavourably received she ends up herself becoming imprisoned and will presumably also be subject to torture.

Essentially the film consists of a series of vignettes, often separated by a black screen largely based on Western stereotypes about Latin America. For example, the dictator talks about how he loves his people, that they are like children and so on. As with *Three Sad Tigers,* Ruiz uses these apparently superficial stereotypes to reveal gestures that constitute a political cartography of the effects of economic and political dependency. Anomalous as the film might have been in the context of Allende's Chile, where it was viewed as being totally disconnected from political reality, subsequent events, not only the Pinochet coup but the ascendancy of military dictatorships and torture throughout Latin America show the film to be extremely perspicacious and even prophetic. Crucial in this is the implication of the Western media in the 'conditions of existence of Latin America' implying that for the West, the rest of the world does indeed exist to provide horrific news stories for media consumption. In this regard, despite the radical differences in style, the film is not that far removed from the Cuban film *Memorias del subdesarrollo* (*Memores of Underdevelopment,* Alea, 1968), in its presentation of the effects of unequal relations of continental dependency, albeit in more abstract and allegorical form. However, as Ian Christie points out, the film also resonates both with Ruiz's origins as an absurdist playwright and his later development as a 'European' filmmaker, especially in its deployment of absurd and surreal scenes such as the rattling of sabres, the singing of the dictator and the enactment of torture scenes based on magical realist novels (Christie 2004b).

Towards the end of the Allende period, it seems Ruiz's filmmaking, after the didactic projects such as *The Expropriation* and *Socialist Realism,* was returning towards equally anomalous terrain in his adaptation of *Palomita Blanca* (1971), a melodramatic and, in Ruiz's own account, reactionary populist novel. However, this project was interrupted due to the Pinochet coup after which Ruiz soon left the country in circumstances which he presents as fortuitous but not dramatic, despite the fact that given the dictatorship's 'interest' in other cultural figures on the left including filmmakers, some of whom were imprisoned, tortured and killed, meant that Ruiz himself, could well have been a future target of the dictatorship. In any event it was clear that the new Chilean cinema had become impossible within Chile and Ruiz, along with many of his contemporaries, could only continue his work in a diasporic setting; in Ruiz's case, Paris, the 'capital of cinema' and a favoured site of Chilean and Latin American exile.

PART 2: FROM THE 'DIALECTICS OF EXILE' TO THE *TABLEAU VIVANT*

The 'Dialectics of Exile'

> The best school for dialectics is emigration. The most penetrating dialecticians are exiles. There are changes that have forced them into exile, and they are interested only in changes. (Brecht cited in Ruiz, *Diálogos de exilados, Dialogues of Exiles* 1975).

Ruiz's first film in France, (*Dialogues of Exiles,* 1975) seems to have been designed so as to be incomprehensible to anyone outside the world of Chilean refugees from the Pinochet coup, who are treated in the film in such an ironic way that it is little surprise that for the most part they were highly provoked by and critical of the film. However, it seems that Ruiz, in the course of making the film, did not consider it a provocation so much as a kind of ethnographic observation of the speech, gestures and behaviours of those in exile, similar to what he had done in relation to different sectors of Chilean society in his earlier films. In a sense it could be argued that this film involved a type of 'objective irony' in that in the time between its production and its very limited release, many of the political projects of the exiles portrayed in the film had disintegrated, thus rendering the film an image of the futilities of exile that was highly aggravating to this particular community. In other words it was the situation of the exiles itself that had become ironic as they strived to continue living in a Chile which no longer existed, despite both historical events and geographical dislocation.

As for Ruiz's own geographical dislocation, according to the director it was only by chance that he wound up settling in Paris. That it could well have been otherwise is evident in that the first two films he made after leaving Chile had nothing to do with France and only appeared after *Dialogues of Exiles* had already been released; the first, *El cuerpo repartido y el mundo al reves/Utopia* (*The Scattered Body and the World Upside Down/Utopia*, 1975), was conceived during the Allende period and was intended to be shot in Peru; in the end it was funded by German television and made in Honduras and then only screened in a mutilated sixty minute version. In fact, one month after the coup and following the arrest of filmmaker Patricio Guzmán, Ruiz claims he had just decided to leave Chile, when he received an invitation from his friend Peter Lilienthal, to come to Germany to make this film for ZDF. Ruiz's departure from Chile, therefore took place relatively undramatically, although even if he had not been arrested, there is no way he could have continued his cinematic activities in Chile. The film concerns two travellers trying to trace the dispersed body parts of a corpse, while at each site a body part is located some aspect of utopian socialism is played out by the local peasants. Despite being one of Ruiz's least seen films, it is nevertheless often referred to as one of his most emblematic films and certainly several elements would reappear in later works. As Gilbert Adair put, 'nothing in his oeuvre could be more certifiably "Ruizian" ' (Adair 1982: 42). The less than satisfactory experience of working with German television dissuaded Ruiz from remaining in Germany and to look for new projects elsewhere. Ruiz's next film *Sotelo* (1976), a short film about the exiled Chilean Painter Raúl Sotomayor or Sotelo was funded by the United Nations High Commission for Refugees in Geneva and focused on the voice of the painter Sotelo rather than his paintings. As such it was a forerunner to several subsequent films by Ruiz portraying artists. Both of these projects were interim ones, which expressed Ruiz's own transitional status between being a Chilean filmmaker in exile and making films that fully engaged with his new context. It was in the midst of these projects, when Ruiz was visiting friends in Paris, that he hit on the idea of making a film about the lives of Chilean exiles at a time when his own exile was as fresh as that of the people represented in the film

Before examining *Dialogues of Exiles* more closely, however, it is worth examining the situation of Chilean cinema in exile at this time. While exile has been a key feature of many Latin American cinemas, Chilean cinema was unique in that in this case an entire cinema that was just starting to develop was forced into exile. According to Zuzana Pick, writing about the decade immediately following the coup, around one hundred and fifty five films were made by Chilean directors in exile in a variety of different international contexts (Pick 1987: 66) and it was only in the late 1970s that any kind of cinema began to re-emerge in Chile and then only sporadically and under the threat of censorship and repression from the Pinochet regime. This exilic cinema while by no means unified in style or content, nevertheless shared general features, which can be characterised in two periods; a working through of the shock of the coup, and an exploration of the dynamics of life in exile. So in a sense it could be said that Ruiz's film was merely anticipating a kind of ethnography of exile that would indeed characterise a good deal of Chilean cinema in exile but only at a later moment in time. However, in 1974, Ruiz's immediate contemporaries were making films under the shadow of the coup such as Littín's *Actas de Marusia* (*Letters from*

Marusia, 1975), which concerned an allegorical account of the massacre of Chilean miners in 1907, or Soto's more direct *Llueve sobre Santiago* (*It's Raining on Santiago*, 1975). Even more powerful than these fictional films was Patricio Guzmán's *The Battle of Chile*, an epic three part documentary that began as a documentary about the third year of the Allende government and became a harrowing record of the coup itself. The footage for this film only survived by being smuggled out of the country to Cuba, where the director was able to edit it in three instalments over the course of the 1970s. It was in relation to films such as these that Ruiz made the following statement that goes some way toward explaining the apparent perversity of making a comedy about Chilean exiles at this particular historical juncture:

> I think there is a version of the 'official art' attitude which sets out to make 'history' exist. They start with the history of Latin America, which is a history of massacres and betrayals and of imperialism, the massacres are mostly hidden and the record of the peasants' and people's movements is equally unknown. So there is an obvious point in revealing this secret history [...] But this is more difficult to accept when it becomes an imperative duty to follow the political line, showing even more massacres and creating a vast funeral ceremony. (Ruiz cited in King: 181–182)

Again it is a question of sacred monsters and a ritualistic repetition of political mantras which is precisely what *Dialogues of Exiles* exposes to a critical and ludic eye. Nevertheless, rather than render the film apolitical, this is merely the abandonment of politics in the sense of an organising historical mythology in favour of a detailed examination of the micropolitical or ethnographic question of how politics is actually lived. For this reason, *Dialogues of Exiles* should not be considered as a break from Ruiz's 'political' Chilean filmmaking, which would come soon afterwards, but more as his last 'non-illusionist' Chilean film in that its scrutiny of the comportment, gestures and speech of exiles is a direct continuation of his Allende period films; what has changed is the context not Ruiz's interest in a 'culture of resistance', or the political unconscious revealed by everyday gestures and behaviours rather than ideological positions. Both the exilic behaviours depicted in the film and its icy reception, certainly render ironic the epigraph from Brecht cited at the beginning of the film. It seems as if Chilean exiles in 1974 were resistant to rather than embracing of change, and instead of combining more than one context productively, as Ruiz would subsequently do, were instead stranded in the void between dreams of the vanished 'former Chile' of Allende, and their adopted home which they were yet to fully inhabit.

Dialogues of Exiles

Dialogues of Exiles has to be understood in relation to the precise and surprising conditions of its production. Ruiz began the film only one month after arriving in Paris, as a new exile himself and used the film to speculate prospectively on the problems the leftist Chilean *émigrés* were likely to face in exile ranging from dealing with overcrowded accommodation, employment problems and dealing with French solidarity organisations to how to continue political engagements after the historical defeat and geographical break precipitated by the Pinochet coup. In a sense it could therefore be understood as a kind of science fiction. However, what accounts for the hostile reception of the film is that all the micropolitical problems it imagined had actually taken place by the time of the film's release, particularly the difficulties in maintaining political commitments in the situation of exile, which objectively gave the film an unintended and unwelcome satirical edge with regard to the community it presents. Nevertheless, viewing the film outside of its immediate context, it is now a fascinating document of both specifically Chilean and more general experiences of exile, a type of 'accented cinema' to use Naficy's term, that makes a virtue out of minimal funding and an improvisational approach to filmmaking that approaches the performative experience of exile itself. As such it is both distinct from Ruiz's earlier 'chaste realism' and the more baroque style he would soon develop and is therefore a pivotal film in Ruiz's career that to a certain extent stands apart for his other work.

The opening scene in the film is, as Zuzana Pick has pointed out (Pick 2004), emblematic of the film as a whole and the existential situation of Chilean exile. Two men are chatting in an office and the first, who appears to be North African is asking the other where the country is that he is from. As a response to all the suggested options, ranging from Italy and Portugal to Indonesia, Mozambique and Angola, the Chilean character always answers in the same way, 'no further, much further away'. This continues until the Algerian character gives up guessing the Chilean's origins while the latter still repeats 'further, much further away'. This not only indicates the displacement of exile but positions exile from Chile as being almost a second degree of exile, as if the distance from Chile was such as to exceed the usual categories and experiences of exile from nearer countries. If there is this doubling of exile, however, it soon reveals itself to be not so much geographical as political in that the Chilean characters in the film are not only spatial exiles but exiles from the no longer existing Chile of Allende, which they nevertheless attempt to perpetuate in the unfavourable conditions of their Parisian exile. This is what adds to the sense of these exiles being 'far away,' not only from their origins but from their adopted reality, or indeed from reality in general.

This double dislocation is reinforced in the film through various anomalies of behaviour and speech that range from a discussion of the differences between the taste of meat in France and Chile that is concluded by discussion of meat consumption in Cuba, through to a hunger strike conducted by a single man, despite it being disapproved of by his comrades. These behaviours generally result in incomprehension from the French leftists who, while full of good intentions and polite conversation, cannot refrain from judging the exiles according to their own, generally bourgeois, European standards and norms of behaviour. For example, shortly after the discussion about meat, a French woman, representing a political organisation that has presumably made the apartment available for the exiles gives a litany of the inappropriate actions the exiles have been indulging in such as making too much noise, not disposing of rubbish properly or letting their children play in the corridor rather than the courtyard. Not even allowing enough time for her speech to be translated, she simply produces a judgemental discourse on the Chileans that they have no opportunity to take in or respond to and then departs. A more humorous incident comes when a doctor who is giving medical advice about the Chilean hunger striker remarks on the overcrowded apartment where the Chileans are staying, saying that someone should help. The Chileans' reply is to ask how many people he will take into his own house, to which the doctor, clearly taken aback to have his sympathy taken so literally, says one and only because he now feels obligated. All of these examples of cross-cultural non-communication could take place in relation to any group of exiles but the extent to which the Chileans are maintaining their former modes of behaviour and expectations, especially in relation to politics, expresses not only a cultural but a political dislocation between the exiles and their hosts; they simply do not share a common praxis whether of everyday life or of political organisation.

While much of the film is episodic and verges on a documentary style, especially since it is interspersed with scenes of the exiles being interviewed about such issues as what they dream about in exile, there is nevertheless a central storyline about the kidnapping of a popular Chilean singer associated with the Pinochet regime, who is on tour in France. This kidnapping is, however, conducted in an anomalous fashion amounting to little more than excessive hospitality. The singer is simply invited to a party to be given for him at the apartment where he will be 'held'; various different people speak with him and ultimately he becomes integrated into the daily lives of the left-wing exiles who he comes to feel an affectionate bond with, which is only partially reciprocated. Soon he is chatting with musicians, singing Boleros and talking about how Chileans are all one big happy family to the irritation of his captors. As the kidnapping progresses it becomes clear that the kidnappers do not really know what goals they can achieve, eventually 'releasing' their hostage in as casual a manner as they captured him by sending him away from a Marxist-Leninist re-education session for reasons of ideological incompatibility; it is only when the singer returns to his hotel that he learns that he has been kidnapped. All these aspects of the central narrative tend to deflate its importance and most of the film is given over to other characters and situations which would normally be presented as peripheral or secondary; Ruiz referred to this as a deliberate strategy of going against the 'habitual pyramid' of commercial cinema that privileges a central story and character over others and it can also be read as a challenge to received ideas about centre and periphery, highly related to the situation of exile itself. Certainly one can see in this strategy the ideas Ruiz would later formulate as a critique of 'central conflict theory' (Ruiz 1995: 9–23) and that would also be crucial to his filmmaking practice in exile.

Key to the film are the relations of the exiles both to the spaces they inhabit and to money. In the principal apartment where the film is set, a seemingly endless series of exiles arrive, struggling to find the necessary floor space in which to lie down. This overpopulation of space seems to have an effect on the space of the apartment itself, which is constantly being modified through the opening and closing of room dividers, continual entrances and exits not only through doors but through windows, all of which express an unstable relationship with the space being inhabited. It also results in uncomfortable relations with neighbours, not only with the French political group that is housing them but also with other exiles. However, these difficult relations are not limited to relations with others but are also apparent in relations between the exiles, which are still conducted in political terms that have little sense outside the former political groupings in Chile. For example, at one point a working class member of a communist organisation objects to a causal conversation between two 'activists' as being too intellectual and therefore alienating the Chilean working class, using the example of one man who did not want to listen to them as evidence for his intervention. Another man soon after accosts one of the men and accuses him of being a CIA agent. In another scene, a woman who does not want to go out with an Algerian man, who even threatens her with a knife, is reprimanded for behaviour that could be construed as racist and therefore give Chileans a bad name, since Chileans never have been and never should be racists; she should therefore overcome her 'individualism' and make the small sacrifice of going out with the Algerian whether she wants to or not. The film is full of such examples that demonstrate the maintenance of former political positions, attitudes and divisions among the Chilean exiles, which no longer make much sense in the new context of exile and from which nothing seems to have been learned.

In terms of money, a controversial series of scenes occurs in which a large sum of money intended for the MIR organisation passes through various hands, each of which deducts a certain amount from it for expenses such as accommodation, telephone bills and so on, drastically reducing the original sum of 10,000 US dollars. This is not the only sum of money that goes missing, however, since another sum of money is given by a French organisation for the airfare of someone in danger in Chile and then nothing is heard again from the recipients of the money. Both these incidents testify once more to a type of flexibility in relations to economic arrangements, in which the exchange of money becomes subject to all kinds of political justifications, and disappoints the strict accountability desired by the French hosts; on the other hand the lack of generosity of the French sympathisers is equally disappointing to the exiles, whose difficulties in everyday life are of little interest to the professional leftists, who prefer to demonstrate their engagement in international politics through fine speeches rather than actions which would actually be directly helpful for the exiles. The film stops short of insinuating that the exiles are simply stealing money destined for political purposes, although it was taken that way by some viewers, who used these examples to argue that the film's negative portrayal 'gave a bad impression of the Chilean émigrés that could be manipulated by right wing and anti-Chilean organisations' (Ruiz, cited in Bax *et al.* 2003: 114).

In short, what the film demonstrates, as a type of prospective critique of exile, is the impossibility and absurdity of maintaining the political investments of the Allende period in the situation of exile, as well as the failures of attempts to form alliances between the Chilean and the French left, due to the incompatibility of their experiences and modes of behaviour and action. However, it does all this on a micropolitical scale in which, as in Ruiz's Allende period films, it is through a minute attention to the details of gestures, behaviours and speech that an ironic politics emerges. This takes place precisely by showing how good political intentions inevitably run aground in the murky realm of everyday life in the conditions of exile. Ruiz wanted to avoid absolutely any analysis of the situation in Chile, partly because that had already been done but mainly in order to make a film about the 'political experience of exile' (2003: 114). However, whereas Ruiz's ironic critique of political stereotypes by means of the everyday or the ethnographic could be accepted during the Allende period as a necessary corrective to taking political dogmas for realities, in the situation of exile, it was received as an unwelcome reflection, a slap in the face for the attempts of the exiles at maintaining political solidarity, which were running into all of the problems that were predicted in the film. And yet Ruiz's intentions were not to attack the exile community so much as to pose some of the essential problems it was likely to face, to make a 'wise, rather than an annoying film,' a confrontation that could just as well have been taken as a positive contribution to the political situation of the exiles. Ruiz's own response to seeing the film was that it was 'healthier than the one we wanted to make at the beginning, the film in which we would have proclaimed that we escaped like lions' (Bonitzer *et al.* 1978: 19). Nevertheless, the end result was that after this film, there was a pronounced break between Ruiz and the Chilean exile community, especially those involved in leftist politics and Ruiz's filmmaking would only resume when he could forge links with French filmmaking institutions, in the first instance meaning L'Institut National de l'Audiovisuel (INA) and *Cahiers du Cinéma*. Nevertheless, even then it was not so much a total break as a passage 'from one institution to another' as an important *Cahiers du Cinéma* interview would put it (Ruiz, Bonitzer *et al.* 1978: 19–23), in which the political aesthetics or the 'chaste realism' of Ruiz's Allende period cinema would be not so much abandoned as transformed.

Ruiz, the INA and Cahiers du Cinéma

One of the problems posed explicitly by *Dialogues of Exiles,* that was no less a problem for Ruiz himself than the exiles who populated his film, was the problem of how to work and make a living in the adopted context of exile. Ruiz claimed his adoption of Paris as a new base was entirely accidental, being based on deciding to make his first major post-Chilean film there and then finding himself with debt substantial enough to preclude relocating elsewhere. He even went so far as to claim that rather than a Chilean or a French film, *Dialogues of Exiles* was a Panamanian one, in other words a transatlantic account of exile that only happened to take place in France. However, once it became clear that Ruiz would be based in France for some time, this necessitated forming new relations to audio-visual institutions in France.

This next step would be realised via two French cinematic 'institutions', namely the influential journal *Cahiers du Cinéma* and the INA. While *Cahiers du Cinéma* may not have written much about Ruiz until the late 1970s, from this point on Ruiz started to forge relationships with some of the key writers from the journal, several of whom would appear in Ruiz's next films. Notable amongst them was Pascal Bonitzer who not only appeared in several of Ruiz's early French films but also wrote about Ruiz and later on wrote scripts for him as well. Another key figure who was highly supportive of Ruiz's films was Serge Daney, the main editor of *Cahiers du Cinéma* in the period of the late 1970s during the review's 'return to cinema' after its militant period of the first half of the decade. For the *Cahiers du Cinéma* of this period, which was notable not only for its attention to marginal and radical forms of cinema ranging from Jean-Luc Godard and Jean-Marie Straub to various exponents of Third Cinema but also for its interest in intellectual figures such as Gilles Deleuze and Michel Foucault, Ruiz was an ideal filmmaker, since he seemed to combine both this philosophical approach to cinema with impeccable political credentials but without any militant dogmatism.[11] As early as 1979, the journal included not only analyses of Ruiz's films but also the director's writing beginning with his article 'Object Relations in the Cinema' and throughout the 1980s and 1990s there would be several special issues devoted to Ruiz and articles even on his most obscure films. From Ruiz's side, he claims that he admired and was amused by the way *Cahiers du Cinéma* would pay so much attention to 'small films' that virtually no-one had seen, such as the early work of Jean-Marie Straub, and produce minute and serious analyses of films that the general public was entirely indifferent to, and devote entire issues to them. He has also stated that despite this cinematic purism the *Cahiers* writers were *bon vivants* and he enjoyed preparing them Chilean dishes which they labelled as being 'avant-garde' (Ruiz in Prieur 2006). This led to Ruiz's decision, when casting his first properly French production, *La vocation suspendue* (*The Suspended Vocation*, 1977), to cast the writer Pascal Bonitzer in one of the principal roles. Pascal Kané also played a role in this film, as did several other *Cahiers* writers and Ruiz claimed that the entire staff of *Cahiers du Cinéma* can be seen constituting the *tableaux vivants* of his subsequent film, *The Hypothesis of the Stolen Painting* (1978).

Once Ruiz's films had been embraced by *Cahiers du Cinéma* and other critics and therefore given some exposure in France, Ruiz showed some of his work to the INA, which was interested in producing work that was neither purely experimental, nor straightforwardly narrative but fell somewhere inbetween these two poles. As this corresponded closely to the type of films Ruiz was interested in making, it became the beginning of a fruitful partnership, beginning with Ruiz making feature films as part of the INA's *Cinema Je* (*Cinema I*) series, followed by several television commissions. Ironically, it was in this period that Ruiz was to become for the first time a state funded filmmaker, which he had never been in socialist Chile, since Chile Films was not able to fund any of his feature films due more to economic than ideological reasons. This arrangement enabled Ruiz to work quickly, making the next project as soon as the previous one was complete or even working on more than one project simultaneously. This manner of working led Ruiz to be described by David Ehrenstein as the Edgar Ulmer of art cinema (Ehrenstein 1984: 96), but while it enabled Ruiz to keep working at an often astonishing pace, it did not always mean his work could be easily seen, since often it was shown neither in cinemas, since it was commissioned for television, nor on television since the end results frequently departed radically from what those who had commissioned the films had been expecting. As we will see this was especially the case for Ruiz's 1979 film on the French elections. Instead Ruiz's cinema from this early period of exile was a cinema of retrospectives, the principal means by which his films have been able to be seen in locations ranging from Paris and Rotterdam to Sydney, from the late 1970s to the present, although certain of his more recent films have benefited from more regular forms of art cinema distribution.

Both of these institutional relationships led to the realisation of Ruiz's next film, *The Suspended Vocation,* an adaptation of the novel of the same name by Pierre Klossowski which, according to Ruiz, was the first film he had made for which there was a script. Before speculating on why Ruiz's entry into French cinema might have been mediated by the seemingly unlikely figure of Pierre Klossowski, it is worth recounting Ruiz's own account of how this happened, an account that he admits has something of Breton's *Nadja* (1928) about it. Turning up the wrong week for a meeting with the *Positif* writer Michel Ciment in a bookstore, Ruiz says he started reading Klossowski's novel, knowing nothing about it and was completely taken in by its presentation as a 'preface' that turns out to be the entire novel. Later that day he ran into a Surrealist friend Goldfayn, who just happened to be dining with Klossowski the next day and said he would mention the idea of adapting *The Suspended Vocation* to him. Ruiz ran into him again on the street a few days later and his friend reported that Klossowski did not see how that kind of novel could be adapted for the screen and instead suggested his novel *The Baphomet*. Ruiz, however, did not see how he could adapt the latter novel (although it would become one of the elements of his subsequent Klossowski-based film) but had a meeting with Klossowski, who agreed on the filming of *The Suspended Vocation*, signing a release form, even though he apparently wrote Ruiz's name as Raül Rouys, possibly one of the prompts for Ruiz to use the name Raoul, when working in France. This version of events is somewhat complicated by Ruiz's claim in another interview that he came across Klossowski's work when reading Deleuze's *The Logic of Sense* in Panama; there is an appendix of this work that deals with Klossowski's works as a type of anti-theology constituting a 'disjunctive syllogism' between bodies and language (Deleuze 1990: 280–301). However, since *The Suspended Vocation* is the one work of Klossowski's *not* mentioned in Deleuze's essay it is not contradictory to accept both of these accounts of Ruiz's encounter with Klossowski's work. At any rate, Ruiz then took the idea to Jean Baronnet, the INA commissioner for the *Camera Je* series, who had already commissioned novel work by Jean-Luc Godard, Paul Leduc and others, and was surprised to have his proposal and subsequently his script accepted and going into production, since at this point he was rather sceptical of being able to continue his cinematic career in France. While working with the INA did necessitate operating with a finished script, there was an almost total freedom to experiment with its contents as was evident from the response of the INA to the finished film. According to Ruiz, when the film was completed, after a big delay due to an actor's strike of several months and during which time Ruiz made the short film *Colloque de chiens* (*Dog's Dialogue,* 1977), the then chair of INA, a Madame Bertain, apparently responded, 'It's wonderful because no-one will get it' which, according to Ruiz, was pretty much what happened. In the meantime, however, *Dog's Dialogue* had somehow managed to win a César award, an amazing feat since it had only been seen by a very small number of people, more or less guaranteeing 'Raoul Ruiz' a future as a 'French' filmmaker, if a highly anomalous one.

The Suspended Vocation

In order to move beyond the merely anecdotal, it is necessary to briefly examine the work of Pierre Klossowski itself and the place of *The Suspended Vocation* within it, in order to bring out the seemingly improbable affinity Ruiz felt with the latter work. Klossowski had cosmopolitan origins with his father being descended from the Polish nobility and his family having associations with such figures as Rainer Maria Rilke and André Gide. Klossowski's intellectual development was galvanised by his encounter with Georges Bataille, with whom he was closely associated throughout the 1930s and with whom he shared a passionate enthusiasm for figures such as Nietzsche and De Sade about whom both men wrote extensively, in Klossowski's case in his volume *Sade my Neighbour* from 1947. Klossowski was also involved with Bataille on several pre-war projects such as the College of Sociology, with Roger Caillois, and the ritual group Acéphale, which had as its goal the performing of a human sacrifice, in line with the centrality of sacrifice to Bataille's theories of eroticism and transgression. However, unlike Bataille, and despite his interest in monstrosity and atheism, Klossowski had a strong interest in theology and after the outbreak of World War II, joined a Dominican seminary and remained there until after the war, causing a break between the two friends, with Bataille referring to Klossowski derogatively as the Christian Klossowski.

In the 1950s, Klossowski's work went through a new phase and beginning with *The Suspended Vocation,* he wrote a series of novels that, while they may not have found a large readership, certainly attracted the attention of the next generation of intellectuals such as Gilles Deleuze, Jean-François Lyotard and Michel Foucault, with whom Klossowski entertained mutually admiring relations. Amongst a wide variety of works, his treatise on Nietzsche, *Nietzsche and the Vicious Circle* was highly influential, as was his distinctive account of simulacra that crossed his theoretical, fictional and later visual work. In the 1960s, Klossowski began producing large pencil drawings, based on scenes that had also animated his writing, in a sense passing over to the side of the simulacra, rather than merely analysing or describing them as he had done previously. By the time Ruiz would encounter him, this was indeed Klossowski's main creative preoccupation and although his drawing continued themes he had developed in his earlier written work, this was only going as far back as the *Laws of Hospitality* series of novels, oriented around the figure of Roberte, in turn based on his wife Denise Morin-Sinclair. For Klossowski, *The Suspended Vocation,* his first novel which dealt with the period in which he was involved both with the Dominican seminary and the resistance, was a settling of accounts necessary in order to recommence both his life and his work, both of which would, from then on, take place under the ambivalent 'sign' of Roberte. While theology hardly disappeared from Klossowski's novels, it was inseparable from a De Sade influenced pornography, which Deleuze referred to as meriting 'the more exalted title of "pornology" ' (1989b: 18), the elaboration of a range of obsessive phantasms and simulacra that are absent from Klossowski's first novel. In *The Suspended Vocation,* if there is any eroticism, it is more homo-eroticism and the disagreements it presents are not between the body and the spirit, or the Church and lay existence but rather between different factions within the church, its matriarchal and patriarchal currents and heresies, which are at once suggestive of Mediaeval quarrels and contemporary political conflicts.

The Suspended Vocation novel presents itself as part of the genre of modern 'confessional' Christian literature, in which the troubled path to faith of an in this case anonymous believer is detailed, in the hope of convincing susceptible non-believers and confirming for believers the miracles of the Christian faith. More accurately the book is the equally anonymous preface to such an account but one which in its detailed description of the absent work ends up substituting for it entirely, in a procedure worthy of Borges and later to be taken up by the Polish science fiction writer Stanisław Lem. This is the trap in which Ruiz says he himself was caught when reading the book for the first time and which first provoked the idea of adapting it as a film, given Ruiz's fondness for unconventional narrative structures. The doubling in the book does not end with that of the preface and the absent work which it reflects; it is also evident in the 'quarrels' that make up its subject matter between one side referred to as the 'Parti Noir' or the Inquisition and the Matriarchal 'devotion' which are less clearly defined sides of a dispute so much as virtual poles exercising a spiritual influence on the institution of the church both in general and in the instances of specific monasteries, convents and other ecclesiastical spaces. There is also the doubling of this quarrel within the church with actual historical events since both the events recounted within *The Suspended Vocation* and indeed Klossowski's own experiences within the church take place in the clearly defined period of Nazi occupation, with abundant references to occupied zones, interrogations, torture and resistance, albeit always refracted through the prism of the church.

This brief introduction to this highly anomalous novel, even in relation to the later work of Klossowski, may give some further indications of why it would appeal to Ruiz as the subject of his 'first' French film. First of all, there is the strange combination of theology and politics that was also part of Ruiz's own formation and in a highly resonant manner since *The Suspended Vocation* is less interested in the content of the theological disputes it presents than in their form, their instantiation within different institutional structures and the kinds of rhetorics they give rise to. In other words, theology is treated on a level of abstraction that is in communication with the logical paradoxes of philosophy, while at the same time directly related to politics. This gives some explanation to the often repeated and at first glance astonishing statements of Ruiz that within this novel he was able to detect the conflicts between the various factions of the Chilean left. On closer examination, this becomes a less extraordinary claim not only because of the prevalence of Marxists with Catholic backgrounds in Chile and other Latin American countries who 'converted' from one church to another but rather because Klossowski's novel was sufficiently abstract to be able to resonate with the dynamics of any institution plagued by the vicious circles of internal divisions.

Klossowski's own position within French intellectual and cultural life was grasped by Ruiz in a particularly perceptive way; the baroque construction of *The Suspended Vocation* and indeed all of Klossowski's writing has an outsider quality in relation to French literary traditions, despite being well disguised in the most bourgeois possible

French. One could point to Klossowski's Polish origins as one explanation for such a baroque sensibility, as well as his cosmopolitan upbringing which was more European than especially French, not to mention his forebears' diverse intellectual interests which include a famous treatise on Alchemy. In short, Klossowski was a type of insider/outsider in French culture who, whatever his links with figures ranging from André Gide and Bataille to the Catholic intelligentsia, dissimulated through an extreme erudition, all the more diabolical, perverse and heretical tendencies, which would be given free reign in his later porno-theological writings and especially in his drawings. In *The Suspended Vocation,* however, all these forces are kept in a unique tension, facilitated through a baroque textual machinery by means of which a supposedly confessional literary genre is transformed into a device for generalising the functioning of any institutional apparatus under siege and was therefore as applicable to the torturous dynamics of the Allende-era Chilean left as to the Catholic church; in this sense, Klossowski's *The Suspended Vocation* became the perfect vehicle for the expression of Ruiz's own 'suspended vocation' as a leftist filmmaker. Following Ruiz's own statements about being drawn to the novel as a way of expressing the situation of the Chilean left, one can find some justification for reading the film as a remake of *Dialogues of Exiles* but now in a coded form, as a sign that a certain conception of political cinema for Ruiz was no longer possible except via an allegorical form that he would develop throughout the 1980s in proximity to the rhetorics of the baroque, the surreal and even the Magical Realism that he had previously condemned as kitsch populism, without fully identifying with any of these procedures. All of which renders *The Suspended Vocation* as pivotal a film in Ruiz's oeuvre as *Dialogues of Exiles,* as the other side of a transformation begun in the earlier film.

Another aspect of the work that seems to have attracted Ruiz was the sheer impossibility of transforming its *mise-en-abyme* literary structure into cinema; how to translate a work that capitalises on the possibilities of absence facilitated by literary language by in essence making the whole work the absent object of exegesis and commentary into a medium defined by the presence of real objects in front of the camera, which according to the credo of Bazinian realism is definitive of cinematic representation as such? Ruiz's response was to use the materiality of film itself against this realist hypothesis and as a way recapitulating, in a manner appropriate to cinema, the literary mechanisms employed in the novel. In the place of the doubling of a preface and a non-existent work, Ruiz substituted a film edited together out of two supposed anterior versions of *The Suspended Vocation* made at different times, with different actors and for different ideological purposes; a 'pious' black and white version filmed in the 1940s and a subversive 'new wave' version filmed in the 1960s. Footage from both versions are edited together to constitute the third version, the one presented to the viewer by taking the 'most positive' elements of both preceding versions. In this way cinematic editing is used to denaturalise photographic realism since the gaps between the two versions, not only in terms of narrative content but also aesthetics, performances, settings and colour versus black and white, problematise any ideas about a 'true version' thereby setting up a similarly undecidable structure to the novel. The end result is that it takes several viewings to have any clear idea of what is actually transpiring in the film and even then the viewer has the impression of having flicked between two different films with a similar content rather than having watched any single unified film.

To make this work, Ruiz worked with several collaborators including writers from *Cahiers du Cinéma* such as Pascal Bonitzer, who played the leading role in the 'new wave' sections of the film and for the first time the Chilean composer Jorge Arriagada, who would do the scores for most of Ruiz's subsequent feature films. Even more importantly, Ruiz collaborated with cinematographer Sacha Vierny, who had been especially associated with 'Left Bank' New Wave filmmakers such as Chris Marker and especially Alain Resnais, as well as shooting Buñuel's *Belle de Jour* (1967), and would subsequently be the cinematographer for many of Peter Greenaway's films. This collaboration, which would last through Ruiz's first three French feature films including both Klossowski related films, enabled Ruiz to not merely complicate the narratives of his films but to do so via rich and ambiguous images that were themselves doubles or pastiches of earlier films. In *The Suspended Vocation* these were pastiches of Catholic films Ruiz remembered from his childhood, early Bresson films and films featuring the actor Pierre Fresnay, usually as a priest or an aristocrat. According to Ruiz, since the lighting of these films was already a pastiche of the Catholic mass, *Suspended Vocation* was therefore composed visually of pastiches of pastiches, referring directly to both other films and the scenography of the Catholic mass. Its images are therefore as much a site of ambivalent doubling as its double editing structure comprising two different versions of the same story with unstable relations between them. The specific use of French language in the film dialogue was the effect of the translation of Ruiz's Spanish into French by the poet Luis Dallafior, who had already collaborated with Ruiz on *Dialogues of Exiles*. Ruiz described the language of the latter as a careful, worked over French and Ruiz specifically instructed him to use rhetoric and to avoid street language, since he was entirely familiar with the former and unaccustomed to the latter. The result was a highly artificial, writerly language, entirely appropriate to the film that was such a successful pastiche of Klossowski's style that few could identify which was the created dialogue and which parts direct quotations form the novel. This artificiality was not limited to the dialogue but also characterised the performances in the film. Ruiz combined in the film actors and non-professional actors, not as in neo-realist films, in order to generate a greater sense of authentic realism but rather for the opposite purpose of maintaining a high level of artificiality, in particular asking the non-professional actors not to act but to simply be themselves and thereby generate a distance between their performances and the roles they are incarnating.

The result of all of the above elements is less a Brechtian distancing from the norms of realism than a simulacral, baroque doubling of the already simulacral original novel. In the film, as we trace the progress of the main character Jerome through a series of tests, ordeals and trials of faith, taking place in a range of ecclesiastical settings, it is impossible not to doubt that the film is really about what it explicitly presents, that is a series of seemingly anachronistic conflicts taking place within the Catholic church, between Patriarchal and Matriarchal currents, or between inquisition and revelation that despite the modern setting are essentially Mediaeval disputes. At the same time the film clearly references, through the filter of the Church, modern questions of politics and aesthetics which resonate not only with the Nazi occupation of Paris and its resistance but also with more contemporary political and aesthetic experiences. For example, at one monastery a key issue concerns a mural in a multiplicity of styles, overseen by a monk who is also a gifted artist but one who has chosen to sacrifice any aesthetic unity of style in order to enable the maximum participation in the creation of the work of art; a situation not unlike that of cinema under the Allende period. However, the interpretation of this work of art proves to be a minefield to the extent that when Jerome offers his suggestions for improving it, this is considered highly heretical and he is immediately expelled from the monastery. In this way the interpretation of the mural engages with contemporary debates about the relations between politics and aesthetics; should classical aesthetic principles be abandoned in order to politicise aesthetics as in the avant-garde, or should aesthetics be autonomous from the political as in the ideals of high modernism? This quarrel, like the others in the film is not resolved but is instead complicated, for example, by the imbrication of both aesthetics and politics with other elements such as the desire for abstract perfection on the part of Jerome, or the corporeal desires of the painter Malagrida who he later encounters, whose artistic decadence is bound up with his erotic and sentimental relations to an adopted street urchin. Within such a closed institution there is no possibility of aesthetic autonomy but only betrayal or heresy as Jerome constantly discovers. This is also expressed on the level of the narrative in that rather than driving the story, Jerome is rather driven by a series of events whose dynamism is that of the vicious circle of the institution itself; Ruiz has described this as the Kafkaesque dynamics of the story that decentre the individual in favour of the institution. However, at the same time, Jerome acts as if he really were in charge of his own destiny and therefore in a sense simulates himself as a free agent while dissimulating an experience of following rather than generating a series of ambiguous signs and events that he will never entirely catch up with.

Timothy Corrigan, one of the few English language commentators on this film made a direct comparison between the dispersal evident in the film, between different versions, performers and spiritual tendencies and Ruiz's own suspended vocation as a cinematic auteur. Firstly he observes that 'the religious blasphemies that appear

Pascal Bonitzer in
The Suspended Vocation

throughout this film are, more than anything else, the blasphemies of figures that refuse to remain stabilised within a textual, religious, or ideological scheme' (1991: 128), or in other words that the abstraction of the apparently ecclesiastical disputes in *The Suspended Vocation* in fact renders them as an aesthetic problem both in the sense of the dispersion of figures in excess of an organising schema and the excess of perceptions over any unified subjective agency: 'the coherence and personal commitment of a vocation becomes hilariously suspended and dispersed by the material of a heterogeneous agency it can never control' (1991: 128). In this latter sense a missed vocation becomes the anachronistic, spiritual equivalent of a highly contemporary experience of political and psychic paranoia. For Corrigan, this sense of a 'suspended vocation' also applies to Ruiz as an auteur, who like the unwitting protagonist of *The Suspended Vocation* 'acts out blasphemies' in relation to the idea of film auteur as the stable origin and locus of meaning of the film text:

> He gleefully suspends himself between the visionary agency of the auteur as artist and the invasions of that position by aleatory events, discourses and situational predicaments that unbalance and often debunk its claims [...] In suspending himself in this way, he literally plays himself out – scatters himself – as a set of formal propositions whose rigorous logic is undercut by the material predicaments that surround and invade that perspective. (1991: 128)

In other words, Ruiz's own vocation as a filmmaker was a suspended one, an 'identity spread across cultures, a vision dispersed through a multitude of industrial conditions and forms, and a voice that addresses an unknown and changing audience' (1991: 128). While this treatment of Ruiz as auteur is subject to a mimetic, poetic exaggeration if applied to his work as a whole, it is certainly expressive of the director's practice at this specific time. The crucial element defining that suspension is precisely the suspension between the different cultural contexts of Allende-era Chile and its political cinema and that of French art cinema in the late 1970s, for which *The Suspended Vocation* served as the perfect bridge at once speaking in a French idiom, while still haunted by the failures of the Chilean left, and meanwhile inventing a new form of cinematic discourse, the baroque, allegorical cinema that Ruiz would further elaborate over the coming decades. Ruiz's suspension is therefore less of the auteur role in general but of the specific passage between being a Chilean and a European auteur, a passage which remains in a remarkable state of tension in *The Suspended Vocation* but reaches a new level of integration in his subsequent Klossowski-inspired film, *The Hypothesis of the Stolen Painting*.

The Hypothesis of the Stolen Painting

> You can say *The Hypothesis of the Stolen Painting* is a detective film because of its riddle. As a rule, in a detective film, as in any gothic system – like Marxism or psychoanalysis – at any rate, in a system where there is a façade and inside a riddle, you enjoy finding the explanation. In a more baroque system, as in the system of *Hypothesis*, you don't enjoy finding the enigma, but rather go from

one level of interpretation to another. It's like the horizon: once you reach the horizon, there's still [another] horizon. (Ruiz 1992: 2)

Immediately upon completion of the filming of *Suspended Vocation,* Ruiz began another project in 'collaboration' with Klossowski but this time one that would attempt to translate the author's aesthetic practices and theories as a whole into a cinematic form. *The Hypothesis of the Stolen Painting* was originally planned as a collaborative documentary on Klossowski's ideas and aesthetic practices, that would take place in Ruiz's words 'in a situation that was befitting to him' (Ruiz 1992: 2) through the cinematic creation of *tableaux vivants*. These *tableaux vivants,* a practice which pervades Klossowski's theoretical and fictional work were, in the film, attributed to the fictitious nineteenth-century painter Tonnerre, whose paintings are obsessively collected by Octave, the central, clearly autobiographical character from Klossowski's novel, *The Revocation of the Edict of Nantes*. Typically, Klossowski also devoted a critical essay to this fictitious painter, 'La *Judith* de Frédérique Tonnerre' (Klossowski 2001: 120–125), which was in fact the direct pretext for the form of Ruiz's film. A *tableau vivant* is the reconstitution of a famous painting using human bodies with the maximum of attention paid to recreating the detail of the original in order to duplicate or intensify its effects. This activity of the nineteenth-century salon can be understood as a highly perverse reproductive technique that instead of making an original more exchangeable through the multiplication of copies, would render it absolutely singular through its corporeal actualisation in 'living material.' Given Klossowski's obsessive interests in art, perversion and mysticism, it is not hard to understand the occult 'aura' that such a practice would exercise on his imagination. So the original idea, which would have required Klossowski to play both himself and his fictional character in order to narrate a series of recreated fictitious paintings attributed to a non-existent painter, and in fact based on obsessive themes from his own work, already had a dizzying blend of truth and fiction, documentation and simulation. In Ruiz's own account of the film, things were complicated further by the fact that Klossowski left suddenly for Italy, leaving Ruiz with a collection of false paintings, some extras and no script.[12] He was left with no option but to improvise a fiction, in which his special kind of Spanish suitable for translation into French became a parody of Klossowski's own archaic, bourgeois style, a free translation of his aesthetic theories into the idiom of the art film, in every possible sense of the expression.

Perhaps provoked by Klossowski's absence, Ruiz organised the film around a constitutive void, namely the idea of the 'stolen painting.' The novelistic paintings attributed to the fictional painter Tonnerre from Klossowski's novel would be examined as a series whose true significance could only be grasped in the relations between them rather than in the 'thematics' of the individual paintings. This turned the project into a strange kind of detective film about art, featuring a single protagonist, 'the collector' as the investigator, and a series of paintings reconstituted as *tableaux vivants* as the suspects. However, just as the collector warns the narrator and the audience about the numerous traps set by the paintings, it would be a mistake to think that this was a film solely, or even primarily about art. Instead, it should be understood as an examination of the creation of theories and theoretical systems that artistic and other phenomena can provoke, about the theoretical monomania that Klossowski is such an exemplary case of.

In Klossowski's novel *The Revocation of the Edict of Nantes* (1959/2002), which was a key source for the film, there is an alternation between two journals, one kept by the perverse Octave and one kept by Roberte, who, along with Octave's unexhibitable collection of paintings by the fictional nineteenth-century academic painter, Tonnerre, form the twin obsessions of his existence. The disturbing fact that the simulacrum of Roberte is a product of Klossowski's own obsession with the physiognomy of his wife, Denise Morin-Sinclair, is perhaps what lead Ruiz to leave this simulacrum aside with the exception of its appearance in the mythological form of Diana the huntress, in favour of that of the Baphomet, the demonic, metamorphic figure par excellence that was the subject of Klossowski's final and most enigmatic novel. The novel *The Baphomet*, first published in 1965, which is set primarily in the atemporal, metaphysical world of 'pure spirits', concerns a ritual supposedly practised by the Templars, based on the sacrifice of a perfect androgynous youth. It is this simulacrum of *The Baphomet* that Ruiz employed to cinematically translate Klossowski's ideas in *The Hypothesis of the Stolen Painting*. By cinematically constructing a series of fictitious paintings as *tableaux vivants*, whose inter-relationships are based around the ritual of the Baphomet, Ruiz was not so much making a film about Klossowski's theories as directly enacting them. Certainly a cinematic *tableau vivant* does not produce an identical effect to a live one, but in its ambiguous intermediate status between pictorial and a cinematic image, as an image that is in apparent stasis, and yet breathes and pulsates, it enacts a similar type of suspension of life as the practice of *tableaux vivants* itself.

In addition to this, in its ability to provoke theoretical activity through being part of a series, the use of *tableaux vivants* in *Hypothesis* is clearly allegorical of the power of both pictorial and cinematic images to provoke thought, to generate complex levels of interpretation. Furthermore, in its aporetic structure it is an attempt to examine the void at the centre of all systems whether philosophical or aesthetic, the point at which they open out onto an unspecifiable, chaotic outside. This is in accordance with Ruiz's own approach to cinema, which is to view films not as self-enclosed entities but as open systems that constantly evoke other films and images to infinity. In Ruiz's *Poetics of Cinema*, Ruiz adapts Benjamin's idea of the optical unconscious as the basis for a wide range of speculations on the nature of primarily cinematic images. Benjamin's idea that there is an unconscious of images, that is a paradoxical 'corpus of signs capable of conspiring against visual conventions' (1995: 32), is used by Ruiz in order to affirm a heretical, simulacral approach to cinematic images in both practice and theory. The cinema, for Ruiz, in its overproduction of signs always overflows whatever normative intentions might be imposed on it in the interests of standardisation: the various theses on the cinema as a hegemonic 'culture industry' only deal with the conscious intentions of mainstream cinema, rather than the unconscious and accidental effects that this cinema continually produces. In this sense cinematic images can function in a similar manner to *tableaux vivants*: rather than the unambiguous representation of a particular time and place, they are potentially nothing more than suspended poses and scenes opening out onto infinite relations with other images. In the original practice of *tableaux vivants* a suspension of time was enacted through the relationship set up between the original models who posed for the artist and the re-constitution of the same poses in the present. The cinema, like the practice of *tableaux vivants*, is an art of demonic repetition, of simulation, but it extends the powers of repetition from a simple doubling into a wild proliferation of images. It is this cinematic power of simulacral repetition, and the sense that what is repeated is other to what the images appear to represent, that is developed in *The Hypothesis of the Stolen Painting* through the cinematic exploration of its precursor, the *tableau vivant*.

The apparent simplicity of the collection of Tonnerre's paintings presented in the film is deceptive, and problematised from the outset by the conjecture of the stolen painting. As each painting is reconstructed as a *tableau vivant*, linked by some seemingly insignificant detail of lighting or gesture to the next in the series, various complications arise: are these relations that the collector indicates not purely arbitrary, when all kinds of other relations between the paintings seem to exist? Does each successive painting not seem to repeat, or even to contain within it elements of the previous ones? Passing over the substantial problems involved with the hypothesis of the missing fourth painting, which would have been the central one in the series, when we come to the fifth painting things become considerably more complicated. We are told that this painting, entitled *The Scandal* composed of nine miniature melodramatic scenes from family life arranged to be read like the face of a clock, also has its basis in an actual scandal featuring the very models 'from a respected family' who posed for the painting. We also learn that the events and rumours surrounding this scandal were re-iterated in a '*roman-à-clef*' that appears to incorporate all the narratives suggested by all the paintings up until this point, even, surprisingly, including the first one of the mythological scene of Diana and Actaeon. Furthermore, as the collector recites the incredibly perverse and complicated plot of the novel, it becomes clear that the series of paintings are all interwoven with a different series corresponding to what the collector has already referred to as 'the ceremony'. This ceremonial series is what the collector was referring to when he stated at the beginning of the film that the paintings do not show but rather 'make allusion'; namely, that instead of a simple series of paintings there are the two series of the paintings reconstructed as *tableaux vivants* and the series of gestures that make up the ceremony itself, which is increasingly revealed to be the Rite of the Baphomet. Some indication of how the communication between the two series operates is given by the seemingly chaotic nature of the sixth painting, in which figures from all the other paintings, and some figures we have not seen before (whose presence is explained through the hypothesis of the stolen painting), are arranged in groups of three. This chaotic assemblage is explained as being the tracing of gestures from the previous painting, all of which form circular curves.

The apparent resolution of the enigma in terms of the re-enactment of the ceremony of the Baphomet, however, remains highly problematic, not least because of the paradoxical role of the missing painting. The stolen painting is the absent centre, the mysterious point that belongs to both series and yet is given in neither. What the film demonstrates is that this empty space, rather than being a lack, is precisely what generates the endless theoretical speculation about the paintings, the ceremony and their

Jean Rougeul in *The Hypothesis of the Stolen Painting*

The rite of the Baphomet in *The Hypothesis of the Stolen Painting*

inter-relationship that the paintings provoke. Considering that its connection to the preceding painting was a mask, and what follows it is the representation of a scandal involving the ceremony, it is implied that the missing painting is the key to the ceremony itself. There is both an empty place between the two adjacent paintings, which can never be specified, and the mask, itself an allegory of the irreducible gap between the two series of appearance and the real, which is an occupant without a place.[13]

Nevertheless, in a sense the repetition of this paradoxical missing element *is* the ceremony, in that it makes the series of *tableaux vivants* and the series of ceremonial gestures communicate by endlessly diverging, and thus generates an experience of the ceremony in the viewer, however inchoate and incomplete this experience might be. In witnessing the very suspended gestures of the *tableaux vivants*, which are the simulation of a ceremony that exceeds rational explanation, the potential of works of art to suspend spatio-temporal relations is directly performed through cinematic means: what the film demonstrates, above all, is the power of the cinema to hold life in suspension, to offer life as a spectacle to itself in a demonic doubling of the affective power of the *tableau vivant*. As such the film offers to the viewer a simulacrum in which the singular phantasm that was the object of the ceremony of the Baphomet, or at the very least a heretical neo-baroque tendency in contemporary aesthetics, is actualised.

As with the earlier *Suspended Vocation,* Sacha Vierny's black and white cinematography was a key means for achieving this cinematic transposition of Klossowski's aesthetics and as in the previous film this was also done through allusions both to the history of art and to the history of cinema. According to Pascal Bonitzer the whole visual style of the film is a homage to the work of the cinematographer, Henri Alekan, and especially that used for Cocteau's *La belle et la bête* (*Beauty and the Beast,* 1946). It is interesting to note that Alekan, who Ruiz has referred to entirely positively as a 'maniac' would be the cinematographer for Ruiz's next project, *Chambord.* Another indispensable contribution was from the actor Jean Rougeul, who a decade previously had played a key role in Fellini's *8½* (1963), as Mastroianni's overly intellectual scriptwriter. Delivering a difficult and monomaniacal script parodying Klossowski's own hyper-bourgeois style, talking while moving about the house and in one instance while sleeping, this performer gave the film in Bonitzer's words, 'a finesse and credibility without which the enterprise would have risked not "passing the bar"' (Bonitzer cited in Bax *et al.* 2003: 121). Commenting on the death of this actor soon afterwards, Bonitzer goes on to reflect that for him this now feels like part of the film, showing that it is 'not only a meditation on "figuration" but also and correlatively a meditation on death' (ibid.). After all the very use of *tableaux vivants* within a cinematic framework is necessarily to pose questions about the relations between stasis and movement, life and death; what is a *tableau vivant* if not an impossible exchange between a dead, past representation and living bodies, who sacrifice their present liveliness in order to re-animate the dead past, a sacrifice echoing the theme of the Baphomet that lies at the heart of the series of *tableaux vivants* that constitute the film?

Despite, or perhaps because of this simulation of Klossowski's thought and aesthetics it was much less pleasing to Klossowski than Ruiz's earlier film. Part of this is due to the fact that Ruiz's film is highly parodic of images that for Klossowski have a quasi-sacred role in his aesthetic system. This was especially the case in the first painting of 'Diana and Actaeon', the only painting that relates, however, obliquely to the figure of Roberte. Ruiz chose to represent Actaeon, the wounded hunter as carrying a broken bow, an unforgivable sacrilege in Klossowski's eyes but one that expresses Ruiz's strong tendency towards pastiche and parody and the refusal to treat any system as sacred. Nevertheless, this same tendency is no doubt what gave the film a larger international success and critical reception than any of Ruiz's previous work. While many critics such as Amy Taubin were highly bemused by the film, it nevertheless fascinated both popular and academic film critics and drew many people's attention to Ruiz's work, often for the first time. This film also had a significant impact on art cinema, particularly evident in Godard's *Passion* (1980), made shortly afterwards, as well as much of the work of Peter Greenaway, both of which feature *tableaux vivants* prominently, without treating them in as radically simulacral a manner as Ruiz's film does. This is largely because Godard and Greenaway present their *tableaux vivants* as incarnations of the actual history of art, whereas Klossowski and Ruiz's use of *tableaux vivants* were based on an already simulated model, hence not leading back to any kind of classicist affirmation of art historical traditions but rather in the direction of their parodic decomposition.

While the film's critical attention is fully justified, it is regrettable that many of these critics lost interest in Ruiz shortly afterwards, since the simulacral aesthetics, *tableaux vivants* and ideas about art and cinema as complex multiple systems elaborated in *Hypothesis* would continue to be elaborated in diverse ways in Ruiz's subsequent films, right up until his final works. Certainly many of these elements can be seen in Ruiz's far lesser-known works produced mostly for television commissions at the end of the 1970s with which this chapter will conclude.

Ruiz at the INA at the end of the 1970s: A Castle, A History Guide, *and* Elections

Thanks to the success of *The Hypothesis of the Stolen Painting,* Ruiz had begun to receive international critical attention and was certainly considered one of the most important directors working in France by film critics, as evidenced by the frequent articles and special issues of *Cahiers du Cinéma* and other cinema journals devoted to his films. At the same time, Ruiz's cinema at this time could hardly be seen outside of retrospectives, even in France. Although both *The Hypothesis of the Stolen Painting* and *Suspended Vocation* had been commissioned as films and more or less corresponded to the definition of feature films at least in terms of running time, many of Ruiz's other projects at this time were so anomalous in terms of formats, genre and content that in many cases it was years before these works were either broadcast or screened.

To give an idea of this kind of anomaly, it is worth looking briefly at the film that was sandwiched between the two Klossowski films, *Dog's Dialogue*, the one that remarkably won a César award, even if this film did in fact manage to be screened in cinemas, if only to a small audience. This film combined the popular conventions of the photo-roman with a bizarre story, worthy of the most delirious Brazilian *telenovela*, all the while situating its excessive narrative between sequences of barking dogs, the only moving pictures in first part of the film. After the first sequence of barking dogs, a voice-over narrator recounts a story, beginning from the premise of the line 'The woman who lives in this house and that calls you her daughter is not your mother', the kind of 'false family past' scenario that will characterise several of Ruiz's subsequent films. This premise is a *détournement* of a line from Buñuel's *Le charme discret de la bourgeoisie* (*The Discreet Charm of the Bourgeoisie,* 1972) and as in this latter film, it becomes the basis for a series of repetitions and variations rather than linear development. However, rather than attacking the absurd rituals of the bourgeoisie, *Dog's Dialogue* deals with banal and popular stereotypes and gestures, pushing a low degraded media form into abstraction precisely through these acts of repetition and narrative excess. Ranging over prostitution, murder, identity shifts and sex changes, as well as everyday desires for wealth, happiness, to start a business, find a lover or have children, the narrative repeats certain key lines and gestures but applied to different characters before returning in circular fashion to another variation on the false origins that began the story.

In this way the film is less an example of Surrealism than a kind of pop art that in performing acts of repetition and seriality on the already serial and repetitive form of the photo-roman, enacts an immanent engagement with forms of mass produced popular culture, without, however, judging them in the name of superior aesthetic values. On the contrary, it is a case of discerning within the most banal forms, strange potentials and a reading of the ritualised gestures and stereotypes of contemporary life. Nevertheless, the interruptions of the barking dogs that suggest that it is they who are recounting these strange tales of their masters, do serve as a kind of Brechtian device, making the audience aware of how these absolutely absurd and contrived tales have nevertheless been fully capturing their attention. Later on in the film, these sequences are supplemented by scenes of a typical French neighbourhood, giving the film an almost ethnographic quality. Ruiz also introduces one of his obsessive themes, namely that of the dispersed body; in this case, a woman is murdered by her lover and her body parts dismembered and dispersed at various locations across a small village, one of the few scenes to be shown in cinematic movement rather than by the series of still images. However, this dispersed body nevertheless manages to 'speak' given that the murderer, owing to his orderly nature, has placed them at exactly the same distance from the café where they both lived and worked, thereby implicating himself in the crime. As the film progresses, the still images hone in more and more on the variations of stereotyped gestures, from situations of affection to those of violence and at times there are deliberate discrepancies between what is seen and what is being described. This obsessive interest in gestures, stereotypes and the suspension afforded by the still image, makes the film much more related than it first appears to be, to the use of *tableaux vivants* in *The Hypothesis of the Stolen Painting*. In fact the real subject of the film is precisely the relation between stasis and movement and the discernment of repetitive and generic gestures that are nevertheless experienced as real and believable.

The film can also be seen as a kind of ironic commentary on the artistic use of these kinds of conventions in films such as Chris Marker's *La Jetée* (1962), deflating their pretensions and revealing them to be little more than variations on the stereotypes of the photo-roman form. How is it possible to categorise a film such as this that while referencing a range of narratives, genres and media formats does not coincide completely with anything but itself? This was a key problem surrounding Ruiz's work at the end of the 1970s, which while for the most part commissioned for the INA was only rarely actually shown at the intended time and sometimes was never shown on television at all. To understand Ruiz's work for the INA, it is necessary to recall that this was a quite singular audiovisual institution, that not only combined the two functions of responsibility for French audiovisual media archives and the commissioning of experimental works but also tended to combine these two functions by letting avant-garde filmmakers use the archives as the basis for new work, a conjunction that not only Ruiz but other innovative filmmakers benefited from. The INA was a state-funded experimental TV producer and the state run channels were obliged to show 60 hours of its content per year, as a way of ensuring audiovisual diversity in French television. Filmmakers who benefited from this set-up form an impressive list and included Jacques Rivette, Chris Marker, Marguerite Duras, Joris Ivens, Maurice Pialat, René Allio and Jean-Marie Straub and Danièle Huillet amongst others. According to Susan Boyd-Bowman, the brief of the INA was not only to commission feature films but especially to 'invent new modes of television expression and to apply new techniques' (Boyd-Bowman 1987: 105), a brief that was clearly compatible with Ruiz's idiosyncratic approach to audiovisual production. In essence the INA applied the same 'auteurism' that had become dominant in French cinema to television production, bringing in outsider auteurs and more or less giving them free rein to be as creative as possible. Nevertheless this was not necessarily embraced by the state television channels, leading to significant tensions between the INA and its distribution, with the effect that many programmes were either screened at inconvenient times, several years later or not at all. This led to a shift in emphasis in the INA which, after succeeding in getting Godard's *Six Fois Deux* series screened in 1976 on FR3, had encountered a lot of resistance on the part of television channels and reframed their activities as a cross between creativity and commerce, experimentation and the maintenance of a popular audience.

One way the INA attempted to do this was through a kind of magazine format, at the same time making use of the audiovisual archives, thereby combining both of its main functions. The first of these series was the 1975–76 series *Hieroglyphs* that was followed by *Rue des Archives* to which Ruiz made a key contribution and *Juste une Image*, based on the famous Godard quotation from *Le vent d'est* (*Wind from the East*, 1969), 'This is not a just image, it's just an image.' The *Hieroglyphs* shows would typically show a range of short experimental works ranging from excerpts from feature films to televisual experiments, interspersed with commentary. The third series was much more sophisticated and dispensed with commentary in favour of a stream of audiovisual images that commented on the various regimes of audiovisual production and aspired to the condition of being an 'imaginary cinémathèque', expressed in purely visual terms (Boyd-Bowman 1987: 112–14). The content could consist of video art, filmmakers' works in progress, archival photographs, animation and dynamic moments from the televisual or cinematic past. In this way each episode was itself a work of bricolage, corresponding quite closely to Ruiz's own practice as a filmmaker. As such it constituted a baroque 'optical unconscious' of audiovisual media, prefiguring the use of this concept that Ruiz would later make in *Poetics of Cinema* (1995), as the passage of the same images from one work to another.

However, the series that Ruiz contributed to, *Rue des Archives* was very different to these two series. As the title suggests it was a series based on the archives, exclusively the French televisual archives and entirely shot on video and so unlike the other series there was no material from the history of cinema or commissioned work. Nevertheless, as Ruiz's *Petit manuel d'histoire de France* (*A Short Guide to French History*, 1979) demonstrates, this did not render the series any less experimental. The idea behind the series was to give the spectator the impression of strolling around this 'vast collective memory' (INA cited in Boyd-Bowman 1987: 109) without being organised by conventional categories like genres, themes and historical periods; in other word it was from the outset a Borgesian project and so one uniquely suited to Ruiz. Ruiz was approached for this second series in 1979 and commissioned to make two episodes on the topic of French history, obviously a subject the producers felt could be best handled by a foreigner.

Ruiz fulfilled this commission in his own way jumping between different historical epochs or showing the same historical personage such as Joan of Arc via five different performers. Ruiz also went beyond the discrete sequences favoured by other directors and montaged several images within the same frame as an audiovisual approximation of the multiple interpretations of history through a kind of quasi-live mixing. This gave the sense of the event being portrayed as being haunted by other events, not just different versions of the same events but parallel events suggesting other possible or virtual histories haunting the actual one being presented. For Ruiz, French history, not only in its televisual but in its academic form, was composed less of hieroglyphs than of stereotypes which pervaded radically different works regardless of their author's intentions or political orientation. Ruiz therefore used as the soundtrack school history textbooks as read out for the first time by a variety of children (in a homage to or parody of Godard's INA television work), accompanied by associated and equally stereotyped televisual images, to fully bring out the sense of French history as the stereotyped *mise-en-scène* of the history of the French state. However, this political thesis was in fact overwhelmed by a type of audiovisual delirium so that by the time it came to the presentation of Napoleon, Ruiz's guide had rendered the history it was presenting almost incoherent. According to Jonathan Rosenbaum the programme at this point becomes 'a helter-skelter slag-heap of near subliminal flashes, one shot per era, which effectively reduces all of French history to a hysterical flood of incoherent clichés' (Rosenbaum 1995: 226).

While this sequence was not typical of the episodes as a whole and might well express Ruiz's attitude towards the history of France, the question remains of what a viewer could possibly make of this wild pastiche operating on the borders of the perceptible: at times there is simply no way to orient oneself within the text and therefore it undermines any relation to the viewer and the communication of a coherent idea or message about French history. But this would be to misunderstand what Ruiz was attempting in these programmes. Rather than delivering a pre-constituted 'real' content, Ruiz was rather investigating the form of the televisual, its stereotypes, rules and limitations but also its dynamisms, rhythms and its specific photographic unconscious. Also, as Jill Forbes points out, the politics of these programmes was not so much about a particular interpretation of the history of France but about the pedagogical and ideological structures of documentary narratives in general: 'it uses the juxtaposition and confrontation of already existing texts to question the nature of all narratives of history so as to show their relativism and, indeed, to question the value attributed to documents by virtue of their entry into the archive' (Forbes 1992: 41). In this respect, A *Short Guide to French History* continues the audiovisual questioning of rhetorics of the image begun in *The Hypothesis of the Stolen Painting* and that is also evident in other works commissioned by the INA such as Ruiz's 'documentary' on the local elections, produced in the same year. Regardless of the comprehensibility of this programme for a contemporary audience, it certainly functioned as a type of laboratory for Ruiz to develop his audiovisual repertoire as would his other television projects at this time.

Prior to this Ruiz had worked on a very different television project for the series *Un Homme, Un Château (A Man, A Castle)* producing an enigmatic work whose full title translates as *The Divisions of Nature: A Man, A Castle, 'Chambord'* (1978). As we have already seen, Ruiz had paid homage to the cinematography of Henri Alekan in his Klossowski films; for *Chambord,* Ruiz worked with Alekan, something the director himself described as a unique experience: 'I wasn't used to someone who begins by measuring the light of the sun and who gets up at five every morning to check the point at which the sun will rise. It was a discipline I wasn't familiar with' (Ruiz, cited in Bax *et al.* 2003: 121). Ruiz says that it was Alekan's fanaticism about light that dictated the way they worked with images on this film and it was Alekan who taught him how to work with filters, in this case monochromatic colour ones. In addition to its technical experimentation with light and colour, the film can be understood as an experimentation with 'point of view', or presenting three entirely distinct ways of seeing the same object.

The initial idea for the project was to present the Chambord castle via three distinct ideological perspectives, that of a Thomist philosopher, that of a romantic and that of 'someone like Baudrillard' (2003: 121). In the voice-over this resulted in respective pastiches of Pascal, Fichte and a contemporary tourist guide. However, the main object of the film was an experimentation with three different visual styles, injecting the maximum amount of artifice and denaturalising the realist pretensions of both the touristic gaze and the other perspectives presented in the film. According to Ruiz, 'the entire film was entirely made from the starting point of optical experiences and tricks, optical deformations' (2003: 121). For example, in the first part of the film, they used the perceptual effects of the colour blue, fog and filters, in order to construct the sense of a metaphysical castle, floating in the air; in the second romantic section, warmer filters were used, tending towards red, along with increasingly kaleidoscopic effects, distancing the castle still further from the demands of realism. The artifice of these first two sections has the effect of denaturalising the realist touristic gaze presented in the final part of the film, exposing it as being as much a 'visual rhetoric' and no less artificial than the preceding sections. In other words the film, both in its excessive visual styles and their relations with the equally constructed and rhetorical textual pastiches, generates what Christine Buci-Glucksmann has called a 'shipwreck of the real' (2004: 35). She then goes on to pose the essential question raised by the film, concerning Ruiz's three versions of Chambord and where this leaves the 'real' object:

> What remains of the object in this generalised mannerism? Perhaps simply a castle of effects. Chambord floats in the air, cut off from the ground by colour-fields; it fragments under the effect of prisms; it drowns via an effect of ice melting in front of the lens; Chambord no longer exists. (Ibid.)

In one sense, the visual excess of *Chambord* was just another example in the sequence of Ruiz's television commissions, a playful response to the demand for production within a format, in this case a man and a castle, that simply went further than other examples in its exploration of both the rhetorics and artifice of the image and the possibility of image-text relations that seem to express in a Foucauldian manner that 'speaking is not seeing'.[14] At the same time it was a type of political attack on the banality of the touristic gaze, not through a straight critique but by opening it up to other modes of perception, other forces, thereby destabilising its pretensions to the natural and the real. Finally, this project gave Ruiz the not insignificant opportunity to develop the kind of visual artifice and play that would be given a different expression in his feature films of the 1980s, which would also be characterised by tricks, false perspectives, chromatic filters and many of the other techniques already evident in *Chambord*. For Ruiz the political aspect of this film and its aesthetic deformations are inseparable at least from the point of view of the mode of cinematic work that was employed: 'It was the first time I made use of 16mm as if it was 35mm ... It was also the first time I discovered the possibilities of changing the light during the shot. This is also very good from a political point of view since it integrates the work of the technicians and electricians who have to concentrate during the take' (Ruiz in Bax *et al.* 2004: 121). While this is, of course, another Ruizian joke, it does contain a serious point, namely that any attempts to make a political cinema needs to take into account both modes of production and modes of perception, hence the inseparability between aesthetics and politics that would continue to characterise the director's work. However radical *Chambord* was in its destruction or rather explosion of the real object, Ruiz's next project for INA, *De grands événements et des gens ordinaires* (*Of Great Events and Ordinary People: The Elections,* 1979), went further still in its complete deconstruction of the televisual codes of documentary which became, inadvertently, the real subject of the film.

The 'great events' referred to in the title was an ironic reference to the lack of interest being taken in the local elections by the inhabitants of Ruiz's 11th *arrondissement*; according to Ruiz eighty per cent of the people approached to take part in the documentary declined, mirroring the lack of interest in the elections themselves. In fact, even the electoral results were a disappointment, since the anticipated dramatic turn towards the left failed to materialise. Ruiz's response to these difficulties was to shift the focus of the film from the elections themselves to the problem of their televisual representation, thereby undoing almost every cliché of the televisual documentary, as well as posing some acute questions about the failures of representation more generally in both the political and aesthetic senses of the term. In Adrian Martin's words, this work 'is the best, and certainly the funniest, of self-reflexive deconstructions of the documentary form' (Martin 2004).

The film takes apart the documentary form by presenting itself as a series of versions consisting for most of its duration as the rushes taken on each day of filming the project, to a series of increasingly shorter edits, dramatising in the process the falsification inherent in all documentary filmmaking. During the 'rushes' section, the objectives of each day's filming are announced but it is soon revealed that there is often a large gap between these objectives and what actually takes place during the shooting. For example, when they plan to film customers in a café to provide 'local character', we are informed in voice-over that none of the cafés in the district would let them film there, so they had to go to one in a completely different district, the sort of falsified trick of realism that would usually be disguised rather than highlighted. This is only the most obvious example of a constant gap between visible objects and their description as provided by the voice-over; this is a film which, in Foucauldian terms, speaking never entirely corresponds to seeing. More than this, the standard tropes of the television documentary are constantly undone through making them explicit, as when the voice-over announces as we see a variety of objects on a table, 'A series of biographical objects to complete the generic convention'. When it comes to interviews it is clear that the neighbourhood's inhabitants have little understanding of the mechanism of the election, do not know who the candidates are, or have any clear idea what effects the electoral results will have on their lives. More than this, the presentation in the film of these opinions shows that the order they are presented in is enough to completely manipulate their meaning, again drawing attention to the falsification inherent in the documentary form. For the second day of shooting which will concentrate on 'posters, the voting office, an interview with a tailor and TV', we are informed that 'we will show posters to indicate the passing of time' this time subverting the pseudo temporality produced through posters as indexes of the passage of time. At the same time attention is drawn to antagonisms between the filmmaker and the subjects as a tailor 'looks down' on the filmmaker because of his foreign accent while the latter loses interest as the tailor drifts from the point. However, as interviews are repeated this unsatisfactory level of interaction turns out to be the norm rather than the exception. Experts are also interviewed, including a number of sociologists, as well as a round table discussion on documentary film comprised of *Cahiers* critics, both of which emphasise the conventions involved in both electoral and documentary representation. Meanwhile, after yet another series of banal shots of the neighbourhood the voice-over intones: 'the everyday to the point of absurdity.'

Once all the nine days of rushes have been compiled we are shown excerpts from them which we are told are not the same images but 'the same order, the same film but shorter'. Indeed some of the images are not recognisable from the already witnessed rushes, leading the narrator to comment that some of the images seem to come from other films. What this indicates is not merely the obvious point that finished documentaries falsify their contents by organising them according to absurd conventions but that they are structurally false because they pretend to show reality in process whereas in fact they are a type of pre-processed reality, the (film) 'reel' rather than the 'real'. To emphasise this arbitrary nature of the documentary shaping of the real, this edited version is exactly six minutes, whereas the previous material was sixty minutes and is followed by an even shorter version of one minute. As such it enacts an implosion of the documentary form itself which is seen to consist of so many rhetorical fictions, used to construct a real whose model is the conventions of documentary itself and nothing else. More than this, throughout the film other perspectives have constantly been creeping in, turning it into an impossible inventory of the everyday that constantly exceeds the conventions it is supposed to be serving or even their deconstruction; for example in the sequences of 'secondary elements' such as camera movements or gestures that might be useful in the finished film.

The film is also under the sign of Jean Baudrillard's theories of simulation and in fact Baudrillard contributed one of the voices that make up the voice-over. Simulation in the film is present both in relation to the elections themselves, whose reality the film is shown to be constructing out of a range of heterogeneous materials, but also in the presentation of documentary itself as necessarily an art of simulation, of the rhetorical presentation of diverse fragments as an organic whole, by the means of a range of conventions, tricks and falsifications. That this is not an empty exercise in free play is indicated by the ending of the film which subverts Chris Marker's *Le Joli Mai* (1963), which had asserted a series of statements of the order: 'while one person is in jail, I am not free' and so forth. Ruiz turns this militant mantra on its head by asserting that in the world of documentary, the opposite is the case: 'While poverty exists we continue to be rich, while sadness exists, we continue to be happy, while prisons exist, we continue to be free' all accompanied by ethnographic stock footage. This ending is nothing less than a denunciation of the illusions of militant documentary's truth claims, that argues that these militant documentaries are formally no different to the most banal TV documentary, such as the one parodied in Ruiz's film. For Ruiz it is not sufficient to change the content of documentaries or even their form if one continues to accept their rhetorical truth claims, the idea of giving some indexical access to a pre-given reality, whether this supposed truth is a reactionary or a militant one. Martin is therefore correct to emphasise that this is an absolutely anti-Bazinian film that refuses any relation between filming and 'reality' and any understanding of documentary except as a particularly pernicious form of fiction or simulation. It is perhaps hardly surprising that after this series of aberrant television 'documentaries' all of which in different ways enact the 'shipwreck of the real' referred to by Buci-Glucksmann in relation to *Chambord* that Ruiz would move instead to projects that allowed him to fully explore the powers of cinematic falsification through the series of 'wild fictions' that characterised most of his work in the 1980s. This phase in Ruiz's work that will be the subject of the next chapter will be examined under the rubric of a 'cinema of piracy' in multiple senses of the term, indicating both a type of subject matter and an aesthetic procedure of appropriation and bricolage. In this way, while Ruiz's work in this decade will be seen as premised on the destruction of the pretensions of militant cinema and documentary truth and realism, it will still be read as no less political, even if this politics is now a politics of the cinematic image or of the 'reel' rather than one that claims any transparent access to the 'real'.

Notes

1. For a treatment of Chilean political history see Brian Loveman (1988), *Chile: The Legacy of Hispanic Capitalism*, New York: Oxford University Press.
2. This manifesto was translated as 'Film Makers and the Popular Government Political Manifesto', in Chanan 1976: 83–4.
3. While King attributes this statement to the AT&T communications network, in Naomi Klein's recent book, *The Shock Doctrine* (2007), there is reference to a declassified CIA document in which Nixon gave this order to the head of the CIA, Richard Helms on September 15, 1970. Klein 2007: 64, 474.
4. On the concept of the biographical legend in relation to Roman Polanski see Ewa Mazierska (2007), *Roman Polanski: The Cinema of a Cultural Traveller*. London: I.B. Tauris.
5. According to Jonathan Rosenbaum, this was facilitated by a Rockefeller grant. That Ruiz, a teenage law and theology student would be receiving a Rockefeller

grant is by no means the most improbable element in Ruiz's biographical legend. See Rosenbaum 1995: 223.

6   On one occasion Ruiz commented that if he had not been a filmmaker he would have been a Pole, attesting to his perception of Poles as having inherent baroque or surreal tendencies, a baroque of everyday life that he also ascribes to Chilean culture.

7   See Bertolt Brecht, 'On Gestic Music', in *Brecht on Theatre,* (Brecht 1978: 104–106).

8   This confusion continues to to this day since the only available DVD versions of the film, attributed to Ruiz, turn out to be the already mentioned Mexican western.

9   Where French texts are cited in this book they are translated by the author unless otherwise indicated.

10 See Franz Kafka (2007), 'In the Penal Colony', in: *Metamorphosis and Other Stories,* Trans. Michael Hoffmann, London: Penguin Classics, 147–180.

11 For an account of *Cahiers Du Cinéma* during 'the Daney years', see Emilie Bickerton (2009), *A Short History of Cahiers Du Cinéma,* London, New York: Verso, 87–107.

12 Klossowski's absence has also been explained as being due to his involvement in a series of films with Pierre Zucca, based around the figure of Roberte, in which Klossowski and his wife played the leading roles. These films were far more 'faithful' treatments of Klossowski's works than Ruiz's film.

13 In this respect there is a strong relationship between the structure of this film and Gilles Deleuze's account of the series in *The Logic of Sense*. See Deleuze 1990: 36–41. See also Goddard 2002: 75–84.

14 This Foucauldian theme was first developed in relation to aesthetic practices such as Raymond Roussel's writing strategies and René Magritte's *This is not a Pipe,* before being applied more systematically in *The Order of Things*. See Foucault 2000: 21–32, 187–203 and Foucault 1970: 46–77.

CHAPTER TWO

The Cinema of Piracy, the Sea and Spectral Voyages: Ruiz's Neo-Baroque Cinema of the 1980s

Introduction: The Surreal, the (Cinematic) Baroque, and the Neo-Baroque Reconsidered

While it is not possible to identify any discrete break in Ruiz's work as dramatic as the one that took place in 1973, there is nevertheless the palpable emergence of new tendencies in Ruiz's cinema from the beginning of the 1980s. Part of this shift is simply that after an eclectic range of projects, mostly commissioned for television in the late 1970s, Ruiz in the 1980s returned fully to cinema, making a series of feature films, in a variety of geographic locations, that have come to be seen as definitive of his cinematic aesthetics. Accompanying this shift was an aesthetic reorientation towards the styles referred to in the introduction, namely Magical Realism, Surrealism and the baroque, styles with which Ruiz has frequently been associated if not assimilated into. This is not to say that these styles were completely absent from Ruiz's work in the 1970s; *The Hypothesis of the Stolen Painting*, for example, was explicitly referred to by Ruiz as a baroque system, the complexity of which was irreducible to any linear schema. Similarly the film *Chambord* developed many of the visual techniques, such as the use of monochromatic filters and light variations that would reappear in some of Ruiz's films of the 1980s such as *La ville des pirates* (*City of Pirates*, 1983). However, as with many of Ruiz's projects at this time, both these works only developed certain aspects of the baroque, focusing either on narrative organisation or visual rhetorics, rather than fully articulating the baroque or rather neo-baroque style that would characterise many of the films of the 1980s.

This is not to reduce the work of the late 1970s to the status of being mere studies for a future cinema at that time not yet possible due to economic constraints but certainly many of the techniques and strategies that were tried out by Ruiz in the late 1970s were developed in a less constrained, less 'chaste' way in Ruiz's cinema of the 1980s. This shift also impacts upon the relations between aesthetics and politics in

Ruiz's work and certainly the most common impression is that the political concerns that had been crucial for Ruiz's Chilean cinema and had continued as a referent in at least some of his work in France, such as *Dialogues of Exiles* or *The Elections,* are definitively abandoned in the 1980s in favour of an aestheticist, purely artistic cinema, with little or no obvious relations to politics. Certainly works like *The Elections* were scathingly critical of the pretensions of militant cinemas but this critique was already evident in Ruiz's work even at its most 'political' in Chile. However, being critical of the dominant modes of political cinema did not mean a total abandonment of the political field but rather a reorientation in relation to it. First of all this is in terms of a focus not on politics as such but the specific politics of the cinematic image, a political and ethical concern not only in the 1980s but throughout Ruiz's career as is clearly evident in his polemical critique of 'central conflict theory', that constitutes the first chapter of *Poetics of Cinema* (Ruiz 1995: 9–23). This politics of the image is not unrelated to broader political issues such as neo-colonialism and the conditions of artistic production under capitalism. However, by focusing on and challenging regimes of the image, Ruiz was able to withdraw from the world-transforming hubris of most militant cinemas that fully believe themselves capable of intervening in the real world. Instead, Ruiz's films intervene in modes of perception and visual rhetorics, domains which visual practices are capable of affecting, as this is their own *modus operandi* and therefore a more pragmatic and modest domain for 'political cinema'. However, since this politics of perception brings politics and aesthetics into close proximity, it often risks seeming to be merely aesthetic, which is indeed the way most of Ruiz's cinema from the 1980s has been interpreted. Nevertheless, I would argue there are sufficient clues in Ruiz's work to assert the continuation of a radical politics of the image, even if this politics now takes place in the context of 'wild fictions' rather than in proximity to documentary or any other form of realism.

It is precisely this interrogation of modes of perception that brought Ruiz's cinema back into contact with the aesthetic styles of Magical Realism and Surrealism. This was a return, since these aesthetics had characterised Ruiz's earliest forays into cinema such as *The Widow's Tango*. However, while certain of Ruiz's films of the 1980s clearly engage with both Magical Realism and Surrealism, they treat these styles as visual and thematic resources, rather than naively subscribing to them. This is relatively uncontroversial in relation to Magical Realism and there is clearly a huge difference between Ruiz's 1980s films and the aesthetics of Garcia Márquez or some of Littín's exilic films such as *Alsino y el cóndor* (*Alsino and the Condor,* 1982) but there is a much stronger tendency to assimilate Ruiz's films into the aesthetics of Surrealism. Michael Richardson in his recent book *Surrealism and Cinema* defines the difference between Magical Realism and Surrealism in the following terms: 'Magical Realism [...] merely seeks to broaden realism's frame of reference. In contrast, surrealism endeavours to shatter the bonds of realism, to discover and investigate *another* reality' (2006: 149, emphasis in original). Especially considering Richardson's statement that 'magical realism should be seen as having no more link with surrealism than does socialist realism or naturalism' (ibid.) it might seem more plausible to situate Ruiz's work within the terms of Surrealism as Adrian Martin has done and as Richardson also does in a more guarded way in his book. Certainly insofar as Surrealism consists in denouncing all forms of realism and searching for ways to open up other realities, this would certainly seem to be expressed in Ruiz's cinema of the 1980s, which leads Richardson to argue that Ruiz's films and statements 'suggest an attitude closer to a genuinely surrealist one than Ruiz might believe' (2006: 150). However, after reading Ruiz's films of the 1980s in surrealist terms, Richardson is forced to concede that if Ruiz is a surrealist he is a baroque, heretical one 'because he uses surrealist devices for purposes that are not against surrealism but outside of it' (2006: 163). This takes up an argument already made by Laleen Jayamanne that it is precisely the devices and tricks of Surrealism that interest Ruiz the most but, against Richardson, she argues that his use of Surrealism rejects the metaphysics and ideals of Surrealism and indeed is a type of critique or deflation of these ideals through the appropriation of Surrealism's most kitsch effects. In this light, Surrealism would be for Ruiz just one more appropriable set of visual rhetorics, with no more or less importance than Magical Realism, or indeed the clichéd devices of popular cultural forms such as the photo-roman.

Frequently these problems in characterising Ruiz's aesthetics are resolved in favour of defining Ruiz in terms of the baroque, but as a singularly slippery and much abused art historical concept, this raises the question of what type of baroque we are talking about. Buci-Glucksmann, for example, appropriating Deleuze's characterisation of 'modern' cinema as a cinema of seeing rather than acting suggests that the cinema as a whole is baroque, or certainly some of its key exemplars such as the films of Welles and Fellini to which the term baroque is indeed frequently applied. However, comparing the effects of techniques such as depth of field in Welles and Ruiz, Buci-Glucksmann argues that with Ruiz we have a type of second degree baroque, or baroque of the baroque, in that rather than being presented with distorted perspectives of a pre-existing reality, in Ruiz's work this assumed reality is subtracted, leaving us with the shadows of shadows or the ghosts of fictions. This echoes the distinction made elsewhere by Deleuze between the classical baroque of the seventeenth century, whose multiple levels could all be ultimately encompassed in the singular point of view of God as in Leibniz's philosophy and the modern neo-baroque aesthetics of Borges, in which incompossible realities co-exist in in a single 'motley' world.[1] In a recent work on Ruiz, Richard Bégin has made a similar argument, arguing that Ruiz's cinema has to be understood as a specifically 'cinematographic baroque,' in the following terms:

> In the cinema of Raoul Ruiz, the symptoms of the baroque manifest themselves in the manner of an auto-representation of diegetic perception, and still more, in the signalling or the *mise-en-signe* [putting into sign] of cinematographic fabulation. (Bégin 2009: 30)

In other words what distinguishes the baroque style, or in Bégin's terms the 'baroque expressivity' (2009: 28) of Ruiz's cinema is less a set of clearly identifiable techniques than a tendency to underline the artificiality of all cinematic fabulation, to render baroque cinema itself, rather than just the differentiation of a certain baroque authorial style whether it be that of Welles, Fellini, or Greenaway from realist forms of cinema.

This second degree, cinematographic, neo or hyper-baroque of Ruiz can be further elucidated, however, by the concept of cartography and it is surely no coincidence that one of the first films made by Ruiz in the 1980s and the film that I would argue fully announces this new baroque orientation in Ruiz's work was the short film *Zig-Zag*, which was analysed in the introduction.[2] The focus on cartography in Ruiz's cinema of the 1980s is the sign of a more spatial orientation that was not developed in order to lend authenticity through the incorporation of real rather than virtual places but rather in order to develop new forms or rather territories for cinematic invention. All of this is already clear in *Zig-Zag*, which uses cartography not as a representational practice but rather as a device for articulating multiple levels of action and relations between objects including human bodies. Mapping in this film is presented as a delirious game and one that blurs the boundaries between both 'real' and virtual spaces, as well as between theoretical reflection, films and spatial exploration. As such it sets up a type of rubric for many of Ruiz's films of the 1980s that can usefully be read as so many instances of 'impossible cartography' in which cinema is used as a mapping device, again in an exploratory and experimental rather than mimetic sense of the cartographic, as so many mobile mappings of new and unpredictable cinematic spaces.

Related to this sense of the cartographic is what could be called a cinema of piracy, drawing on the multiple senses of this term. Already it has been clear that Ruiz was both a *bricoleur* and a 'thief of thoughts and images', whose films tended to be pastiches of other films, styles and rhetorics rather than proposing any fixed or stable aesthetic principles. As such, Ruiz's multiple practices of pastiche and simulation can be seen as a type of deliberate piracy, even in the legal sense of this term, or in other words the appropriation, repetition and transformation of existing cultural artefacts and styles. Piracy also indicates a type of postcolonial relation to cultural traditions and especially to European cultural heritage which at once expresses a will to plunder its riches and a lack of reverence for established cultural values and the distinctions between 'treasured' and debased objects; an approach that also accounts for Ruiz's indifference and lack of distinction between revered styles such as Surrealism or debased ones like the photo-roman. However, in the 1980s, piracy becomes in Ruiz's cinema, not only a *modus operandi* but an explicit thematic, with several films dealing with pirates and pirate narratives, as well as the related domains of sea stories, ships of the dead and children's tales. Ruiz was, of course, hardly alone in this enterprise in the period of 'high postmodernism', and similar fascinations with both cultural and literal piracy can be seen in the work of writers like Kathy Acker and Hakim Bey, to name just two examples.[3] However, in Ruiz's work this is not merely the celebration of appropriation and bricolage that would increasingly constitute the so-called hacker ethic of emergent digital culture; nor was it the mere repetition of the swashbuckling myth of outlaw masculinity that perhaps received its ultimate expression in the Hollywood *Pirates of the Caribbean* franchise (2003, 2006, 2007, 2011). Instead, Ruiz's pirate films express the search for an outside, a space of passage, beyond both European and Latin American traditions and cultural objects, the idea that by passing through the most clichéd forms of narrative, myth and folklore it might be possible to arrive at an open space that is directly associated by Ruiz with the sea. It is surely no accident that it is in this precise period that Ruiz moved both from televisual to truly cinematic projects as well as from working predominantly in France to a variety of European and international locations, particularly Portugal, facilitated by Ruiz's beginning of a long term working relationship with the Portuguese film producer Paulo Branco. This was not a purely pragmatic move, even if Portugal at this time was considered one of the most economical countries in Europe for producing art cinema and therefore attracted several other European auteur filmmakers such as Wim Wenders; for Ruiz, Portugal was also a passage to the ocean, indeed the only European coast that fully meets the Atlantic, just this side of Latin America and therefore constitutes a type of substitute for Chile's South Western 'littoral' that faces the Pacific; or as Ruiz has stated, Portugal operates in his cinema precisely as a bridge to Chile. This is not merely due to the geographical coincidence of being a narrow strip of land on the south west corner of a continent, directly facing the ocean but also to a range of atmospheric resonances with cultural as much as geographical dimensions. All of this would be incorporated into the impossible cartographies expressed in the series of films that Ruiz would film in Portugal during the 1980s, beginning with the aptly named *The Territory.*

The Territories and Negative Anthropology of Ruiz: The Territory and The Roof of the Whale

Despite the relative frequency of the concepts of territory and cartography being used to account for Ruiz's cinema, there is remarkably little critical engagement with the film *The Territory*, that began his new cycle of feature films in the 1980s, along with his important collaborations with both the Portuguese producer Paulo Branco and the English writer Gilbert Adair. Even the latter who recounts writing the script with Ruiz 'in a hotel room in Sintra' (Adair 1982: 40) is not especially forthcoming about the film except to describe it as a 'philosophical exploitation movie' and to state that it was filmed under 'hair-raising circumstances' (ibid.) without elucidating further what these circumstances were. The film seems to be shrouded in a kind of mystery concerning its production, for example, concerning the involvement of Roger Corman. While Corman is listed as one of the producers in the film's data, and Adair claims that Ruiz was able to persuade him to invest in the film, according to Adrian Martin, his sole contribution was to write a telegram saying that 'this movie must be very, very disgusting' (Corman cited in Martin 2004). Similarly there is the story that the entire cast and crew was appropriated by Wenders for his *Der Stand der Dinge* (*The State of Things*, 1982) that was shot shortly afterwards and featured Corman playing a lawyer and with which indeed many of Ruiz's crew and cast were involved including Branco and the co-producer Pierre Cottrell, along with the cinematographer Henri Alekan and much of the principal cast. From Wenders' perspective, however, we get a different account of the situation as recounted by Alexander Graf, who seems not to want to mention Ruiz by name: 'The story is based on … the situation he [Wenders] found when he visited a director in Portugal to charitably bring black and white film stock to a stranded film-crew whose finances were exhausted: their story became the background to the story for *The State of Things*, in which he films the crew – some of whom were borrowed from the real stranded crew – in the act of waiting' (Graf 2002: 44). Could it be that Wenders' most self-reflexive film about the plight of being a European auteur at the mercy of Hollywood and its market forces, might be based on a not-too-charitable act of appropriation of the work of a much more truly 'outside' filmmaker, the suppression of whose name in Graf's account gives the impression of being both an act of Eurocentric colonial violence and the reduction of the other to the nameless anonymity of the recipient of an act of generosity (a theme that would resurface subsequently in Ruiz's *Three Lives and Only One Death* and other works). While this is apparently the thesis of the never completed Jon Jost documentary *In Corman's Territory?* that apparently presented Ruiz as a third world subversive being 'cannibalised' by the system, as represented by Corman and Wenders, Ruiz, according to Martin, denied the prevalent myth that Wenders 'stole' *The Territory* from him. Indeed this kind of slippage and migration of characters between different films by different directors could itself be seen as corresponding closely to Ruiz's concept of the 'photographic unconscious' that will be dealt with in the next chapter.

Whatever the case, *The Territory* was clearly made on a virtually non-existent budget and was only able to be released in 1983 at the same time as the much more widely distributed *Three Crowns of the Sailor* (*Les trois couronnes du matelot*, 1983). Appropriately enough considering its production conditions, it concerns a group of tourists who become stranded in an anomalous zone, a forest park, from which there seems to be no escape, as it constitutes a kind of labyrinth. The tourists soon resort to bizarre behaviours culminating in cannibalism. Based in part on recent news stories about the passengers of crashed planes in the Andes turning to cannibalism before even running out of food, on one level the film uses cannibalism as a critical mirror for examining the mores of contemporary consumer society. However, more than this, it is a type of dark utopia that explores an alternative society, in which the rules of civilisation have been suspended. While commentators on the film have alluded to the 'Zone' of Tarkovsky's *Stalker* (1979) which was released shortly before the shooting of Ruiz's film, *The Territory* can only have a parodic relation to this film, since its 'mysticism' is very far removed from the Christian-derived moral one of Tarkovsky and is rather more related to ethnological or Bataillean questions of sacrifice, survival and the origins of the social.

A more productive intertext is Buñuel's *El ángel exterminador* (*The Exterminating Angel*, 1962), the most explicitly Surrealist of his Mexican films. In this film, the upper class guests at a mansion find they are mysteriously unable to leave it, not because of any actual barrier but because of a mysterious failure of the will. Abandoned by their servants to their own devices, all they have left are their absurd social rituals and conventions, which quickly begin to be subverted and degraded, culminating ultimately in acts of suicide and cannibalism. Superficially *The Territory* appears very close to this scenario and it is quite extraordinary that commentators on the film, who even contrast Ruiz explicitly with Buñuel like Buci-Glucksmann, have not mentioned this seeming parallelism between the two films. However, whereas *The Exterminating Angel* uses surrealist devices to present a clear social critique of the upper classes that is, as Richardson suggests, a direct adaptation of Hegel's Master-Slave dialectic (2006: 36), Ruiz's film instead presents an undecidable and anomalous domain, where it is concerned less with the question of the degradation of an old order than the creation of a new micro-society, or of society itself. Even cannibalism assumes an entirely different function in the two films; whereas in *The Exterminating Angel* it functions as a mere index of the decadence and moral vacuity of the bourgeoisie, in *The Territory*, it is the object of a strange affirmation, as the sign of a new mode of human existence, even if it is produced via a similar suspension of spatio-temporal and therefore social norms. Ultimately the key difference between the films is that between the degradation of the urbane interior of a mansion that perfectly encapsulates the social habits of its occupants and an exterior space of the forest in which the tourists become lost in *The Territory*. In the latter film, the tourists are 'strangers in a strange land', already potentially lost, and subject to external forces of an alien nature which brings *The Territory* into greater proximity with the aesthetics of the horror film than those of Surrealism.

In the beginning of the film, the tone is certainly more that of a low budget exploitation movie than an art film. While the French, English and American characters speak in a banal way about their impending trip into the forest a dinner is prepared of a whole pig, to which one of the children reacts in revulsion, thus signposting the future development of narrative events. The expedition is at first marked by generic events such as trouble with the guide Gilbert and the sense that their path is taking them in circles since they are crossing the same landmarks. When the body of Gilbert is found the film starts to acquire a more macabre atmosphere, as the characters argue with one another while attempting to find ways out of the park such as going to higher ground or walking in a straight line, none of which make any difference to the circularity of their wanderings. A key moment comes when they encounter a map of the park in which its nature as an impossible labyrinth is made clear; the map inverts, in a series of concentric figures, the park's situation of being within the province, within the country, and within Europe, so that the park contains first the province, then the country and finally Europe, a clear example of a Ruizian impossible cartography. Another key example comes when they encounter two men having a picnic of bread and cheese at an abandoned dam. While at first seizing upon this as their salvation, the characters soon discover that it is useless to try to talk to these men as they not only lack a common language but the men seem to be inhabiting a different space; certainly they seem unable to comprehend in any way the 'plight' of the trapped tourists and are no more useful when questioned later in the house of their friend by those searching for the missing visitors.

While Gilbert is dead he is no less central to the story as the tourists keep re-encountering his corpse which they wrap in plastic. After the children are seen playing happily inside this plastic, the adult characters move quickly from the difficult task of hunting small animals for food to the decision to consume Gilbert's body, from which only one of the adults, Françoise, abstains. More interestingly a type of religion, spearheaded by the American, Peter, starts to develop around these acts of cannibalism, making it clear that Françoise who has become ostracised from the group will be the first living victim of this rite. According to Peter, 'just as Jesus Christ shared his flesh, so should we'. Later in a highly comical scene the two men start fighting for who will become the next gift of food, a battle decided when Peter has a heart attack. When the tourists are finally rescued, the survivors become media celebrities, an existence so appalling to the one surviving child, Ron, that he chooses to go back to the territory. However, this account of the narrative of the film does not do justice to its aesthetics in which the territory is depicted in an increasingly luminous and non-naturalistic way via the uses of filters, fog, strange camera angles and towards the end allegorical images of human skulls and stars. It is as if the more the characters leave behind their banal middle class lifestyles and habits, the more the style of the film departs its initial realism, in favour of an allegorical style which suggests that this is not a descent into an animalistic form of survival so much as the invention of a new society and form of life.

More light can be shed on the film via reference to Ruiz's filmography. After all, his films of the late 1970s also concerned the suspension of social norms through the creation of specific environments ranging from the monastic spaces of *Suspended Vocation* to the mansion populated with *tableaux vivants* in *The Hypothesis of the Stolen Painting*, to the living-dead ludic world of *Zig-Zag*. All of these films can be seen as the exploration or mapping of labyrinthine territories, in order to elaborate their particular systems, all of which are predicated on the suspension of spatio-temporal and therefore sociocultural norms. *The Territory* makes this mapping operation even more explicit and clearly Ruiz was hoping that the film would also succeed in suspending the distinctions between commercial and artistic cinema, by being at once a Roger Corman exploitation film and a philosophical parable about the origins of human society. The financial difficulties surrounding the production only adds another layer to a film that was already about a type of crisis of sociality and the possibilities of survival, explored in a much less imaginative way in Wender's *The State of Things* in which the science fiction film within the film is called, appropriately enough, *The Survivors*. The prescience of *The Territory* was to combine the banal with the fantastic so that when the viewer finally sees edible human flesh as a type of *sashimi*, drying on a washing line, this seems less a shock device than a purely logical and everyday aspect of the micro-society created within the territory, in which everyday habits are combined with drastic new behaviours, in a manner largely devoid of any drama. *The Territory* seems to be one of the examples of Ruiz anticipating subsequent developments of mainstream media culture, in this case the rituals of reality TV, whose exemplars such as *Survivor* are based on similar, if more constrained and less extreme premises. What distinguishes Ruiz's film most of all from any of these intertexts is a type of ethnographic approach to his protagonists, a form of 'negative anthropology' that insists that we do not know what human beings are capable of, given a 'territory' in which habitual laws are suspended and other human potentials as epitomised by cannibalism can be realised. This ethnographic dimension to Ruiz's work would be given a more direct expression in his subsequent film, made the same year in The Netherlands, *Het dak van de Walvis* (*The Roof of the Whale*, 1981).

If *The Territory* was an excursion into the low cultural domain of the B movie, a territory that Ruiz would make several further voyages into, notably in *Shattered Image* (1998), *The Roof of the Whale* (1981) was definitely an art film, with a much clearer relation to the political questions that characterised his Chilean cinema. It has an especially close relation to *The Penal Colony*, not merely for addressing similar questions of cultural imperialism but also for presenting a fictitious cross-cultural encounter in which language, or more specifically plurilingualism, plays a key role. As such, more obviously than in Ruiz's other films from around this time, the problematics of exile are clearly inscribed in this film, albeit in a non-linear and fabulated form.

The encounter presented in the film is between a French anthropologist and his family and a tribe of Patagonian Indians, whose last surviving members have just been 'discovered'. The anthropologist is particularly interested in learning and formalising the Indian's language, however this language, at least as described by the Indians themselves, seems to consist entirely of a single phrase, '*yamas gutan*', which when used in different contexts is able to express the entire sense of the world. When the anthropologist points to different objects and asks the Indians to name them, this single phrase, spoken with different inflections is always given as an answer. What is more the meanings attributed to this polysemiotic signifier turn out to be far from stable and in fact the meanings seem to change almost daily, leading the anthropologist to abandon his interpretative endeavours. As such, on one level the film is a type of parodic treatment of the problematics of cross cultural 'first contact' in which, in Latin America as well as in other colonial settings, the efforts of anthropologists to understand native cultures, however well-intentioned, are inevitably linked to the destruction of these very cultures.

Taking place in five languages including the fictitious monolingual one spoken by the Indians, the film was shot on an island close to Rotterdam which, as filmed by Alekan, stands in remarkably well for a fictional Patagonia. However, the film is by no means a narrative about this encounter but rather uses it to stage a series of variations, which Rosenbaum refers to as 'a prodigious stream of visual, verbal and conceptual ideas centring around this theme' (Rosenbaum 1995: 231). In other words while both the complicit dynamics of first contact and ethnography and its critique are all present in the film, they do not exhaust its generative meanings which include philosophical speculation on the nature and origins of language, as well as on cinematic language. This led several commentators to see the film as a meta-cinematic work; for example, Louis Skorecki referred to the film as 'the most child-like film in the world, the least perverse, the most fluid. The childhood of its subject, of its themes, of its games, is that of cinema itself, which is suddenly rejuvenated by fifty years, that is to say it rediscovers the magic of the first recorded words' (Skorecki 1983: 34). This is not merely about verbal language, however, but an enactment of all ways of making sense of the world, including through images and sounds. The implication of the errors made by the anthropologist in interpreting the speech of the Indians is equally applicable to the images in the films which 'lose their weight of reality, and become as if dreamt, doubtful, perhaps even false' (ibid.).

Again it is a case of different rhetorics which cross between verbal and visual forms of expression, not to integrate them but rather in a form of mutual contamination leading to their further separation and questioning. The film therefore strangely accords with Michel Foucault's project of radically distinguishing verbal and written statements from visual and spatial *dispositifs* in order to analyse the workings of 'Power/Knowledge'. Ruiz's aims are clearly different and yet they proceed by a resonant method that instead of emphasising finished constituted perceptions focuses on their arbitrary and often falsified process of constitution, which nevertheless produces real effects; is not the cinema, for Ruiz a mechanism based on just such false premises which, rather than undermining its effectiveness and power actually makes it possible in the first place? It is in this regard that the oft-noted visual excess of the film, the use of artificial coloured filters and other trick devices seemingly unnecessary for a film about language can perhaps best be situated; in the sense that the anthropologist's attempts at comprehending the 'world-view' of the Indians by deciphering their language will inevitably fail since not only is their language untranslatable from its original context but also any such encounter is inevitably a game in which the 'objects' of ethnographic inquiry are dissimulating themselves, and this dissimulation is inevitably subject to further distortions in its interpretation. This can be read, as it is by Hamid Naficy, as an effort on the part of the Indians to evade capture in Western grids of interpretation: 'by remaining unintelligible, they become a moving target that cannot be comprehended and apprehended' (Naficy 2001: 50). This game of dissimulation is then echoed in the artifice of the images via which it is presented to the viewer, which is no less riddled with cross cultural misunderstandings and projections of meaning. It is perhaps on this formal level that the problematics of exile, dealt with more explicitly in *Dialogues of Exiles* and *Three Crowns of the Sailor* function as another allegorical level of the film in which Ruiz's situation as a Latin American filmmaker working in Europe is replicated by the situation of the Patagonians who find themselves under the ethnographic gaze of the French anthropologist and his family. That this is not completely far-fetched is supported by the story Ruiz apparently related in an interview with *Cahiers du Cinéma* cited by Adair, in which he described three 'Chilean' attitudes towards colonisation: Lautaro who studied the Spaniard's methods for no better reason than turning them against the colonisers, Jimmy Button who, adopted on board the Beagle, learned English in three weeks, went to Oxford and was admitted to the bar only to forget everything on his return to Latin America and Valderomat [sic], who was the darling of the salons before drowning himself in a sewer. When asked who he identified with, Ruiz apparently replied 'I have the feeling I drift from one to the other…' (Ruiz in Adair 1982: 44).[4] In other words, Ruiz's cinema of this period expressed these problematics of decentred relations between colonised and coloniser, centre and periphery, all the elements that make up what Naficy refers to as 'accented cinema'. In fact Naficy cites this film as a prime example of one of the key strategies of accented cinema, namely the multilingualism of exilic films which 'is driven by the many languages of the filmmakers and their crew, the stories they portray and the situated audiences whom they address' (Naficy: 49–50). However, as the above citation makes clear, Ruiz's version of accented cinema is uniquely complex and multiple, avoiding the adoption of a fixed position in favour of fluid relations both to Chile and to Europe, relations that would be expressed in a less opaque manner in Ruiz's next major film, *Three Crowns of the Sailor*.

Three Crowns of the Sailor

Before moving onto *Three Crowns of the Sailor*, it is necessary to emphasise that the production of these 'major' feature films by Ruiz, was accompanied by the continued production of other projects, several of them commissioned by various television stations, commissions the pace of which had hardly abated from the late 1970s. For example in 1980, Ruiz made, in addition to the short film *Zig-Zag* analysed earlier, 'La Nouvelle Ville', a film about the architect Patkai, 'Pages of a Catalogue/Dali' and 'Fahlstrom' for the Pompidou Centre, 'Musée Dali', the experimental video 'The Image in Silence' for the TV series *Télétests* and the four episode TV series *Le Borgne* (*The One-Eyed Man*), and he made a similar number of shorter projects in 1982, including 'La Classification des Plantes' ('The Classification of Plants') and 'Querelle des Jardins' ('The Dispute of Gardens') two very different projects for the Antenne 2 *Botaniques* series and 'Ombres chinoises' ('Chinese Shadows') under the pseudonym Wang Shi Shen for the *Juste une Image* series. It was only in 1981 that this extraordinary production rate slowed down slightly with a single short being produced, 'Images de Sable' ('Images of Sand') about a Dutch sandcastle artist, although Ruiz did shoot two feature films that year. In part this can be seen as the continuation of the mode of working already developed in Chile of working on several different levels and modes of production simultaneously, although now without the same political motivations. At the same time it is an expression of Ruiz's vocation as a cinematic *bricoleur*, never refusing a commission but frequently diverting it from its initial conception as was clearly evident in the case of *The Elections*. In some cases too, it has to be remembered that any distinction between major and minor works by Ruiz has an arbitrary dimension and in some cases is retrospective; for example, *Three Crowns of the Sailor* was a television commission that was only released as a 35mm film because its commissioners were so pleased with the results. For Ruiz, in contrast, the TV series *The One-Eyed Man*, described by Michel Chion as a 'Bardo film' (Chion 1983: 39) which was never developed beyond four episodes of the twenty that he originally envisaged, was far more central to his aesthetic concerns.

More than this, while *Three Crowns of the Sailor* was and remains one of Ruiz's most popular films with both critics and audiences, it is nevertheless one of the films which he was least satisfied with and which he seemed almost to have an animosity towards: 'It's a film I don't like much. There was a complicity on my part, with what was expected of me. The most grating thing was its success!' (Ruiz cited in Ruiz and Peeters 2002: 24). What Ruiz objected to in the film is that to him the images were merely the realisation of a fully developed script rather than its at least practical subversion in the process of shooting, as was the case with *The Hypothesis of the Stolen Painting* and would be the case with his next major film, *La ville des pirates* (*City of Pirates*). However, more than any of Ruiz's other projects until then, this was the film that fully announced Ruiz's 1980s cinema of piracy, both in its reference to tales of the sea and to its specific manner of combining and pastiching multiple sources both Latin American and European. As such it fulfils the function of being a vital step in Ruiz's aesthetic trajectory in the 1980s and definitely warrants further investigation.

Three Crowns of the Sailor as already indicated is a complex pastiche and combination of multiple sources including but not limited to Coleridge's 'Rime of the Ancient Mariner', Isak Dinesen's *The Immortal Story,* via its cinematic adaptation by Welles (*Histoire immortelle,* 1968) and popular legends of ghost ships of both a Chilean and European provenance, not to mention other literary influences like Edgar Allan Poe and Robert Louis Stevenson. Perhaps inspired by *The Immortal Story,* the film seems to aspire to be a pastiche of *all* the stories about ghost ships which have been told in myriad forms in diverse contexts ranging from popular folklore to high modernist literature and cinema. The film explicitly presents itself from the beginning as a complex maze of storytelling; in a colour pre-credits sequence, to the sound of Latin American accordion music, we see a glass of red wine and a hand that is writing a first person account of a sea voyage to the West Indies. Then, during the credits we see an old-fashioned ship sailing on an impossibly purple sea (which we might assume corresponds to the already narrated voyage). However, after the credits we see instead deep focus black and white images and hear the narration of a student who has just arbitrarily murdered his professor and 'teacher in the art of polishing diamonds', seemingly for no particular reason. This narrated act of murder is confirmed by the images we see, whose deep focus cinematography evokes the atmosphere of Wellesian film noir, while the narration evokes modernist literature. However at a certain point the narration abruptly changes and we hear the line, 'Tadeusz, who referred to himself in the third person'. Already we have several problems in locating any stable point of view; if we are now seeing the point of view of Tadeusz from this third person narration, what are we to make of the preceding first person narration, an uncertainty of subjective identity that is only amplified throughout the film? 'Tadeusz' now meets the sailor and after an absurdly logical exchange of dialogue, this leads to a scene of storytelling in which part of the price (the other part being the three Danish Crowns) that the student must pay for being rescued from danger (although it is suggested that in fact Tadeusz has already himself been killed by a stray bullet), is to listen to the story recounted by the sailor, which begins in the Chilean port of Valparaíso.

The rest of the film involves a relay between these two scenes, the first scene of storytelling shot in black and white and taking place in a spectral night-club and the second in colour of the fantastic story that is being told. However, this doubling is complicated by the fact that characters within the narrated story tend also to narrate other stories with all these layers of narration having multiple resonances with each other, but also by the interruptions of the first scene. These interruptions have the tendency to remind the viewer that these fantastic tales are already known; the student is constantly becoming impatient with the story, whose tale of a ship of the dead, of strange rituals amongst seamen, of meeting exotic characters in picturesque ports is already a kind of cliché, a familiar genre of conventional stories while the student is impatient to get to the more interesting and original aspects. This sets up a *mise-en-abyme* structure whereby the viewer is doubled by the student who embodies both the fascination and boredom with these kinds of stories, the credulity and incredulity they inspire, the impatience to get to the end of the tale and the experience of being caught up in the world of the story, which in the student's case is made literal by his doubling of the role of the sailor since he too has a place on the Fuchalense, or the ship of the dead.

The scene of fabulation in *Three Crowns of the Sailor*

The sailor and his sweetheart in *Three Crowns of the Sailor*

The other key aspect of this film is that through its deliberate use of clichéd genres and narratives, of the types of story that everyone has heard before, it taps into a modern collective imagination of movement and subjective dislocation, that it is then able to play with. Key to this is the deployment of doubling so that narrative events never have the linear effects we are anticipating but rather tend towards repetition. For example, when the sailor's friend, who refers to himself constantly as 'the other', commits suicide in protest at the cruelties of the officers, an evocation of Eisenstein's *Bronenosets Potyomkin* (*Battleship Potemkin,* 1927), the narrator is surprised to find him alive and well the next day saying that it was not he who jumped but the other. This doubling and dislocation of subjectivity reaches its apotheosis when the narrator himself becomes possessed by 'the other' or an alien perspective and it is only with great difficulty that he is able to maintain any sense of subjective identity and avoid himself jumping overboard.

This spectral subjectivity is clearly an artificial consequence of the narrative cliché of the ship of the dead, which in its presentation of a limbo state between life and death (and these spectral figures are surprisingly corporeal with their constant eating, various sores and diseases, and mysterious tattoos), allows for a complication and multiplication of problems of identity. But this limbo, 'bardo' state is also precisely that of diaspora and exile in which one must at the very least double one's identity in relation to both one's country of origin and the newly-adopted cultural context. The limbo state presented in the film therefore directly inscribes the experience of diaspora, rather than representing it as narrative content. In this regard one could view the artificial attempts of the narrator to create social bonds by inventing a hybrid family consisting of the 'virgin' prostitute who becomes his 'sweetheart', the young old man that he adopts as his son in Singapore and so on as similarly expressing the subjective experience of diaspora not as one of melancholy or loss but as one of a social creativity in movement, that is nevertheless haunted by the former experience of native collectivity.

Another point to make about this film is on the level of economics and exchange indicated by the title. Throughout the film there are complex exchanges of money which seem to reject the idea of money as an abstract universal equivalent but rather see it, instantiated in particular currencies, as a form of inexchangeable singularity. First of all, the sailor demands from the student three Danish crowns, rejecting the student's offer of larger (stolen) sums of money in other currencies which the student admits are worthless. Then there is the meeting of the sailor with the blind man who gives the sailor money, simply in order to borrow it from him again in order to buy them both drinks. And since every gift must be returned he then proceeds to return this gift in the form of information about the legendary Fuchalense. Finally, when the sailor wants to give Maria the money necessary for her to repay her father's debts and therefore to escape a life of prostitution, he borrows the exact sum from the petty officer in a variety of anachronistic and fantastic currencies, all of which must eventually be returned in exactly the same currencies and denominations since these bills are 'family heirlooms'. This is why the sailor needs the three Danish crowns. In all these cases, there is a strange economics at work that associates the exchange of money with that of stories while at the same time rejecting the capitalist abstraction of this exchange, the idea that any story can be exchanged for an abstract sum of money. Rather what is at stake is a kind of gift economy, in which singular stories play a vital role in the relations between human lives and money, so that currencies themselves seem to take on the vital qualities of singularity, while life becomes infinitely multiple and exchangeable. On the one hand this could be seen as Ruiz's version of Klossowski's utopian and Sadean idea of 'living currency',[5] in which human beings become themselves a form of money but on the other it is an implicit critique of the narrow economics of Hollywood cinema and its ethos that all stories are transparent and exchangeable for an abstract price; one could make a comparison in this regard with Godard's *Éloge de l'amour* (*In Praise of Love*, 2001) that also critiques the exchangeability of stories and money. Instead, as with Ruiz's critique of central conflict theory, this film argues for a cinema that through multiplying existing narratives, leads to a more open cinematic economy that has the paradoxical result of achieving a much greater level of singularity. In this way the film itself functions as if it were a uniquely disruptive and inexchangeable currency, in relation to normative models of both cinematic production and narrative construction. This is one way of characterising what I am calling Ruiz's cinema of piracy.

This aspect of the film has been brought out by some key post-colonial readings of the film by Zuzana Pick and Laleen Jayamanne, which are worth examining in more detail. In Pick's book, *The New Latin American Cinema,* she objects to the abstracting of Ruiz's work from its exilic conditions by critics such as Jonathan Rosenbaum who famously described Ruiz's earlier Chilean cinema, very little of which he had actually seen, as 'pre-Ruizian' (Rosenbaum 1995: 227). In contrast, Pick reads *Three Crowns of the Sailor* as being haunted by specifically Chilean sources such as the Chiloéan legends of the phantom ship, the Caleuche, which she argues is the direct inspiration for the Fuchalense. Considering that Chiloé was the coastal area of Chile that Ruiz himself originated from and that his father was a sea captain who no doubt would have recounted stories such as these, this seems a credible hypothesis. However, what she is really arguing is that the film, despite its European referents, is one in which 'the disembodied and phantasmagoric subjectivity of exile is replotted through the imaginary of popular culture' (Pick 1993: 183). In other words what Pick refers to as the various 'stylistic tics' of the film (ibid.), its use of dated techniques such as gels and excessive depth of field, its anachronistic use of voice-over, and its setting in exotic third world ports, are all products of the displacement characteristic of exile, in which home and cultural identity is displaced into a variety of locations. This is especially apparent in the sailor's attempt to create a surrogate family that includes the adoption of a child who is in fact an old man in Singapore and his attempt to pay the debts of a child prostitute he encounters in Tangiers.

Beyond the exoticism of the film's referents can be seen the exile's attempt to reconstitute a sense of identity at a distance from cultural origins, a reading that is reinforced in the film when the sailor returns to Valparaíso only to find his house is boarded up, his mother dead and that his sister has committed suicide; a return that can certainly be read as an allegory of the fate of contemporary Chile under Pinochet, as well as being a generic element of fables of the sea. Therefore, according to Pick, the film expresses a distinct sense of being in the world, which 'represents a self-reflective style of imaging whereby regional signifiers are reterritorialised and cultural identity ceases being solely attached to geographical codes ... Hence the "mise-en-spectacle" of exile is located in a metafictional territory where subjectivity nourishes itself in the criss-crossing of parody and utopia' (ibid.). In other words, the film is a type of exilic cartography, a deterrritorialised and redrawn map in which stable relations between centre and periphery, the real and the imaginary, the first and third worlds, geographical and fictional space are re-imagined from a mobile, displaced perspective.

Similarly, Jayamanne rejects the reading of Ruiz in Eurocentric terms, specifically as a surrealist, making explicit reference to his positioning as such in a retrospective in Australia curated by Adrian Martin. The assimilation of Ruiz into Surrealism is for Jayamanne to occlude Ruiz's much stronger relations with the baroque and not the high European baroque of Spain but the living tradition of the popular baroque in Latin America. In contrast to Martin's claim that Ruiz embodies a deep surrealist impulse, in contrast to the mere clichéd and stereotypical shock effects to which Surrealism is sometimes reduced, Jayamanne suggests the opposite, namely that it is precisely these superficial aspects of Surrealism that interest Ruiz and that he makes use of as part of 'his own allegorical practice' (Jayamanne 1996: 224). In other words, Ruiz's practice is fundamentally at odds with surrealist metaphysics and instead of seeking to make everything simple, it instead follows a baroque impulse of making everything more complex. This is related to the question of exile not just because the baroque is a living tradition in Latin America but because the practice of allegory itself is expressive of a rupture with identity that in Ruiz's case was not so much willed as the involuntary effect of the rupture with his homeland after the Pinochet coup.

According to Jayamanne, 'it is from a position of loss of country, language and identity that Ruiz begins to recover the loss by allegorising the moment of rupture in a film like *Three Crowns of the Sailor*' (1996: 236). She relates this experience to the Portuguese word 'Saudade' which while roughly translatable as nostalgia, in fact indicates a nostalgia for something that never was, whose non-existence is both cause for sadness and relief, at least in Ruiz's gloss on the term. In other words, the past is not an imaginary plenitude, a real to be regained even in the imagination, but a space of virtuality to be reinvented or transformed through the powers of allegorical creation. The feminine figures that populate the film such as the 'transvestite' femme fatale who strips off even her organs and the mother for hire who all the sailors want access to and who allegorises memory are perfect examples of an allegorical practice with a clear diasporic 'accent', an accent entirely lacking in European Surrealism. The fact that these allegories tend to destabilise the mythic symbols of the feminine as both femme fatale and the mother in the direction of an allegory of memory as an act of writing, are not the least of the salutory affects of the distancing of Ruiz from surrealist aesthetics enacted by Jayamanne in this essay. Both these readings clearly indicate that it is very risky to separate out a European, surrealist Ruiz from his Chilean origins and instead favour the concept of a Ruizian continuum that is nevertheless subject to creative differentiations, twists and turns that certainly characterise his trajectory over the course of the 1980s. With this caveat in mind, it is now possible to proceed to Ruiz's next film, *The City of Pirates,* a film that has been particularly generative of surrealist readings of Ruiz's work.

The Voyages of 'Captain Ruiz': From City of Pirates to Treasure Island

From the perspective of French and international film criticism, the overwhelmingly positive critical response to the release of *Three Crowns of the Sailor* was to turn 1983 into a veritable year of Ruiz, as exemplified by the two special issues of the leading French film journals *Cahiers du Cinéma* and *Positif* being devoted to his work. The former special issue featured several long interviews with Ruiz, engagements with his recent films by critics as renowned as Serge Daney and Michel Chion, and a bio-filmography in the form of a snakes and ladders game as a homage to Ruiz's short *Zig-Zag* (1980) that also referred to this game. Around this time there were also notable accounts of Ruiz in Anglo-American film journals like *Sight and Sound* and interviews and essays by leading critics such as Ian Christie and Jonathan Rosenbaum. The latter went so far in a report from the Rotterdam film festival in 1982 that 'like Godard and Rivette in the 1960s and 1970s, Ruiz "can simply do no wrong"' (cited in Adair 1984: 162). Ruiz's collaborator and commentator Gilbert Adair in the same article in which he cited this 'perilously hubristic attitude' (ibid.), goes on to state the following about the director's work at this time: 'There now exists a Ruiz-effect, a Ruiz-system, a Ruiz myth. As an artist, he has become subject to what could be described as the Law of Increasing Returns, to the point where, were he to append his signature to a frying-pan, lets say, it would oblige us to revise our perception of both the utensil itself and Ruiz's career – and perhaps of the world...' (ibid.). Such critical hyperbole could not last indefinitely, of course and by the late 1980s Rosenbaum referred to Ruiz's 1987 productions as showing 'a certain running down of inspiration and suggest[ing] a temporary exhaustion' (Rosenbaum 1995: 233). Nevertheless, the period of the mid-1980s was a remarkably productive and consistent one in Ruiz's career and one in which Ruiz showed, despite radically different projects, a singular focus on a cluster of themes around the sea, adventure, voyages, pirates and childhood. Anticipating this tendency, Danièle Dubroux's contribution to the special issue was entitled 'Les Explorations du Capitaine Ruiz' (The Explorations of Captain Ruiz), and viewed Ruiz's filmography as analogous to that of an explorer of uncharted territories: 'Each of Ruiz's films indeed proposes an exploration in the geographical sense of the term: a forest (*The Territory*), a town (*The One Eyed Man, Zig-Zag*), a garden (*The Dispute of Gardens*), a castle (*Chambord*), a painting (*The Hypothesis of the Stolen Painting*), but above all, an exploration of all the narrative possibilities, and all the visual and aural techniques that the cinema allows, with its accidents along the way, surprises and discoveries' (Dubroux 1983: 33). In other words, Ruiz's cinema can be seen as a type of cartography but a uniquely cinematic one that instead of exploring 'real' spaces, instead maps the potentials of the second order space of cinema itself and is therefore a type of virtual or impossible cartography. While this citation certainly gives an apt approach to Ruiz's films up to *Three Crowns of the Sailor,* it is even more appropriate to the films that would immediately follow it, especially Ruiz's next major work, *City of Pirates,* which can also be read as Ruiz's reaction against the success of *Three Crowns of the Sailor,* in which he made a sea story in the way he would like, with many more inventions, accidents, suspensions and aporias than the preceding film.

City of Pirates was filmed again in Portugal and according to Ruiz was the result of a strange process, partly based on a traumatic response to his first trip to Chile since the coup and partly an extension of the already developing obsession with the sea that had informed *Three Crowns of the Sailor.* In that film, Portugal, as Europe's southernmost opening to the Atlantic ocean, had already functioned as the allegory of the 'Littoral', substituting for both Valparaíso and a variety of other 'exotic' ports; in *City of Pirates* however, this allegorical function is intensified, and the Portuguese coast becomes a dreamt or *displaced* Chile, to use Adrian Martin's term, whose oneiric and allegorical logic dispenses with any need for a direct narrative or precise geographical referent: 'a constant referral elsewhere in terms of the action's origin or destination, its animating impulse or its ultimate meaning [...] the *entire tale,* its theorem of people, places and events, is always potentially "about something else", a distorted reflection of an elsewhere (such as, in Ruiz's case, far-off Chile)' (Martin 2004: 48, 49). In the same essay Martin also refers to Ruiz's practice of 'micro-fictions' (51), the art of putting at least two stories into a single film, or conversely the dispersal of similar motifs across multiple films. These practices, which correspond to Ruiz's account of the centripetal and centrifugal functions of the shot, will be explored more fully in the next chapter; for now, however, it is worth noting that *City of Pirates* was one of the first of Ruiz's films to systematically apply this principle since there are two distinct stories, with overlapping characters and no indication given that one has passed from the space of one story to the next. Ruiz's own account of the making of the film clearly indicates it was a very different situation to working with the highly polished script of *Three Crowns of the Sailor*:

> We had a script, in a sense, but it was written in an almost automatic way. I arranged some dramaturgical elements, some disparate ideas almost completely disconnected from one another. … There was a ball, a knife, a chessboard, an old radio, jewellery. All the objects were there, just like the characters … and once [the] story was constructed, I deliberately removed certain given elements of the script. (Ruiz in Ruiz and Peeters 2004: 26).

The proximity of this film to a type of cinematic automatic writing, deliberately unworking the script, has enabled its reading in proximity to both psychoanalysis and Surrealism, for example in Martin's already cited article, 'Displacements' to an idea of Ruiz's 'film-work' in proximity to Freud's analysis of the dream-work in *The Interpretation of Dreams* and Michael Richardson discerns in the film a 'surrealist mythology' (2006: 154), in the film's reference to Isidore Ducasse (the name of one of the main characters is Isidore) and a similar violent unmooring of the world's bearings as Buñuel's *L'Age d'Or* (*The Golden Age*, 1930).[6] However, for Richardson, 'the real surrealist provenance of the film lies in the mode of storytelling and the faith it has in chance to imbue imaginative wanderings with meaning' (2006: 155). Writing at the time of the film's release, Paul Hammond opened his account of the film by stating that 'Raúl Ruiz's *City of Pirates* is (de)composed under the sign of Surrealism, with its trust in ecstasy, scandal, the call of the wild, mystification, prophetic dreams, humour, the uncanny. Given the surprising swerves and disorientations evoking Buñuel and Dalí, and the confidence in a poetic discourse recalling Eluard and Péret, one wonders if Ruiz didn't elaborate his scenario using the Surrealist mode of automatic writing' (Hammond, 2004). Bearing in mind that for Ruiz Surrealism is more or less a specific, modern variant of the baroque, one might read the film less as surrealist than of making use of particular surrealist procedures for the specific purpose of destabilising normative narrative forms and opening up cinematic potentials beyond the telling of a single, organic story, knowable in its entirety. In fact Ruiz refers in a recent interview to making the film in a '*piscine surrealist*', a surrealist pool. If this film is in proximity to Surrealism therefore, it would certainly be less to a mainstream Surrealism's celebration of the marvellous than to the heretical surrealists like Bataille, whose ellipses and emphasis on 'the night' of unknowing, seem to employ similarly subtractive methods to Ruiz. Nevertheless, Ruiz's particular way of exploring the relations between processes such as automatic writing and the multiple potential relations between images is at the same time fully consistent with Buci-Glucksmann's concept of the baroque eye of the camera, in which Surrealism is not so much excluded as incorporated as one visual rhetoric among others, one way of fabricating allegories and exploring and elaborating unforeseen cinematic spaces.

City of Pirates, while not pastiching literary sources as explicitly as *Three Crowns of the Sailor,* was nevertheless inspired by numerous other narratives. First of all, Ruiz had been preparing another film based on a story of two children discovering a deserted island and finding there a children's graveyard, whose origins lay in the repression of a child revolt, a tale Ruiz associated with Jean Vigo's *Zero de Conduite* (1933).[7] This film was abandoned just before shooting was due to commence, so Ruiz decided to play with these and other images of childhood, including some with a surrealist or quasi-surrealist provenance, like the Genetian idea of the child assassin, as well as the motif of the murderous maid that so attracted Breton and other surrealists. Added to this was Antoine De Saint-Exupery's story *Le Petit Prince* (*The Little Prince,* 1995) that Ruiz had a strong antipathy towards and seemed to want to create a counter-mythology to, using these darker images of childhood. All of this was combined with what Ruiz has referred to as the '*cauchemars de sieste*' (siesta nightmares) inspired by his visit to Chile. Ruiz stated that Chile under the dictatorship appeared to him as a heightened, intensified version of itself, which he went so far as to describe as a kind of 'epiphany' and his siestas there were troubled by dreams that had a Walt Disney quality to them. A final element that came into the end of the film was a news story about some Chilean policemen who liked to kill couples when they were in the act of making love. According to Ruiz the method of making this film was also very unusual and certainly corresponded to surrealist practices of automatic writing. With all the elements assembled, the objects, the characters and the décors, Ruiz would write the script each day immediately after the siesta; hence, in effect, *dream* the script rather than writing it, validating Martin's idea that the work on this film bore a close resemblance to the Freudian idea of dream work.

Consider, for example, the opening sequence of the film. Rather than the beginning of any story, the scene presents an array of initially disconnected elements that only gradually come into relation with one another. However, in this process the film tends to become more rather than less bizarre and works to open up a mysterious cinematic space out of apparently banal and simple elements: a kitchen, a terrace, some knives, a bouncing ball, a couple and a maid. After opening shots of the sea with highly artificial coloured filters in which the tide seems to be moving in two directions at once, a visual refrain that punctuates the film, there is a complex sequence containing a number of elements that seem to exist in separate spaces to each other. There is a radio switched on at the beginning of the sequence by the maid, Isidore, to which no-one is listening. Meanwhile the maid is recounting the sorrows of her broken heart in a series of clichés and in the terms of popular melodrama. Meanwhile, a woman of about the same age is pacing in the kitchen also reciting banal statements but of a more bourgeois variety. There are also two knives on a table in front of the radio, one of which is absently picked up by Isidore, perfectly justified by this being a kitchen and yet given a disturbing prominence in the frame. Meanwhile the camera, rather than following the movements of the characters who keep disappearing from the frame seems to be following its own logic, and especially to be seeking out the sea that lies beyond a partially open window that is ultimately shut by Isidore. At the same time, a male voice can be heard calling Isidore's name but receives no response from either of the on-screen figures; so far there is no indication of how all these elements will be combined. Following this sequence shot, there is an abrupt cut to a shot in which depth of field is used to present the woman in the foreground, obsessively washing a glass and entreating Isidore in the background to 'forget him' while the latter clearly remains inconsolable.

The scene then shifts to the terrace and the mobile close up of a tray of coffee and breakfast that Isidore is bringing to the couple we presume to be her employers. However, this initially banal scene is rendered through an alternation of shots that become increasingly bizarre, and use depth of field to present extremely magnified objects in the foreground of the image, completely distorting any type of natural perception. These include an extreme close-up of the woman's hand with cigarette in a long holder with Isidore in the background facing the sea, a shot of a drinking glass with an iced drink in front of an image of the woman, a shot of a plate of potatoes in extreme close up in front of a white bouncing ball in the middle ground with the man in the background, a shot from under the glass table via some fruit to the head of the man and so on. The visual culmination of this sequence of increasingly absurd and improbable point of view shots is an entirely impossible shot from inside the male character's mouth beyond whose teeth the woman's face can be seen.

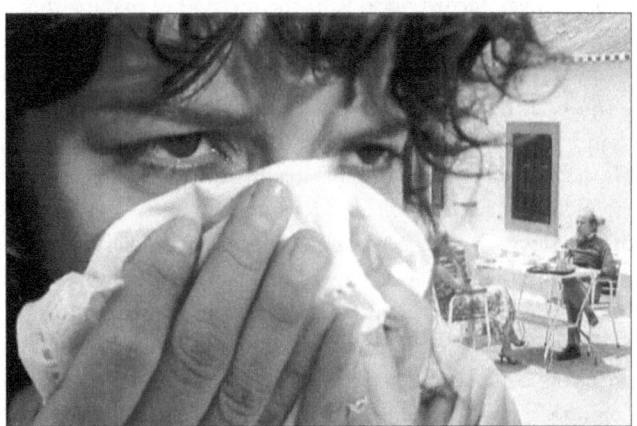

City of Pirates,
Terrace scene 1, Isidore

City of Pirates,
Terrace scene 3, toothache

During this visually remarkable sequence the conversation has consisted of apparent *non sequiturs* and poetic statements such as 'how sad it is, the coffee of exile' while a key figure in the scene is the bouncing ball which is not only self-moving but seen by the couple in a matter of fact way as being their lost son. They also discuss both having to move house and the man's toothache, which provides a type of justification for the impossible shot referred to above. This description, which only very partially does justice to this opening sequence, can give some idea of Ruiz's way of working in this film in which one is following a series of associations between the visual and sonic components constituted by the objects, characters, décors, and the cinematic shots and movements themselves, whose meaning, if there is any, is yet to be determined. To complicate things still further, key elements of the story, such as it is, are deliberately suppressed. For example, while we assume that these characters permanently live in the house they are occupying, in fact, they are merely some type of guardians, who move from house to house, according to the rule that whenever the man gets a toothache, they have to move. With this arbitrary but nevertheless explanatory key omitted, the following scene in which the characters are seen throwing their suitcases through the open window of another house has no justification whatsoever. Nevertheless, this is precisely what Ruiz was aiming at, since for him, even suppressed, subtracted scenes play a role in the effects generated by a film and in a sense because of films being composed of the montage of multiple spatio-temporal fragments *every* shot has a suppressed, subtracted before and after that continues to play a role in a film despite not being perceived by the spectator; Ruiz is therefore just making this process explicit, according to his formula, for 250 shots, 250 films.

It is sequences like the above that led commentators like Adair to declare that in this film 'the cinema virtually renounces its role as a recording medium' (1984: 161), meaning that everything that appears in the film, including its shots of nature, seem to be invented on the spot and yet create an entirely consistent if hypnotic and oneiric world. There is, however, a type of narrative that emerges in the form of the sudden appearance of an angelic or demonic child who precipitates with Isidore's complicity the brutal murder of the couple and then 'elopes' with her to a semi-mythical island. Once on the island, the child unceremoniously abandons Isidore, who becomes the prey and prisoner of a psychotic loner, thus entering the space of an entirely distinct story. Ultimately, Isidore returns to the space of the first story and is exonerated for the murder of the couple, since it was in fact perpetrated by the police. Childhood, desire, violence and death are all articulated via these tales that nevertheless have a haunting and hypnotic atmosphere and visual richness that overrides the actual stories, which are reduced to a mere pretext or even red herrings, serving simply as the basis for a rich series of articulations of the possibilities of cinematic language. Colour, for example, is both extraordinary and excessive in the film, from the multi-coloured tinted seascapes to the costumes of the characters and the artificial lighting used in almost every scene. However, rather than communicate any symbolic meaning, this use of colour generates an intensified vision of the world, whose only meaning might lie in the allegorical sense that what we are seeing is a refracted vision of another reality, that might correspond to Ruiz's initial wish to call the film *Impressions of Chile*. In fact, the way the film operates is at once to frustrate the desire for narrative meaning while nevertheless evoking several tales, providing openings for an entirely different mode of relating to cinematic images as a type of associative exploration of an invented cinematic space. While this could indeed be related to the idea of surrealist automatic writing, it can also be productively understood as a type of audiovisual cartography, an impossible cartography in the sense that it presents movements and perspectives that are only possible cinematically – for example, the point of view from within the mouth of a character suffering from toothache – but that nevertheless generate their own consistent reality. This is provided that this reality is entered into in an experimental or ludic rather than judgemental manner by the spectator. This is no doubt why this film by Ruiz is so frustrating for some critics and certainly did not generate as widespread an enthusiastic critical response as his previous film but at the same time is considered one of the most perfectly realised Ruiz films by those critics most attuned to his work; to describe a film as Ruizian is more or less the equivalent of evoking *City of Pirates* as perhaps the most poetic and hypnotic point of Ruiz's entire career.

The following work in this 'series', *Les Destins de Manoel* (*Manoel's Destinies*, 1985) was produced in multiple forms as both a four-part Portuguese and three part French TV series, as well as a feature film version, none of which seem to be identical; a multiple manner of working that is by no means unique in Ruiz's career and also characterised his recent film *Mistérios de Lisboa* (*Mysteries of Lisbon*, 2010). The first part or episode of the TV version of *Manoel's Destinies*, 'The Destinies of Manoel', uses repetition to generate a non-linear or rather multi-linear narrative in which on the way to school Manoel is called by a voice which he follows into a vacant courtyard behind his house, the camera lingering on a series of actions that initiate the adventure; climbing a wall, crossing a field, entering and exiting a dark passageway. On the first occasion he follows this path he meets an older version of himself who informs him that the choice he will make will influence his destiny and that of his family; when he returns home it is night and giant shadows are projected on the walls of his house. This sequence is repeated with variations, in one of which he encounters an old fisherman who takes him out on a boat and recounts wild stories of the sea. It soon becomes clear that these repeated journeys are not following a chronological order but rather present three alternate destinies according to the choices Manoel makes in response to this call of the unknown, of stories, of the sea. In one series, his mother, despairing of her son's aberrant behaviour commits suicide; in the second series, Manoel stays away from the mysterious zone and becomes a brilliant student leading to his father's suicide at having to pay exorbitant school fees; in the third variation his efforts to save his parents results in his own death. However, this does not stop these series from continuing their repetitions the 'next' day.

More important than the narrative events themselves is this structure of variations that more resembles a piece of music than a chronological narrative. In the subsequent episodes of the series the action shifts to other locations, a school trip to a forest, a stay at his aunt's house, without losing the sense of multiple possible worlds already established in the first episode. The spaces traversed by Manoel are less physical spaces than spaces of fabulation, in which the multiple possibilities of story-telling are played out in all their variations. More than this there is a continual crossing between stories, and this sense of passage is embodied in the figure of the sea captain/ferryman in the third episode who states 'crossing borders is my business'. While Richardson states that the film unravels towards the end, it would be more accurate to say that the film/series becomes increasingly detached from a direct relation to any linear story, even a multiple one and becomes an exploration of the powers of cinematic images themselves, with all their crossings, transmissions and interferences. For Fergus Daly the film 'takes us on a search through the worlds of, firstly, the storyteller, the philosophical weaver of words and worlds; secondly, the calculating and computing laboratory of science; and, thirdly, the generating sources of creativity, of art and life' (Daly 2004) and it is certainly the case that this is one of Ruiz's works that most demonstrates the powers of images to generate multiple stories and meanings, even at the risk of these meanings becoming lost in an overwhelmingly complex audiovisual flow of images and events, uncontainable in any single narrative.

This ludic play with visual fabulation, in proximity to childhood games, pirates and sea stories would reach its apotheosis in the relatively big budget France/Great Britain/USA co-production of *Treasure Island*, featuring stars such as Martin Landau, Jean-Pierre Léaud and Anna Karina, made in 1985 but not released until 1991 and even then certainly not as the 'blockbuster' that its US backers must have been hoping for. One can certainly see why Ruiz in this period might have been drawn to Stevenson's classic story not merely for its tales of piracy and adventure on the high seas but more so for its presentation of the relations between childhood imagination and adult cynicism as two distinct worlds that nevertheless impinge upon one another without ever being fused into one. As Richardson points out, *Treasure Island* was a novel that 'enchanted the Surrealists' (Richardson 2006: 155) and Ruiz's film certainly emphasises the breaking down of the barriers between reality and the imagination that was no doubt what made the novel appealing to this movement. Yet *Treasure Island* is not as close to classical Surrealism as *City of Pirates* and not only because in the place of 'cinematic automatic writing' it takes on the more conventional task of literary adaptation. It is rather that the film, despite its apparent anachronism, takes on a far more contemporary engagement with media and especially with the idea of the game than would even have been possible in the classic period of Surrealism, in a way that fully engages with both postmodernism and new media in the form of video games that were just beginning to be developed at that time. It is in this film that Ruiz's cinema most approaches the ideas of piracy embodied in the postmodern fiction of writers like Kathy Acker, whose privileged *modus operandi* was to inhabit the spaces of pre-existing, anachronistic fictions by deliberate acts of plagiarism, in order to deconstruct their workings and use them as tools for destabilising organisations of gender, desire and subjectivity. This is not to say that Ruiz was in some way influenced by postmodern writers like Acker; it is rather a case of affinity as is borne out by Ruiz's subsequent collaboration with the postmodern performance group 'The Kitchen' for *The Golden Boat* (1990) a film in which Acker also participated. Nevertheless if many of Ruiz's films of the early 1980s and before had been characterised by pastiche and the reworking of found fictional materials, in *Treasure Island* this reaches a climax in which an anachronistic fictional construct becomes a device for a type of media engagement with more in common with the future development of video and media art than with classical conceptions of cinema.

This reading of the film is confirmed by the opening images which seem to come from an African civil war, complete with running natives, gunshots, screams and fire. These sequences are preceded by the title, 'My tale begins with a misunderstanding', which indeed proves to to be the case since these images are in fact from the favourite TV series that the main character 'Jim Hawkins' is watching. Subsequent to the release of the film but presumably written beforehand was a novel by Ruiz, *In Pursuit of Treasure Island* (Ruiz 2008), that while pursuing related strategies to the film in its appropriation and decentring of Stevenson's text is also marked by key differences. One of these differences is that in the place of this TV sequence there are numerous accounts of reading, including of a book of memoirs written by a female African escaped slave. Both the book and the film present characters who are haunted and possessed by pre-existing fictions but it is significant that in the film these are at least in part audiovisual ones and therefore a more contemporary 'media ecology' than that presented in the book. As this television transmission is interrupted by a power cut, we are informed that its tale of a *coup d'etat*, diamonds and treachery continued in Jim's head. In other words while we may be aware that stories originate elsewhere and come to us from the outside it is we who continue them as they take possession of our imaginations; so before even introducing any of the elements of *Treasure Island*, the key theme of possession by prior stories that make up not only Ruiz's film but in a more implicit way the original novel itself is already well established. This corresponds well with Serge Daney's poetic description of the film:

> Take a child and make sure that he is dreaming; wake him up and tell him a story. Cradle him with your most beautiful voice-over, make it insidious. It must be that once asleep again, the child is able to dream the story that you have breathed into him. It must be that when he awakes he feels that its the story he has chosen and not the inverse. *The Immortal Story* was the title of one of Welles' last films; but every story is immortal say all of Ruiz's stories. From which come so many delights, then too many delights, then terror. (Serge Daney, cited in *Le Cinéma de Raoul Ruiz* [website])

What follows is what the viewer mistakenly believes to be Jim's story, that is the story of Treasure Island itself; the arrival of a seafaring stranger, strange nocturnal conversations about diamonds, treasure maps and an expedition to retrieve them and so many other elements that even in the original novel were already well established tropes of what we might call after Ruiz, Welles and Dinesen/Blixen an immortal story. As Matthieu Lindon put it in a contemporaneous review in *Libération*, 'more than a century after its appearance, Stevenson's novel has transformed itself into such a myth that it and all that it represents, the time of childhood and first reading experiences, has become a treasure in itself, in search of which every adult has a thousand reasons to pursue' (Lindon cited in Bax *et al.* 2003: 145). While Ruiz's cinematic treatment of the elements of the novel is done with his customary decentred visual flair, especially in its presentation of perverse familiar relationships and childhood desire and curiosity precipitating increased exposure to a violent adult world, what is most distinctive in his approach to the story only becomes gradually apparent. At a certain point in the film it starts to become clear that all the strange and violent adult behaviour that Jim has been spying on, even including the murder of his father, has been nothing but a lure, the attempt to seduce him via a romantic yet incomplete tale into playing the role of Jim Hawkins which is revealed to be less his personal identity than a pre-established and necessary role in what is shown to be not *Treasure Island* itself but a Treasure Island game. As in the cartographic game in *Zig-Zag* this is a game played in real spaces with real lives and deaths but it is no less fictional than the novel on which it is based, while the latter is increasingly read not as a fiction but rather as an instruction manual for how to operate successfully in the Treasure Island game.

All of this starts to become clear when a young man, a writer played by Jean-Pierre Léaud arrives on the island and seems to know everything about Jim. The casting of Léaud works perfectly in this role since Jim and the writer are different temporal aspects of the same character, his past and future respectively, since the writer is also the voice-over narrator of the film and therefore a future Jim Hawkins recounting the past adventures that the young Jim Hawkins is about to live through. Léaud's performance cannot help but recall his roles for Truffaut and Godard as the New Wave child actor *par excellence* in films such as *Les quatre cents coups* (*The 400 Blows*, 1959), especially in relation to Poupaud who performed a similar series of roles in Ruiz's films of the 1980s. As Cyril Béghin puts it, together they constitute a Janus figure that is crucial to the film: 'Jim/Melvil Poupaud has another voice than his own, that of an older actor, Jean-Pierre Léaud, who looks at him via his past with Truffaut towards the future of the young actor (Poupaud, like Léaud with the director of *The 400 Blows*, has made a series of films with Ruiz, since child-hood). Then Léaud appears, playing the role of a writer in trouble, a sort of proto-Stevenson who doesn't stop telling Jim that he has been waiting for him, to put an end to his writing' (Béghine 2004). This is only one layer of paradoxical meta-fiction out of which the film as a whole is constructed as a series of multi-layered performances whose basis lies in 'immortal fictions' rather than any pre-existent reality.

These meta-fictional aspects of the film in which it is less the case of characters living out a real story so much as characters attempting to impose on Jim an already scripted yet malleable story, a story that he has to willingly participate in, enables all kinds of strange, paradoxical effects and Ruizian jokes such as the pirate who while stating menacingly that 'you can't make an omelette without breaking eggs', actually proceeds to do so. There is also a good deal of cruelty ranging from the father driven to suicide or perhaps murdered right in front of Jim to his beating by the pirates as a just punishment for his treatment of the blind man with the complicity of his mother and the captain. But since his parents and all the other characters are playing the roles of characters from *Treasure Island*, all of this is just role playing designed to entice Jim further into the game, to entice him to provide the directions of a map that he is completely ignorant of. After the death of his father, all this is made explicit and the characters are shown dissecting the pages of *Treasure Island* for clues as to how best play the Treasure Island game: 'Captain: "Read this book carefully – on that is based the fate of Western civilisation" ', spoken as the captain is dying after having murdered Jim's cat 'as a joke'.

At the same time the Oedipal coordinates that open the film, the weak and implicitly detested father, the dominant and desired mother, the intrusion of the stranger as castrating outside threat and paternal superego, are increasingly dispersed throughout the social field with everyone claiming patrimony over Jim. It is as if the father function becomes so generalised as to be co-extensive with the novel itself, which is after all, Jim's true progenitor. Similarly when they finally embark on the voyage to Treasure Island and are taken over by another vessel, they do not need to explain anything since the captain of this vessel is a fan of literature and is already completely familiar with every detail of their story. Or else this too is a role and this captain, Benito Cyreno, another literary reference, just another mask for another player in the game. As Helen, Jim's Aunt, also the femme fatale-like object of his desire, who surprisingly turns up on the ship explains it: 'They have no morality because they're playing a game. They don't care about money or danger, which makes them 10 times more dangerous, I hope I manage to kill them all.' The gunfights, scenes of torture and so on that ensue are all equally fake even though they can have real consequences and this is perhaps the point. At the same time the narrator, who is also the writer and therefore another Jim Hawkins, maintains that 'everything happens as it had been written', and that 'everything depends on two factors: the book and the game'. Everything happens as it was written and yet since the text is submitted to the logic of the game how it will have been written depends on how the game is played, which has a degree of contingency that the book will be forced to adapt to. As such it has a lot in common with video games, then a relatively new phenomena in which generic narrative fragments are pre-designed and activated by particular sequences and at the same time subject to a range of possible alternatives depending on how the game is actually played.

This ludic structure is not, however, simply the borrowing of and reinvention of one media form, the videogame in this case combined with literature, in the terms of another, cinema, as could be argued of game-related films like Cronenberg's *eXistenZ* (1999); at least the implication in Ruiz's film is that games are a serious matter. At the end of the film it is revealed that the Treasure Island game was invented by a professor of 'Polemology' which is the study of human conflict and war and indeed it is claimed at the end of the film that 'the world is not at war, the world is playing an enormous global game, there are rules but the rules are secret'. While this may just sound like a conspiracy theory of the type advanced in Robert Anton Wilson and Robert O'Shea's *Illuminatus* trilogy, the mainstream Hollywood film *The Da Vinci Code* (2006) or even Ruiz's own *The Hypothesis of the Stolen Painting*, at the same time it recognises the ways in which contemporary violence, including military violence are increasingly based on game models and simulations, as the banal examples of the use of video games for military training purposes, or the enacting of cruel games of torture both taken from the current war in Iraq are clear instances of. Everything may be a game and even, as Ruiz has suggested elsewhere as a cosmological principle he subscribes to, the entire world might be created as a joke (Ruiz 1999: 66), but it is a deadly serious one for those whose fate it is to play within it. In the Ruizian universe the ludic is therefore raised to this cosmological level and this is perhaps nowhere played out as explicitly as it is in *Treasure Island*. In this sense it is not far-fetched to argue that far from being a fantasy adventure film, a harmless film for children, *Treasure Island* is in fact one of Ruiz's most *political* or at least ethical films, especially in its presentation of the resistance to imposed narratives of competitiveness and death, which it is not a distortion to read as a form of resistance to so many deadly violent games that are played out not only in films and in other forms of entertainment but in the world at large; this is only to assimilate the film to Ruiz's subsequent arguments against 'central conflict theory' which will be engaged with more fully in the next chapter.

Ruiz's Spectral Journeys: Memory of Appearances, A TV Dante, Dark at Noon

This cluster of tropes of the sea, piracy, childhood and adventure became increasingly abandoned in Ruiz's cinema of the late 1980s and certainly after the at once aesthetic high point and, in respect of the idea of major Hollywood film distribution, disappointment of *Treasure Island*, it is hard to see how Ruiz could have gone any further in this precise domain. In this sense, in the absence of the film being released, Ruiz's novel, *In Search of Treasure Island*, which is even more disorienting and dispersive than the film, constitutes the ultimate statement of this complex in Ruiz's work, despite the resurfacing of some of its elements such as the sea and childhood. At any rate, as usual this is far from the only domain of work Ruiz had been pursuing in the mid-1980s and in this last section of the chapter we will examine another cluster of films which, without abandoning the idea of piracy on a structural level, can better be characterised as spectral journeys taking on a variety of forms from one project to the next and yet also exhibiting a perceptible stylistic consistency.

Prior to this, it is worth pointing out some of the other tendencies exhibited in Ruiz's mid-1980s films that are continued and extended in these films from the second half of the decade. One of the key characteristics of the director's work in this decade was a tendency towards a transmedia practice that while remaining focused on cinema also traversed a number of other aesthetic domains. We have already seen crossings with literature and television in *Treasure Island* not to mention Ruiz's television work of the 1970s; in other projects of the 1980s we also find direct engagements with theatre, with films of Racine's *Bérénice* (1983) and Shakespeare's *Richard III* (1986), as well as *La présence réelle* (*The Real Presence*, 1984) at once the portrait of a precariously employed actor and a documentary about the Avignon festival, and the film *Mémoire des apparences* (*Memory of Appearances*, 1986) which incorporated scenes from Ruiz's own theatrical production of Calderón's *La vida es sueño* (*Life is a Dream*, 1636); *Mammame* (1985), which presents a dance performance choreographed by Jean-Claude Gallotta; *A TV Dante* (1989) which was commissioned by Channel 4 in its more experimental phase and followed on from a previous episode done by Peter Greenaway; *The Golden Boat* (1990) which was a film made in cooperation with the New York performance art group, The Kitchen and also a transposition of both US and Mexican soap operas; and finally the beginning of the 1990s saw Ruiz's first forays into installation art with *The Expulsion of the Moors* (1990) which was exhibited in Boston, Santa Barbara, Valencia and Paris. It should also be mentioned that Ruiz was at this time further diversifying his cinematic activity by taking on the role of co-director at the Maison de la Culture at Le Havre from 1985, during which time he produced several of his own films alongside live productions, as well as producing some films of his contemporaries.[8]

There is much that could be said about these trans-disciplinary explorations, occurring as they did in the decade in which many of Ruiz's contemporaries such as Godard or Wenders were lamenting the state of cinema in its submission to market forces and domination by television. On one level Ruiz's multi-disciplinary work can be seen as a pragmatic affirmation that it is always possible to create in whatever medium or context is available, if not a film then a play, an installation, a performance, a work for television or some crossing between these domains without the slightest trace of ontological anxiety about the medium specificity of cinema. In this respect, Ruiz's aesthetic wanderings mirror the contemporaneous development of Raymond Bellour's concept of '*Entre-Images*' which under the pressure of both television and video art, sought to reposition cinematic images as one form of technical and aesthetic image amongst a diverse field of media practices including not only photography and video but also painting, poetry and philosophy in which we are no longer certain exactly what constitutes an image (Bellour 1999: 9). Ruiz's transmedia voyages, however, have less to do with stories of what is or was cinema, as Godard would subsequently investigate in *Histoire(s) du Cinéma* (*Historie(s) of Cinema*, 1989/1998), but rather about the powers of creativity across media in which cinema is caught up. In this respect, far from being a threatening enemy, television, for example, was often a way of continuing Ruiz's prolific output, with its own fascinating logistics to explore, as was already evident in Ruiz's INA projects of the 1970s. Beyond this, it is possible to see in Ruiz's transmedia experimentation another trajectory which is that of the spectral; already Ruiz's work had evidenced a long-term interest in spectres, shadows, marginal phenomena and anomalies and these interests certainly intensified during the 1980s. It is as if to complement the cartographies of 'real' spaces in the films just discussed, Ruiz was pursuing at the same time other journeys into more shadowy regions, even if this meant staying in one place in a geographical sense.

In *L'éveillé du pont de l'Alma* (*The Sleepwalker of Alma Bridge,* 1984), for example, a collection of characters intersect around the narrow terrain surrounding the bridge in question; nevertheless the film is full of passages between sleep and wakefulness, life and death, presence and absence so that it becomes every bit as much a film of voyages as Ruiz's 'pirate' films of the same period: a stationary voyage in other words, in which the phantom-like characters are no less mobile. Two insomniacs, a boxer and a professor who meet on the Alma bridge and have interminable philosophical conversations, observe and rape a pregnant woman, Violette, the first in a series of victims. After giving birth, she commits suicide by throwing herself in the Seine but keeps returning both in the form of a subsequent victim and in the visions of her surviving son, who is aware of the identities of the perpetrators since his mother maintains communication with him. At the same times this is, as Pascal Bonitzer commented, a film about theories: theories of paternity and origins but also of metaphysics as embodied by the string of questions the child poses to his father that follow a logic of infinite regress: 'Papa, let's be serious ...you know that Christ came to save us and that he was born of a virgin. What is a virgin? A virgin is a woman who has not had relations. What are relations? Relations consist in a very strong embrace but at the same time it's a message signed by a minister. What is a minister? It is a functionary who works within a mystery. What is a mystery? It's a little fish.' This obscure line of questioning is something Ruiz would elaborate on later in *Poetics of Cinema* in the relations between 'ministry and mystery' or institutions and belief but it functions in the film to forge a series of connections between diurnal, rational theory and a somnambulist, watery domain of spectres, revenants and shadows. The whole film becomes bathed in a spectral ambience in which sleep, dream and wakefulness, the bridge and the river, insomnia and theory as well as life and death become indiscernible and interchangeable. Another example that could be singled out from the same period would be the short film 'Voyage of a Hand' ('Voyage d'une main', 1984), based loosely on the writings of the Polish baroque writer Count Jan Potocki, in which a disembodied hand travels various exotic locations throughout the world accompanied by a black statuette, which is ultimately melted down into a cannonball with which the main character commits suicide (based on an actual yet surreal detail of the death of Potocki himself). This film condenses and carries to a point of absurdity the kind of impossible, spectral cartography Ruiz was pursuing at this time in a number of his films. In the rest of this section we will explore three of these spectral journeys, namely *Memory of Appearances*, *A TV Dante,* the project made for Channel 4, and *L'oeil qui ment* (*Dark at Noon*, 1992), which are key instances of these spectral aesthetics that constituted Ruiz's filmmaking at the end of the 1980s.

Memory of Appearances is definitely one of Ruiz's most fully realised films of the 1980s, a film which combines a high level of formal abstraction, with several of Ruiz's obsessive concerns, notably with memory, inter-relations between cinema and theatre and their respective signs and I would also argue, signalled a re-engagement, however obliquely, with specifically Latin American questions of the politics of exile and return. The textual pretext for this film was the Calderón play (or rather plays since there are two distinct versions written at the beginning and end of the playwright's creative life), *Life is a Dream,* which Ruiz had adapted for the Avignon festival as a piece of theatre already given the same title of the film, *Mémoire des Apparences*. The original play is a highly oneiric and baroque work in which the main protagonist, the Polish prince Sigismond is caught up in a labyrinthine play of dream and reality, so that he remains unsure if he is a prince deprived of his position and unfairly imprisoned or conversely a prisoner merely dreaming he is a prince; furthermore the play poses the question as to whether there is any distinction between these two interpretations since life itself is perhaps merely one dream amongst others. In the film, however, the play is merely one of the components of a uniquely Ruizian assemblage that directly links up the oneiric qualities and power relations of the play with the contemporary politics of Latin American dictatorships and their resistances as well as the dreamlike conditions of exile via a complex mnemotechnical system as Lesley Stern (1995) and other commentators have pointed out.

Essentially there are three levels presented within the film. On the first level, Ignacio Vega, teacher of Spanish, who as a teenager had achieved the impressive feat of memorising the entire play, *Life is a Dream,* in 1974 used it as a mnemonic device to memorise the names of militants, their addresses and armed operations. On his capture by the forces of the junta he was obliged to forget all this information which also had the effect that he completely forgot the play as well. Ten years later, presumably on release from imprisonment, he makes contact with an old friend and member of the militant network and must try to remember this vital, political information. He finds, going to a provincial movie theatre in his old neighbourhood that is still playing the same films he dimly remembered from childhood, that watching these films operates as a memory trigger, releasing memories both of lines from the play and the associated names of militants. In order to facilitate this process, he starts going every day to the movie theatre, 'despite the risks', in order to retrieve this information. The second layer within the film consists of the films he views in the movie theatre, corresponding to a number of genres recreated in an abstract manner through the use of coloured filters and other devices. Finally there is the level of the play itself, whose dialogue is first heard superimposed over that of the films before being fully visualised in a markedly different, more static style to that of the filmic sequences. As the film progresses, the pretext of the play comes to be increasingly dominant so that at times the film tends towards a theatrical adaptation at the risk of forgetting the context in which it is being remembered, despite a high level of interference between all these different levels. As Didier Plassard puts it, 'these three levels are clearly enough marked in the first part of the film: treated as so many heterogeneous filmic materials ... they tend little by little to intersect in the montage and even to be superimposed within the [same] shot, constructing a veritable labyrinth in which the spectator progressively loses all reference' (Plassard 1998: 7).

This complex construction allows for remarkable and diverse range of experimentation with the image while at the same time corresponding to a rigorous logic or system, perhaps the most elaborate system of visual rhetorics used by Ruiz since *The Hypothesis of the Stolen Painting*. For example, the films shown within the movie theatre allow Ruiz to construct a series of pastiches of science fiction, action adventure films like *Iron Man* (1931), pre-war British detective films of unknown provenance and other genre films, all of which are transformed by Ruiz through the use of green or sepia coloured filters, alternations between colour and black and white and exaggerated and stylised forms of *mise-en-scène*. More significantly, this structure allows Ruiz to emphasise the passages between films as the same actors turn up in remarkably different settings, corresponding to Ruiz's own description of his experiences as a child spectator of Hollywood B movies, marvelling at the way actors like Vincent Price would die in one genre film only to be resurrected in another. This passage between the different films within the film also implicates the external reality of the movie auditorium and the 'dream' of the dimly remembered play that they evoke, with some actors passing between all three levels. For example, shortly after Ignacio has seen a glamorous woman in a musical setting in one of the films, accompanied by the line 'images that conjure the face of a woman better forgotten', this 'same' woman materialises in the movie theatre, offering to show Ignacio her scars, one of the many veiled references to torture within the film. At another point in the film a flock of birds is seen flying within the cinema auditorium, corresponding to a just seen cinematic image.

As with other cases of films in which cinematic processes are prominently presented within a film, *Memory of Appearances* functions as a kind of meta-cinema in which the cinematic experiences of the protagonist are in some ways generalisable to cinematic experience itself. Unlike either Godard's *Le Mépris* (*Contempt*, 1964) or Fellini's *8½* (1965), however, the emphasis here is not on cinematic production but on spectatorship, very much corresponding to the theories Ruiz would fully elaborate in *Poetics of Cinema* about delinquent spectatorship and 'the photographic unconscious'. This will be engaged with more in the following chapter but essentially this means the idea of images and signs migrating between heterogeneous films and realities, forming a kind of general unconscious or virtual reserve of images capable of subsequent re-actualisation. The images in the film are therefore very much images of images, rather than images of reality, including the *supposed* 'reality' depicted in the film. *Memory of Appearances* situates these processes of passage and correspondence between diverse images within a mnemotechnical apparatus in part based on Frances Yates' study, *The Art of Memory*. According to Yates, in periods ranging from the Classical period to the Renaissance, architecture, art and design were used for the purposes of evoking particular memories which would otherwise be difficult or impossible to recall in their fullness, thus constituting a now lost art of memory or mnemotechnics. By transferring these dynamics to the cinema, Ruiz seems to be indicating that it too operates in similar ways even if cinema's mnemotechnical properties are for the most part hidden or unconscious. Implicit within these processes of translation between the different image regimes of cinema and theatre, as between architecture and memory is a necessary incompleteness or failure, which is also a direct echo of the project within *The Hypothesis of the Stolen Painting* to fully reveal the truth of the series of paintings via their reanimation as *tableaux vivants*. Just as there is always a missing painting, there is in *Memory of Appearances* the sense that the information that Ignacio seeks to reconstitute via the mnemotechnics of cinema viewing will also never be complete, that the art of memory is precisely an art and never a science, a conclusion reinforced by his tendency to increasingly wander or err within both the cinematic and theatrical texts rather than extract from them the vital and necessary information.

So one of the key aspects of the film is the reconstitution of this 'delinquent' spectatorship in which there is a fluidity of passage between one film and the next, and between one actor and several characters, facilitated by the tendency of Ignacio to fall asleep in one film and awaken in the next, or perhaps to dream he has awakened, where not only the film but the characters inhabiting the movie auditorium are subject to unexpected variations. This extends also to the intercalated remembered or dreamed fragments of the play whose philosophical dialogue pondering the relations between dream and reality are continued in a different mode in conversations taking place within the auditorium, often with the same actors playing related roles between all three narrative spaces. This extends the ambiguity between dream and the reality of the play into a complex passage between different realities which all the characters, including Ignacio, seem to accept in a matter of fact way as the labyrinth it is their task to negotiate. Whether this takes on a comic form such as when Ignacio finds himself involved in a slapstick style Hollywood shoot-out, with various characters leaping over and under seats in the auditorium, or a more tragic and artistic tone, there seems to be no escape from the overall assemblage that superimposes Ignacio's experience, the film fragments and the dreamt play through which conflicts between power and resistance, trust and betrayal are played out.

Nevertheless, while these mnemotechnical dynamics of the film have been evoked by both Stern and Jonathan Rosenbaum, not enough attention has been to the specific context presented within the film, namely that of a former militant in Chile, still attempting to resist the dictatorship, in a context in which such resistance has become barely possible. The dates mentioned in the film are significant in this regard, 1974, just after the coup, around the time of Ruiz's *Dialogues of Exiles,* and ten years later, corresponding roughly to Ruiz's first experience of revisiting Chile that also obliquely informed *City of Pirates*. Relative to this earlier film the references to Chile and its contemporary political history are much more explicit and deserve to be taken seriously despite the phatasmagoric nature of the cinematic construction by means of which they are presented. In this sense *Memory of Appearances* is one of Ruiz's most political films, even if it concerns a politics of memory that is highly ambiguous and far from expressing a strictly definable political position; a political cinema therefore not entirely removed from some of Ruiz's Allende period films such as *The Penal Colony.*

A telling scene within the film in this respect comes when sequences from the action adventure film are accompanied by an excessive screaming that Ignacio intuits are not coming from the image but behind. Clambering over seats, he goes to investigate behind the screen, where he discovers a fully functioning police station where statements are being taken by an officer on an old typewriter. This scene, unlike most of the film, is one of the few to use the kind of bizarre angles that characterised *City of Pirates* with some shots taken from the floor and some from above, and others magnifying the fingers typing out the report on Ignacio. The style in which this scene is presented rules out simply seeing it in any obvious way as the revelation of the truth 'behind the image': the idea that the brutal reality behind the illusions presented in the movie theatre is one of dictatorship suggesting that Ignacio, like Sigismond, may only be dreaming his freedom and in fact his memories may be being provoked under conditions of capture and torture. Rather the set up behind the screen is just another facet of the ambivalent political relations of the whole apparatus of the film in which betrayal and trust, power and subversion, like memory and forgetting, are impossible to fully distinguish. The fact that this scene cuts to another film and then to Ignacio waking up in his room further emphasises the unassignability of any prior reality grounding his experiences in the movie theatre. This undecidability, far from rendering the film apolitical, however, in fact constitutes its very political point; in a context in which contemporary politics has been subject to disappearance and erasure the only way it could be reconstituted would be via a kind of spectral phantasmagoria, an art of political memory, however, any such acts of memory will necessarily be incomplete and insufficient to the realities and lives that have been erased. Nevertheless the film, while emphasising the impossibility and futility of resurrecting past militancy, nevertheless affirms a kind of politics of memory against politically imposed forgetting, an 'obstinate memory' not limited to ideas of political realism but extending into the lost domains of childhood and subjective memory also presented within the film. The mnemotechnical relations between the fragments of film, the play and the surrounding reality imply that there is a relationship between the affirmation of the diversity of and passages between images and the passages operating between lives, even those that have been subject to political disappearance and erasure.

Ruiz's project several years later for Channel 4, *A TV Dante*, also involved a spectral return to Chile but this time parts of it were actually filmed there. Ruiz stated that, incapable of producing his audiovisual interpretation of Dante in the multimedia form adopted by Greenaway for the first instalment, he instead used something he was familiar with, namely cheap horror effects and the political aesthetics of militant films from Latin America. All of this was in the service of an idea that was originally a type of Chilean joke: where do the characters of Dante's *Inferno* find themselves after death? Answer, Santiago de Chile, as the title beginning each Canto informs us. This is not, however, a purely aestheticised Chile devoid of political referents and critique, but rather a deeply political engagement with the problematics of exile and the role of images in relation to a remembered place of origin. Hence Richardson's comment that the film is made 'without making any political point about Pinochet's regime' (2006: 162). Richardson is only half correct since it is very much about the political unconscious of Chile as expressed through cinematic images and its presentation of the country as a latter day hell is as redolent with critical implications for the Chilean political situation as was *Memory of Appearances*. At the same time, *A TV Dante* completely rejects the rhetorics of militant cinema and indeed parodies them within the work. As Ruiz himself memorably described the at once ludic and serious basis for this project: 'If you behave badly in this life, in the after-life, you will become Chilean. It is therefore about Chile and about exile' (Ruiz in Bax *et al.* 2003: 154).

From a formal point of view, this project enabled Ruiz to experiment freely, as Martin (2004) has pointed out, deploying many ways of combining images from Hollywood continuity editing to Soviet montage to US avant-garde associative editing. More than this, the combination of the spoken texts of Dante with images of Chile, both stylised and real, allowed for a more extreme form of disjunction between sound and image than characterised Ruiz's previous films, however complex their audiovisual construction. The soundtrack which is often composed of more than one musical layer, the narrators' voices but also shouting and singing crowds, sound effects and voices with varying relationships to what is currently being seen on the screen, allows for a rhythm of divergence and convergence between sound and image. In this respect, Martin's comparison of Ruiz's strategies with Duras's *India Song* (1975) are very apt and the project also has scenes that seem to embody the latter film's sense of post-colonial exhaustion.

In the beginning of Canto 9, after the title that begins all the Cantos, 'Santiago de Chile', we seem to be in a bureaucratic waiting room, with an official office behind in which a variety of figures including the actor playing Dante are seated and patiently waiting. A relatively conventionally edited series of cuts is interrupted by a series of disturbing images reminding us of where we are; a foot that is on fire, followed by a cup and saucer and a book also on fire, meanwhile a man passes across the room with hideous wounds, in fact his brains seem to be leaking out from his head, followed by another scene of a man with a wounded head drinking what appears to be a glass of wine. When he drinks the liquid pours out through a wound in his neck which he catches in a second glass. When the first glass is empty and the second full he simply reverses their position and drinks the same liquid again. As Jonathan Rosenbaum has indicated (2004: 244), throughout this Canto, if there is any relation between the spoken text and the images it often appears arbitrary such as when the lines 'his speech alarmed me all the more for that' are accompanied by the image of an alarm clock in flames.

Throughout this opening we are presented with a banal reality pierced by what Ruiz described as bad effects from horror movies as clichéd representations of hell; all kinds of flaming objects, people with monstrous wounds to which they do not react, as if the only way to show hell was via a type of sub-zombie movie aesthetic. However, something different starts to happen visually half-way through this Canto; a series of depth of field shots alternate, depicting different figures and spaces, all of which have a statue in the extreme foreground and background. This is a technique which would resurface in *Le temps retrouvé* (*Time Regained*, 1999) and serves to not only break up the distinctions between objects and subjects, the living and the inanimate but also the sense of time. The foregrounding of these statues remind the viewer that all these seemingly animated figures are just shades of their former selves and that the scene is taking place in a bardo like, post-mortem space, in hell in other words, not in the everyday reality that it pretends to resemble. However, just as these effects are producing a maximum of artifice in the image and on the soundtrack we are hearing the first descriptions of the torments of hell, the scene is invaded by wind-blown newspapers, followed by a sudden cut to an aerial view of the city of Santiago de Chile, enveloped in mist with mountains in the background. Next there is a cut to a pile of burning books. This in turn is followed by a series of scenes of a documentary nature; a long tracking shot through a Santiago street where fruit and vegetables are being delivered by workers. At one point during this montage that passes jarringly between the realistic and the highly stylised the following words are spoken: 'surrounds the dreadful city of despair which we can enter by force alone.' This is one of many moments in *A TV Dante* that support its reading as a political allegory, without the object of this allegory being made explicit. The idea of taking the city by force resonates both with the recent political history of both the Popular Unity revolution and the Pinochet coup while at the same time making reference to the fact that after the 1988 referendum was the first time it was possible to return to Chile to make films with any degree of freedom. In other words, Santiago was both taken by force by Pinochet and being taken back by force both on the level of cinematic expression and everyday life. However, it would be a trap to read any of these allegorical moments too literally in terms of recent Chilean history since Ruiz's aesthetics rejects militant polemics and prefers to play with images of Chilean history. For example, when the text refers to three hideous gorgons that to merely cast one's eyes on would precipitate dire suffering and the abandonment of all hope of returning, we see three well-dressed Chilean bourgeois women, chatting happily about Chile, while superimposed in the foreground are giant spiders. This kitsch superimposition deflates any directly symbolic reading of the film while parodying the aesthetics of militant cinema's representations of social classes.

This Canto sets up the aesthetics of the ones that follow in which images of the real and the fantastic, the kitsch and the political collide both with each other and with the textual and other elements of the soundtrack. Along the way are some startling images such as that of a man in a fedora with a half erased face or a warehouse where headless bodies are suspended from the ceiling upside down with their shoes beneath them as the area of hell reserved for suicides. At times there is absolute contradiction between sound and image, as for example, when there are descriptions of gruesome punishments of tormented souls while we see happy children playing along the side of the road following the camera while at other times the text and image come into relation with one another in intriguing ways. In Canto 13, for example, we hear a description of the groans of tormented souls who the narrator at first imagines to be hidden in the forested undergrowth they are traversing. He is then encouraged by the guide Virgil to break off a twig and see what occurs. Meanwhile the narrator has wandered into a clearing where there appears to be a village in front of which a crowd has gathered including a young girl whose singing seems to be enchanting Dante. At the same time he reaches out to tenderly touch her face, there is the textual description of what happens when the narrator breaks off a 'young shoot' which results in bitter complaints since the tormented souls are not *in* the forest but in fact *are* the forest. What we see at this point is a sudden cut where the effects of Dante's touching of the young girl's face are a sprinkling of hideous wounds that increasingly fester. At this point the image fully embodies the text but via an allegorical displacement, whereby the 'theological' dimensions of the text are enacted in a fully social context. What is to be made of these alternations between the real and irreal, the cosmological and the social? Despite Ruiz's refusal of any militant rhetoric, there is a strong allegorical reference in *A TV Dante* between the punishments of the 'lost souls' of the inferno and the punishment and suffering endured by the Chilean people. The frequent scenes of book burning, of flaming crosses, of crowds of people beating against fences and doorways, beyond their kitsch and surreal aspects are also expressive of both real suffering and the desire to escape from an infernal period of history. Similarly the scenes and descriptions of torture and death, while fully in keeping with the textual descriptions of the Inferno, cannot but evoke the recent Chilean history of disappeared people, subject to brutal forms of torture and execution which both in reality and imagination were no less monstrous than those tortures imagined by Dante.

The 14th and final Canto begins by a return to the same aerial view of Santiago but for this Canto the narrators are absent from the screen. It begins as a kind of grotesque cooking show in which disembodied eyes, brains and other pieces of flesh are prepared in a variety of visceral sauces, boiling liquids and covered in seasonings. At once a parody of the television cooking show and a lurid evocation of the worst torments of hell, this sequence is also a refrain of Ruiz's obsessive theme of the scattered, mutilated body and fascination with cheap horror aesthetics that was also apparent in the cannibalism in *The Territory*. It seems to pose the question of at what point does the human body become just another form of consumable flesh, a question equally applicable to the fictional world of Dante and the real world of torture and dismemberment. Soon the various fleshy organs that seem to include brains and hearts are also joined by an amputated human hand all still being coated by sauces and seasonings. This cooking sequence is followed by a series of monstrous portraits: two men in flames superimposed on a bowl whose contents are being stirred, a man with two tongues who genuflects, a woman covered with wounds which are eyes, a bearded man who eats a spider, a man whose facial wounds have sprouted furry protuberances and is breathing in and out in an exaggerated manner. This gallery of grotesques is followed by a sequence of reprised images from the film such as the suspended inverted bodies, followed by repeated earlier shots of trees, a country road and a final panorama of Santiago. What this ending seems to ask is, given the recent and still raw experience of torture and disappearance, evoked both by the gallery of monstrous portraits and the room of 'suicides' both of which can be read as the respective living and dead products of a regime of torture, what is required in order to survive, to go on living in these conditions? The film implies that rather than repeating no longer meaningful gestures and habits, evoked both by the gestures of genuflection and other religious or political habitual reactions of the various lost souls in the work, it is necessary to look directly at the horror, to journey through it and map it, even if paradoxically this can only be done by exceeding the limits of rationality through a kind of mythopoetic, folkloric or allegorical engagement with the past. It is these folkloric dimensions of contemporary Chile that Ruiz would return to much later in his work for Chilean TV beginning with *Cofralandes* (2003) without, however, the Dantean depiction of Chile as a modern Inferno that gave this project its unique allegorical tone.

The final spectral journey that will be examined in this chapter marks perhaps the end of this particularly prolific period of Ruiz's filmmaking and was the last major feature film for several years, a slowing of pace at least by Ruiz's standards that would be followed by a renewed bout of creative energy from the mid-1990s. As such *Dark at Noon* is both a farewell and culmination of Ruiz's work of the 1980s, what we are referring to here as the cinema of piracy and spectral journeys, but also in some respects presages its subsequent transformation. The prologue introducing the main character and narrator of the film as having two passions, miracles and foreign languages could, as Rosenbaum has suggested, be applied to Ruiz's twin obsessions of 'multiple fictions miraculously coexisting in time, multiple cultures linguistically coexisting in space' (Rosenbaum 2004: 247). As with several of Ruiz's films from the 1980s there is a babel of languages, only added to by the coexistence of French and English versions of the film whose actors are French, English and Portuguese. Similarly the fictions on which it is based are also multiple and difficult to trace, combining tales apparently originating from both Borges and Lovecraft that are not credited in the film or any account of it. There is at once a flesh-eating painting, a prevalence of apparitions of the Madonna that has become a banal nuisance, even for the church, and the tale of a factory built according to Bentham's design of the panopticon, an aspect of the film that has not been widely commented upon. Finally the heart of the story and presumably Ruiz's own invention is the tale of two lovers who are united within the body of a third person, a situation complicated by the fact that the English actor John Hurt plays two out of the three characters in this bizarre triangle. Distinguishing between these narrative threads is as sticky an enterprise as attempting to escape the tendrils of the flesh-eating painting depicted several times within the film itself, not least because Ruiz made use of similar subtractive strategies as he did in other of his films such as *City of Pirates*, deliberately withholding some of the information necessary to grasp all of the sense of what is occurring on-screen. Nevertheless *Dark at Noon* is a much closer approximation to a linear narrative and in this sense anticipates several of the films Ruiz would make later in the 1990s.

The film begins when a doctor/researcher Felicien, avid student of foreign languages and researcher of miracles, based in a post-World War 1 invalid hospital where he gets to exercise both passions, is called away to deal with his father's affairs in Portugal, the latter having just died. This narrator is already an ideally liminal Ruizian figure, caught as he is between the worlds of science and faith, 'mystery and ministry', and one who is well disposed to being highly receptive to the anomalous reality he will encounter in Portugal. Once arriving at the site of the 'enterprise', anomalies do not hesitate in making their presence felt; there are peasants sleeping in fields and courtyards, fields of upturned crutches and wild dogs everywhere. When the narrator does finally reach the appointed place, in a manner very much resembling the baroque journeys in Has's films *Rekopis znaleziony w Saragossie* (*The Saragossa Manuscript*, 1965) and *Sanatorium pod klepsydra* (*Sanatorium under the Hour-Glass*, 1973) the house at first seems deserted and then the narrator is addressed cryptically and rudely as follows: 'shut the door and your mouth, it's the same thing anyway.' This interlocutor who is subsequently revealed to be the 'artist', Ellic, then abruptly wishes the narrator a curt goodnight and it is only after a troubled sleep on the floor that he is properly welcomed by his host Anthony, the entrepreneur he had come to see. From this point on we get introduced to the major threads of the story such as the history of the panoptic enterprise of constructing adjustable artificial limbs, its long running battle against the everyday miracles pervading the countryside and start to discover the tangled threads of relations between the four main characters residing in the complex; in addition to Ellic and Anthony, Ines his partner and her uncle the Marquis, the latter apparently reduced to a canine level of behaviour and with a penchant for burying people alive as Felicien will shortly discover.

If the specific provenance of this tale or multiple tales is not clear, its affinity with the weird fiction of H. P. Lovecraft is more so. Several critics have recently pointed out the difference between weird fiction, a genre Lovecraft contributed to the invention of, and fantasy. In particular, whereas fantasy in its usual generic conventions points to some completely other world, weird fiction is notable, according to Mark Fisher, 'for the way in which it stages a conflict between this world and Others' (Fisher 2007). While there are some instances of fantasy in which characters from our world depart for another, it is only in weird fiction that our world is invaded by beings or experiences from other worlds, in which there is interference between worlds, the obsessive theme of Lovecraft's work. In this light it would be possible to characterise several of Ruiz's films in terms of the weird, for example, in addition to *Dark at Noon, Three Lives and Only One Death* which is another collection of 'weird tales'. However, while Ruiz fully takes on Lovecraftian weirdness, he denudes it of both its pathos and its metaphysical coordinates. If Lovecraftian horror already takes place in this world, it nevertheless draws upon the same Christian metaphysics of traditional horror in that the intrusion into this world is presented as an outbreak of evil, the perversion of an otherwise potentially 'good' reality. In *Dark at Noon,* these dynamics are replaced by a world of pure anomaly; there may indeed by some horrific events taking place but the moral coordinates in which they might be assigned a good or evil status are lacking. In this sense, Ruiz's film is arguably more weird than Lovecraft's fiction since there is not even any potential transcendence and even the multiple apparitions and miracles in the film are thoroughly immanent and earthly, even irritating intrusions of other realities within the fabric of heterogeneous reality in the film.

One of the elements the film does share with Lovecraftian fiction is the idea of the limits or even the ruins of rationality. This rationality within the film is worth pausing over, since it is presented in terms of an enterprise constructed according to Bentham's model of the panopticon. This model is of course very familiar since Foucault used it in *Discipline and Punish,* as a diagram of power, enabling the functioning of the modern 'carceral society' through its implementation of spatial mechanisms of surveillance in the architecture of multiple institutions such as prisons, hospitals, factories and schools.[10] However, the panopticon as presented in the film has little to do with this Foucauldian appropriation but rather Bentham's original and delirious idea of a kind of mega-institutional architecture, forming the basis of an enterprise that would be all these institutions at once and others besides, including the church. In point of fact, after the initial description of the panopticon there is little reference to surveillance and the buildings hardly seem to correspond to these multiple functions or to the purpose of surveillance; it is rather presented as a business enterprise at once fulfilling a rational need and the desire to make money through the manufacture of prosthetic limbs for the many injured veterans of World War 1. If anything the narrative surrounding the business, a pastiche of many tales of grand Victorian enterprise, seems to be involved in a conflict over attention rather than concerned with surveillance; while on the one hand there is the tale of immigrants from every country and speaking every language pouring in to make the business function, there are also the persistent superstitious beliefs of the local inhabitants, quickly adopted by the new arrivals, manifested in abundant apparitions of Madonnas and the frequent performing of miracles, rendering the factory and its rationality redundant. This is dramatised when the entire factory burns to the ground, the apparent result of the actions of 'Our Lady of Fires'.

Much of this story only becomes apparent gradually after Felicien has gone through the experience of being buried alive by the Marquis and subject to persistent apparitions and miracles, and despite his earlier intentions becomes determined not to leave until he has penetrated the mystery of these various anomalies. This enlightenment comes about partly through the revelations in a book which is at first blank but on which letters assemble themselves when the correct page is turned to; on the second encounter with this book Felicien's attention is drawn by a giant forefinger that crashes through the ceiling and hovers ominously over his desk. Again this seems to reference Has's *Saragossa Manuscript* in which the entire narrative is prompted by two opposing army officers reading a book in which there are several layers of tales within other tales. In addition to the back story of the prosthetic limbs factory and its struggle against superstition, there is the tale of the strange romance between Anthony and Ines, overseen by the shadowy figure of the Marquis. Despite promising beginnings, involving a genealogical connection with St Just, the Marquis who must give permission for his niece to get married exerts a disturbing influence over this union. During the week-long wedding festivities, while Ines stays in her room, Anthony feels that the festivities also do not concern him but are rather for the benefit of the Marquis. When he next encounters Ines she informs him that they will not sleep together this or any other night, a disappointing outcome only overcome when the two lovers find themselves united but within the body of the Marquis in a kind of perverse gnostic trinity. This unity of three beings within one that is at first suggested by anomalies of overlapping voices and strange behaviours, persists even when Felicien submits the Marquis to medical examination revealing a series of feminine and masculine components, even male and female styles of masturbation.

Subtending this already weird tale is the one of the flesh-eating painting, cared for by Ellic. Despite Ellic's constant invitations to Felicien to examine the painting, he only does so after rescuing the priest who, like himself and presumably for the same reason had been buried alive as future food for the painting. When Felicien goes to examine the painting unannounced, he is caught up in a series of tendrils that seem to shoot out from the paintings surface, performing the same function of a spider's web immobilising and isolating its prey. Ellic is only able to extract him from this web with great difficulty using the complex mechanical machinery operating, as in any good mad scientist tale, as the life support of the living painting, while the latter proves to be in some unexplained way the support of the eternal youth of the Marquis. All of this is referred to throughout the film, for example in the enigmatic lines 'shut the door and your mouth' or the whole idea of the panopticon as a giant body in which the eyes are the head or the brain, thus casting a zone of indistinction between the animate and the inanimate, the living and the dead, rationality and the diabolical.

This account of the narrative of the film is principally done to emphasise its functioning as a complex and weird tale that while abjuring any Christian metaphysics of good and evil, despite its presentation of both Madonnas and monstrous paintings, nevertheless presents a highly anomalous and consistently strange fictional world. Part of this consistency derives not from the tales themselves so much as the vividness of the images and objects by means of which they are presented. The relatively high budget of the film meant that Ruiz was able to use very sensitive film and an Arriflex 535 camera that he described as being the 'Rolls Royce of Cameras'. Since he was often used to using 16mm, this meant that on this film he was able to present a rich tapestry of visual information that is apparent both in the evocation of a particular period and the place of the story, as well as in the special effects, belying Rosenbaum's claim that the bigger budget of the film was of no particular advantage. For example, the series of glowing and smiling Virgins that populate the film, transcend their possible reading as mere kitsch jokes at the expense of Fatima and become intrusions of rich visual artifice into the space of the film, echoing the intrusion of multiple anomalies in the narrative. Other vivid effects include letters rapidly assembling themselves on a blank page, the giant plaster hand crashing through the ceiling and the painting itself which not only gives off a sense of animation through the threads it shoots out into the room in which it is located but also the metamorphoses that take place on its surface. In a sense this 'demonic' painting is almost the inverse of the *tableaux vivants* employed in *The Hypothesis of the Stolen Painting*; in the place of models arranged in the compositional order of a painting, suspending their present life in order to 'animate' a past 'now inanimate' moment, we have a 'living painting' whose metamorphoses feed off the consumption of the life energy of human beings, meanwhile supporting the life of the living corpse that is the Marquis, whose body is the animate 'house' of Anthony and Ines.

Dark at Noon is at once, therefore, one of Ruiz's most occult films and yet also one of his most entertaining and weirdly accessible; as Ruiz himself says it is at once a highly hermetic work and one, with its frequent cosmic jokes about Fatima, and the crisis of the church faced with an over-abundance of miracles, that is not that far removed from the quotidian Surrealism of Monty Python. For Adrian Martin, this film is a prime example of the poetic desire to, following Lezama Lima, 'build a waterfall in a dark room' (Martin 2004), meaning to create something beautiful and fascinating even in an unpromising or unexpected context. This can be seen throughout Ruiz's films of the 1980s but was rarely accomplished in such a full and lush way as it was in *Dark at Noon*. However, whatever Ruiz devotees might have been expecting of this film, it was not yet the commercial breakthrough that would bring Ruiz to the attention of a much wider audience in the second half of the 1990s. Before this, however, Ruiz would take a semi-hiatus from feature film production, at least by his own prolific standards, and turn his attention to other areas such as pedagogy and theory, a re-orientation that would lead directly to a renewed wave of prolific filmmaking resulting in, for at least a decade, a much wider public and commercial recognition of his work.

Notes

1 This distinction between the baroque and the neo-baroque was made by Deleuze in *The Fold*. See Deleuze 1993: 81–81, 136–137.
2 The intriguing and under-explored relations between cinema and cartography were recently engaged with in Tom Conley (2007), *Cinematic Cartography*, Minnesota and London: University of Minnesota Press. However, the highly idiosyncratic deployment of cartography in Ruiz's work is not referred to by Conley.
3 See Kathy Acker (1996), *Pussy, King of the Pirates* and Hakim Bey (2004) 'Pirate Utopias', 97–98 ff.
4 This interview may be somewhat fabulated by Adair but is by no means inconsistent with Ruizian discourse even if, as Pick suggests, one of the figures referred to, Valderomat is in fact, Valderomar, a Peruvian writer. See Pick 1993: 206n.

5   See Pierre Klossowski (1997), *La Monnaie Vivante*. Paris: Rivages Poche.
6   The 'automatism' of Ruiz's Surrealism is further enhanced by the fact that he was apparently unaware that Isidore Ducasse was the author who used the pen-name *Le Comte de Lautréamont* and claims that he genuinely believed at the time that Isidore was a French girl's name.
7   Ruiz would later contribute a section 'Promenade' to a Jean Vigo inspired compendium film, *À Propos de Nice, la Suite* (1995).
8   On this important phase of Ruiz's activity see Serge Toubiana (1985), III, 'Le Havre, ville-studio' and Ian Christie (1987: 96–100), 'Raoul Ruiz and the House of Culture'. According to Christie the dual theatrical versions of *Mémoires des apparences/Memories of Appearances* were the first testing of this new mode of artisinal trasnmedia production at Le Havre (1987: 99).
9   The two volumes of Bellour's writings on 'Entre-Images' have now been partially translated as a single English volume. See Raymond Bellour (2012) *Between-the-Images*, trans. Allyn Hardyck, Zurich/Dijon: JRP/Ringier/Les presses du réel. This translation does not include the chapter referred to here.
10 For Foucault's account of the panopticon see Foucault 1995: 200–2ff.

CHAPTER THREE

Cartographies of Complexity: Ruiz's 'French' Cinema Since the Mid-1990s

Introduction: Ruizian Pedagogy and the Poetics of Cinema Project

This chapter will be focused on one of Ruiz's most productive periods and one in which, at least between 1996 and 2004, represented by the production of the two films *Three Lives and Only One Death* and *Klimt* respectively, his cinema gained a wider and more international public visibility than ever before. This was achieved through a modification of Ruiz's aesthetic procedures to such an extent that some critics saw Ruiz's recent cinema as abandoning its 1980s Surrealism and experimentalism in favour of an adoption of the codes of the French art movie, of becoming a kind of cinema of quality, complete with linear narratives, high production values and big international stars. However, as with Ruiz's other acts of aesthetic metamorphosis, this is no straightforward capitulation to established codes but rather a complex process of adaptation; some of Ruiz's recent films may resemble French art cinema but in most instances this is a way of producing effects that are all the more subversive for being conducted in a more subtle and sophisticated way. Another important point to bear in mind is that throughout this period, Ruiz maintained his tendency to work on a variety of different modes and levels of production producing work ranging from high profile international co-productions like *Le temps retrouvé* (*Time Regained*, 1999) or *Klimt* (2004) to forms of guerilla filmmaking and much more low budget feature films like *Combat d'amour en songe* (*Love Torn in Dream*, 2000), not to mention artistic shorts and at least one B movie. Ruiz himself referred to pursuing less 'exhausting' aesthetic strategies, stating that even he found his earlier films like *The Hypothesis of the Stolen Painting* exhausting, despite or perhaps because of grasping all the multiple dimensions of this complex work. This does not mean that these more recent films are less complex but rather that their complexities are able to coexist with providing more obvious spectatorial pleasures through the adherence to one or several cinematic codes, while at the same time undermining these codes in ways that operate in a more subtle manner than in Ruiz's productions of the 1980s. This why Ruiz's cinema of this period will be treated here as cartographies of complexity, complicating events, identities, national belonging and above all cinematic images. However before addressing these films it is worth looking at the period that immediately preceded their production in which Ruiz was turning his attention to other areas of practice namely pedagogy and theory.

If the period from 1992 to 1995 seems to indicate a slowing down of strictly cinematic activity on Ruiz's part (although he was still producing around three short films per year) this can be accounted for by the fact that he was at this time engaging in a new pedagogical and critical activity as a visiting professor first at Harvard and then Duke University that would continue intermittently up until his appointment as visiting professor at the University of Aberdeen (2007–2009). In between, Ruiz has also engaged with educational institutions in France and Belgium for varying lengths of time. One aspect of this pedagogical activity has been the running of practical filmmaking workshops with students in some cases leading to collaborative films, as in his collaboration with CIFAS in Belgium, resulting in the production with students of *Vertige de la page blanche* (*Vertigo of the Blank Page,* 2003). At the same time, these University appointments have enabled Ruiz to concentrate more intensively on writing, most notably resulting in the publication of his key work of film theory, *Poetics of Cinema* (1995), that was based on the lectures he delivered at Duke University. However, it would give a false impression if this suggests that Ruiz's pedagogical activities were strictly divided between theory and practice. In fact his practical classes involved exposing students to a dizzying array not only of cinema but also of theory and philosophy, while his written work, although the product of time devoted to research, tended to continue his practical engagement as a filmmaker, for example, by laying out potential thought experiments, often supposing the production of possible or impossible imaginary films. Furthermore, Ruiz's writing on cinema considerably pre-dates the *Poetics of Cinema* project, even if it was only with this project that Ruiz had the time to elaborate his thoughts in such a full way. Before turning to this work, it is worth examining a key Ruizian text written much earlier, that in many respects was the seed that would eventually become his *Poetics of Cinema,* namely 'Object Relations in the Cinema' (Ruiz 1981: 87–94).[1] This was not the only early theoretical text of Ruiz's devoted to cinematic aesthetics and similar themes were explored in interviews and other short texts devoted to particular films and especially in the 'Imaginary Dialogues' he conducted with Jean-Louis Schefer shortly afterwards. Nevertheless, 'Object Relations in the Cinema' remains the text in which Ruiz's ideas about cinema were most fully and directly expressed, at least up until the appearance of *Poetics of Cinema.*

'Object Relations in the Cinema' sets out a set of theorems about the relations between cinematic objects, which it then proceeds to investigate via a series of exercises, a procedure also taken up in *Poetics of Cinema.* Proceeding with a Witgensteinian set of definitions concerning vision, cinema, sets and objects, Ruiz's text seeks to elaborate the functions of objects both for human perception and as part of cinema. In

Ruiz's terms 'Objects take on meaning as a result of the correspondence between what we see and our experience' (1981: 87). Ruiz is particularly interested in the relations between objects in the foreground and background of a cinematic image, arguing that there is a tension caused by objects in the background struggling 'of their own accord to emerge out of the background' (ibid.). This leads to a situation in which there is a kind of 'subterranean current' in films in which half of the story is provided by us and half by the objects themselves, whose relations therefore vary according to the interests and associations of different viewers and these relations are only partially controlled by the filmmaker. The art of filmmaking would therefore be the art of elaborating these object relations from set to set in more or less interesting ways. Apart from decentring the act of filmmaking from conventional concerns with narrative, character or even traditional understandings of *mise-en-scène*, this passage clearly anticipates the subsequent exploration of object relations that Ruiz would himself conduct on a practical level in many of his films of the 1980s, for example, in the aberrant use of depth of field and highly magnified foreground objects in films like *City of Pirates*. That this apparently philosophical passage is intended practically is further reinforced by the fact that it is followed by a series of 'exercises' in which the reader is invited to imagine a series of cinematic perceptual experiments that respond to the problematics of object relations that have been elaborated in theory.

This alternation between theoretical elaboration and practical exercises continues through four different sections exploring object relations in different ways. In the second section dealing with 'the simplest relation between two objects' (1981: 89), that is when one object becomes the background or container for another, Ruiz asserts that 'the story represents the way in which objects enter into container/contained relations' (ibid.), further emphasising the displacement of narrative in favour of spatial transformations. By the third section, the text achieves a level of delirious intensity as it seeks to explore the theorem that 'two lovers looking at each other have no off-screen space' (1981: 90). In the following consideration of the relations between different looks, Ruiz proposes a field of looks that encompasses the entire planet; one of the exercises designed to explore this section involves making 'an exhibition of yourself in front of any group of people. Note the objects they look at to avoid seeing this shameful sight' (1981: 91). Despite the clearly comedic aspects of this text, its mode of development sets the tone for Ruiz's future elaborations of theory as well as providing a first sketch of several of the key concerns that would animate *Poetics of Cinema*. In particular it uses the concept of object relations to displace the focus on cinematic narrative in favour of the explorations of the associative dynamics of cinematic images which is key to Ruizian aesthetics in both its cinematic and discursive forms: 'when we show images in association, these images are necessarily linked: two images placed side by side are linked and mutually concerned, though they do not, nevertheless, stop reaching back towards the field that they came from' (1981: 92–93). In *Poetics of Cinema*, this situation would be described in terms of what Ruiz would call the photographic unconscious, operating in excess of the domain of linear narrative which will be critiqued in the first chapter of the latter work as 'central conflict theory'.

The first volume of Ruiz's *Poetics of Cinema* is a rich and complex work that while absolutely refusing disciplinary boundaries has had a considerable impact in the field of film theory and reflection on film more generally, as evidenced by its citation as one of the key works on film in a 2010 survey of critics conducted by *Sight and Sound*. While *Poetics of Cinema 1*, can and usually is read as a stand-alone volume, it was in fact the first of a projected series of three works, of which the first has the subtitle 'Miscellanies', the second, would be called '*Serio Ludens*' (serious play) and be composed of 'parodies and conceptual simulations' (Ruiz 1995: 8), while the third would be devoted to methods and consist of exercises and formulae intended as 'a method of filming' (ibid.). The second volume only appeared eleven years later and while it does indeed contain a number of examples of 'serious play' in the form of elaborate thought experiments, it no longer carries that subtitle and seems to have departed from Ruiz's original intentions. At the same time, the first volume also contains its share of 'serious play' in the form of thought experiments accompanying the more theoretical discourse, demonstrating that for Ruiz theory is never entirely distinct from practice, even if that practice might not necessarily be the practice of cinema but theory itself. Arguably, all of this was embodied in the earlier Ruiz text that was already examined but it is in the first volume of *Poetics of Cinema* that Ruiz's idiosyncratic practice of theory was given its richest and most powerful expression, exceeding anything he wrote before or after. As for the planned third volume, this was being worked on during Ruiz's sojourn in Aberdeen, beginning from annotations on the late theoretical work of Eisenstein, *The Film Sense* (1986), but since his death in 2011, the only plan to publish these notes seems to be for a Spanish volume in Chile with the planned title of *Poetica del Cine 3*. However, Ruiz has written at least one other key theoretical text, 'Six Functions of the Shot' (Ruiz in Bandis *et al.* 2004: 57–68). In what follows it is principally some key concepts from *Poetics of Cinema 1* that will be addressed, therefore, with some reference to other theoretical texts by Ruiz.

In the foreword to *Poetics of Cinema 2* (Ruiz 2007: 10), Ruiz describes the earlier volume as a 'call to arms' and this is certainly true of the first chapter, 'Central Conflict Theory' (1995: 9–23). In this chapter Ruiz contrasts the fairly anarchic impression that US films made on young Chilean spectators with the surprising discovery later on that they were the product of a method of dramatic construction he refers to as 'central conflict theory.' This theory is not a global account of classical Hollywood cinema as can be found in the work of Thomas Schatz (1998) or Bordwell, Staiger and Thompson (1988) but rather a pragmatic tendency evident primarily in scriptwriting manuals that dictates how good movies should be structured; exactly the same model advocated by Robert McKee and others that was parodied in Spike Jonze's film, *Adaptation* (2002). By choosing to target the dominant pragmatic way in which popular narrative cinema is produced, rather than Hollywood as an economic or cultural system, Ruiz moves away from the third cinema ideological critique of US cultural imperialism in the direction of an immanent critique of Hollywood and, by extension, capitalist pragmatism. As such this is a Foucauldian move, inasmuch as it focuses not on an abstract and imagined centre of power but rather on how power is diffused throughout global cinematic production, not ideologically but practically, by the dissemination of certain norms of cinematic construction which are implemented in film schools, funding decisions and dominant industry practices. As such it is not only more incisive than the critique of cultural imperialism but also more productive in that it immediately raises the practical question of how films might be made otherwise.

Essentially, central conflict theory proposes that good films are propelled by a central narrative conflict in which one character wants something and someone else does not want them to have it; all the narrative details will then circulate and either advance or obstruct the resolution of this central conflict. This is problematic for Ruiz since it 'forces us to eliminate all stories which do not include confrontation and to leave aside all those events which require only indifference or detached curiosity like a landscape, a distant storm, or a dinner with friends' (Ruiz 1995: 11). The selectivity of central conflict theory, in keeping both with some versions of Marxist dialectics and American philosophies of action (1995: 15), posits a fundamentally hostile world in which characters attempt to impose their monomaniacal will through a series of strategies aimed towards a goal 'which, if not in itself banal is certainly rendered so' (1995: 11). The problem with this banality is not merely that it is an inadequate account of both human psychology and behaviour but that it has political stakes ranging from its implementation in US foreign policy (and Ruiz has referred in this regard to the recent wars in Iraq as being based on central conflict theory) to its more everyday implementation as a key basis for determining which film projects are worthy of support by funding bodies and film studios.

Ruiz proposes as an antidote to this banal narrative realism what amounts to a 'politics of boredom' that would seek to affirm precisely those moments indicated above whose boredom derives from the fact that that they contribute nothing towards the central conflict and rather tend to become autonomous from the rest of the film and in doing so open up other powers of the cinematic image. Elsewhere (Goddard 2004), I have argued that this constitutes an open or general economy, after Bataille's term in *The Accursed Share* (1991), as opposed to a restricted one in which there is a direct economic exchange between cinematic images and money both in the sense of the funds required to produce them and the commodified pay-off for the spectator of narratives produced according to the restricted economy of central conflict. To use the dynamic model that Ruiz would adopt later, central conflict operates on a tight centripetal circuit, whereas Ruiz is interested in films that fly off their hinges and open themselves to other films, memories and experiences precisely through these centrifugal dynamics.

In *Poetics of Cinema,* one of the ways Ruiz approaches this type of strategy is through the idea of the photographic unconscious, the transformation of Benjamin's concept of the optical unconscious that was elaborated in his famous essay, 'The Work of Art in the Age of Mechanical Reproduction'.[2] In this essay, Benjamin analysed the power of cinema and other modern techniques of image reproduction to disturb the conventions of Western art and its modes of reception, famously through the destruction of the aura. While Benjamin had in mind emergent modes of mass perception made possible via newly-invented photographic, cinematic and other technologically mediated imaging techniques, Ruiz's photographic unconscious is somewhat different to this. In the place of Benjamin's focus on optical techniques such as the close-up to 'surgically' render visible to the masses the previously invisible structures of reality, Ruiz instead uses the photographic unconscious to refer to a 'corpus of signs capable of conspiring against visual conventions' (1995: 32). This is Ruiz's particular interpretation of Benjamin's essay. The subversive corpus of signs that Ruiz refers to, however, only has a latent existence in Benjamin's essay and is really an invention of Ruiz, even if it draws on the powers of cinema and technical reproduction identified by Benjamin. This corpus can take many forms and rather than being a strictly contemporary phenomenon for Ruiz, is no less evident in treatises on Chinese painting, for example, or the ninetheenth-century practice of *tableaux vivants*.

What is central to the concept for Ruiz is the multiplicity of relations between images or between images and other signs that is always in excess of any simple notion of representation. For example, in viewing the photo of 'someone we love', we are prey to a kind of double vision in which 'in the first moment, we recognise what we know, and in the second we no longer know what we are recognising, in a mass of details which remain invisible to the naked eye and which the lens renders eloquent' (1995: 32). For Ruiz, simple misrecognition opens up onto a whole field of interference between signs and images that refuses any enclosure in stable economies of signification. Therefore, if Benjamin's concept of the optical unconscious can be said to express modernist ideas about technological invention and its impact on mass perceptions, Ruiz's photographic unconscious is precisely postmodern in the sense of opening up any individual image to a field of multiplicity in excess of its place within the narrative economy of a particular film, and instead opening it up to multiple relations with *all* the cinematic and other images any given image is capable of evoking. This accounts for the previously cited formula, for 250 shots 250 films, and in general Ruiz's favouring of the multiple and the centrifugal over the centripetal as both an aesthetic tendency of his work and as a politics of the singular image.

Ruiz proposes his concept of the photographic unconscious as much through a series of thought experiments as through logical reasoning and, in a sense, both taken together constitute a type of multi-layered thought in which it is not only the ideas but the manner of their presentation that is baroque. For example, there is the theoretical tale of the blind painter who paints by numbers with the help of assistants and the future collector of this painting who is surprised to recognise himself in it; this being only the beginning of a delirious series of transformations of this painting that manages to interact, *Zelig*-like, with a whole panorama of twentieth-century art and political history. The point is that in order to escape the confines of central conflict narratives and by implication the film theory that contents itself with these kinds of stories, a type of imaginative engagement with images is necessary, in order to grasp them in their full creative multiplicity. In *Poetics of Cinema*, Ruiz proposes a number of ways in which to do this including, for example, the idea of a 'shamanic cinema' is neither the transcendental style of Ozu or Tarkovsky, nor the mythopoetics of US underground filmmakers like Stan Brakhage or Kenneth Anger, nor the utopian productions of various generations of avant-garde filmmakers, but would rather consist in the crafting of singular films, irreducible to genre, story-lines or particular schools; films which are in other words, 'monsters' (1995: 78). While Ruiz refers to this kind of film as the crafting of a poetic object, this has nothing to do with film craft as it is usually understood, even if there is something of the artisanal in Ruiz's description:

> It has some elements of the old-fashioned crafts, for instance, a hands-on approach to celluloid or video, a spirit of inventiveness ... the purpose is to make poetic objects. The rules you need to understand these poetic objects are unique to each film and must be rediscovered by every viewer; ... in short these are films that cannot respond to the question, 'What is this movie about?' (Ruiz 1995: 77)

While this quotation might be taken to be the defence of elitist forms of avant-garde or art cinema, it is telling that nowhere in this chapter does Ruiz propose any kind of canon and indeed the one film singled out as an example of this shamanic cinema is a Hollywood film, Edgar Ulmer's *The Black Cat* (1934), whose poetic qualities arguably derive more from a combination of involuntary narrative, photographic and performative inconsistencies and Ruiz's 'delinquent spectatorship' than they do from any poetic purpose on the part of the filmmakers. Nevertheless, it is a fitting example since what Ruiz is proposing is a practice of singularity in filmmaking that could never be specified as an aesthetic formula, resulting in films whose multiplicity could never reduced to being simply 'about' something other than the multiple relations constructed with other images and films. This is why Ruiz's cinema, as well as being characterised as baroque and cartographic, can also be usefully seen as a cinema of multiplicity and complexity and nowhere more so than in the cinema he produced from the mid-1990s onwards. For this reason, this last chapter will be organised somewhat differently from the preceding ones in that it aims to chart the ways in which Ruiz's films express complexity in relation to a number of dimensions, including those of identity, events and the image itself. In order to do this it will depart somewhat from strict chronology in order to bring out more clearly Ruiz's different strategies for making films that are complex poetic objects, beginning with perhaps the key film in Ruiz's most recent phase of what I am calling his cinema of complexity, namely *Three Lives and Only One Death*.

Cinematic Virtuosity and Multiplicity: Three Lives and Only One Death

In *Three Lives and Only One Death* we are, as in *Dark at Noon*, in the realm of weird tales but this time they are presented by a modern day storyteller, Pierre Bellemare, a French radio personality famous for his colourful recounting of anomalous and mysterious tales taken from both history and everyday life. Ruiz stated that he listened to Bellemare's extraordinary tales as a way of learning French after his arrival in Paris, so it seemed natural to use this familiar voice as a kind of guide to the series of urban legends that make up the film. These stories correspond to what we have already examined as 'immortal stories' meaning tales such as that of a man leaving his apartment for matches only to return twenty years later, or a professor suddenly taking up life as a bum, or a young couple inheriting a mansion from a mysterious benefactor, who find its only occupant to be a majordomo, who in fact is this same benefactor. For this and several of Ruiz's subsequent films he worked with Pascal Bonitzer as a scriptwriter, thereby raising the level of the French dialogue to impeccable art cinema standards, although this is somewhat undermined by having most of the characters speak French in strong foreign accents which are not always their own. Coupled with these stories taken both from news stories and in the latter case from some stories by Nathaniel Hawthorne, was an interest in multiple personality disorder (MPD). Apparently Ruiz was approached by Barbet Schroeder to direct a serious film on this subject, *Never Talk to a Stranger*, but thought that it was better treated comically rather than tragically (Ruiz and anon. 1995: 2). Apparently he even went so far as to meet with US psychiatrists expert in MPD and saw it as being perfectly able to be mixed with 'the telling of several stories which turn out to only be one' (1995: 2). Furthermore, Ruiz goes so far as to see this condition in as much social as psychological terms as, 'the disease of the twenty-first century, a mental or rather moral illness that consists in compartmentalising, in constructing a personality for others ... This becomes a type of tree of personalities' (1995: 2). As Ruiz's interviewer pointed out, this kind of experience is also that of exile and this type of multiplicity of character was hardly new in Ruiz's work. Nevertheless the hypothesis of MPD, which Ruiz sees as a a condition characterised by a certain degree of bad faith, that is a deliberate if unconscious slippage between different roles, formed an ideal basis for linking up the distinct yet interlocking tales that make up *Three Lives and Only One Death*.

The film begins in a radio studio as Bellemare begins to recount the tale of André Parisi, who has woken up with a terrible headache and is hearing the combined sounds of his crying child and a vacuum cleaner operated by his wife Maria. But in the first of many narrative traps, it soon turns out the story is not at all about him but about the enigmatic character he shortly encounters in a local café tabac where he goes to buy cigarettes, Matteo Strano, played by Marcello Mastroianni, who plays the central character in all four of these strange tales purportedly recounted by Bellemare. In fact another of the origins of the film can be traced to Ruiz's desire to work with the Italian actor, famous for his roles in Fellini films such as *La Dolce Vita* (1960) and *8½* but whose performance in this film has more in common with his role in Mikhalkov's 1987 production, *Oci ciornie (Dark Eyes)*, which combined several Chekhov stories within a single narrative. As it happened, Ruiz's film was to be Mastroianni's penultimate cinematic performance. Nevertheless these variations on a single actor's performances and their consequences for the film are only built up as the film progresses. In the beginning we find ourselves in an apparently everyday story in which a family man with a splitting headache encounters an eccentric older man in a café, who insists that they share a drink together and states that he is ready to pay André well for his time and the opportunity to get to know him, although he already seems to know quite a lot about him.

From this point on we are led into an increasingly anomalous world, actualised by a scene of storytelling in some respects evocative of the sailor and the student in *Three Crowns of the Sailor*. However, in the place of strange tales of the sea and exotic journeys, Matteo Strano recounts a tale bounded by the very neighbourhood in which it is told, even though it is nonetheless a strange and exotic journey 'in a certain fashion' as Matteo keeps repeating. The story recounted could be subtitled 'a strange journey in time' since it concerns a day more than twenty years ago when Matteo went out for cigarettes and ended up, on a whim, renting a nearby apartment, the very apartment that André has been gazing at on his way to the café. As Matteo points out, travelling does not have to be to a distant location, a few metres can be sufficient. Matteo insists that this apartment is not only inhabited by fairies but that these fairies have the strange properties of eating time and in fact devoured twenty years of his life in a single night. Furthermore, on another occasion, they locked Matteo within a single instant which he was able to examine from every possible angle and which contained the entire life of the neighbourhood. When Matteo succeeds in activating André's curiosity enough to go to see this bewitched apartment, the latter realises too late that the price for these stories is much higher than he supposed, since Matteo wants him to remain in the apartment, while he takes his place in André's apartment which it has been revealed is in fact the very apartment he left all those years ago. When André refuses this exchange he finds himself with a hammer in his head, thus retrospectively explaining his headache as a premonition, only to be cheerfully buried in the flower garden. Matteo then returns to his former apartment and is greeted without particular surprise by Maria his former wife, with whom he now seems to be resuming their previous relationship.

As Adrian Martin has pointed out, with this film we are in a new regime of Ruiz's cinema; gone are the impossible shots and angles of 1980s films like *City of Pirates* or the gratuitous coloured filters that abounded in many of Ruiz's colour films of this period. Nevertheless, this is not to say we have entered a smooth cinematic realism, devoid of any destabilising optical techniques or effects. Throughout the conversation between André and Matteo, there are subtle dislocations produced by low and high angle shots, circular camera movements and shifting backgrounds that reinforce the sense that all is not as normal as it appears. All of this serves to put us in André's position of the incredulous receiver of fantastic tales believing just enough to want to know more. The disorientation is increased as Matteo's tale becomes illustrated as a space of memory or fabulation in which usual laws of space and time become suspended. For example we see the apartment as he remembers it, full of photos of the newlywed couple he was part of, whose mania for photographing themselves led to Matteo's eventual failure to recognise himself. This sense of misrecognition, that was also discussed in *Poetics of Cinema* is intensified by the way Ruiz shows the photographs to be sliding against the wall, then covered by a moving textured shadow. This shadow could well be that of a curtain moving in the wind but without any diegetic support it becomes a shadow that throws the closed life of the couple, already described as a kind of hell of overindulged intimacy, into doubt.

It is when the scene changes to the bewitched apartment that things really seem to depart from the realm of the normal and the everyday but nevertheless in initially unspectacular ways. First of all Matteo's impression that the dimensions of the apartment keep changing are presented literally as we see the walls of the apartment expanding resulting in a disorientingly unspecified space that prepares the way for the apparition of the 'fairies' that appear first as 'miniature Parisians' as we see photographic representations of the neighbourhood in a circular framed iris image reminiscent of silent movies. Matteo says that within this image he could see the life of the neighbourhood including his own departure to buy cigarettes. Later we see them as twinkling lights, miniature human figures with wings and ultimately as small chickens. There are several clues that indicate that these time-eating fairies have something to do with cinema itself. Apart from their initial silent movie appearance, there is another sequence, this time with a red filter, in which after waking up twenty years later with no memory of the intervening time, Matteo sees an image of these last twenty years in monochrome with multiple superimpositions of speeded-up movements that Matteo says are extremely difficult to read. This is echoed in a later animated scene in which as an analogue of the fairies consumption of time, we see them devouring newsprint, which is presented as the rapid disintegration of a pile of newspapers, page by page as if eaten away by some acidic agent. Surprisingly when we return to the scene of story-telling this too is bathed in red which, while it could be justified by the setting sun rather indicates a contamination between the magical world of the fairies and that of the scene of story-telling. In addition, there is a 'photograph' that Matteo shows André as proof which looks like a still picture but on closer inspection contains multiple small movements. This is echoed in another 'trick' played by the fairies in which Matteo finds himself for several months trapped within a single moment, witnessing the coming and going of events not only those that actually happened but also virtual events which could have taken place but in that specific moment were still potential. This is presented first of all in a shot in which Matteo seems to be wandering through a photograph but then via a series of *tableaux vivants* in which the trembling of the poses of the models indicates the instability of any given moment when examined more closely, evoking also the *tableaux vivants* of *The Hypothesis of the Stolen Painting*.

One obvious aspect of all these sequences is that they revisit the experimental techniques Ruiz had employed throughout his earlier career, the use of filters, time and speed variations and *tableaux vivants*, only this time this is done in a relatively more conventional manner as the characteristics of a magical other space within an otherwise more stable reality. Nevertheless, as we have seen, from the beginning this apparently stable reality is contaminated by this other space of the fantastic, and the fantastic itself is remarkably everyday, consisting of nothing other than a variety of ways in which to perceive a particular neighbourhood. More than this, everything about this first tale is highly evocative of cinematic experience. First of all there is the exchange of stories for money, in Matteo's offer to pay for André's company but really this turns out to be misleading since it is Matteo who is telling the stories and André the one who will pay. Furthermore, Matteo behaves very much like someone who is 'pitching' a story to a potential audience, attempting to entice André into a fantastic other world, inciting his curiosity to see and know more in the manner of both a cinematic trailer and a classical story-teller. As with a Hollywood trailer we are led into the tale by means of both a voice and a play of spectacular images, although in this case what makes the images spectacular is their anomalies. In the end André cannot resist the desire to see the fairies for himself, which means paying the ultimate price of admission. Another cinematic aspect is the idea of the consumption of time; what after all is the cinema and other media entertainment if not a way of consuming time, of being both present and absent, or present in the absent, virtual space of the screen? In this sequence, it is not only Matteo who loses time, whose time is consumed by these flickering fairies; André, and by implication the viewer, faces the same fate as he loses track of the day by spending time in the fantastic world of the story and ultimately he will forget himself completely to become trapped in the story itself. It would be inaccurate to take these analogies too literally since this would belie the light tone of this sequence, despite its culmination in a fairly gory death; more importantly Ruiz is clearly playing a game with the power of stories and of cinema, just as was the case in those other immortal stories that constituted his 1980s cinema of piracy. What has changed, however, is the way that the game is being played, in that the delirious techniques so characteristic of Ruiz's earlier work are now framed within a believable, even realistic world, making this film pass for a relatively 'normal' production. However, this is just as deceptive as the conclusion of this story in which Matteo returns to his ex-wife who greets him without surprise and, as we are informed at the end of the story by Bellemare, the two then live happily until their death. The appropriately named Matteo Strano seems a little too strange, not to mention prone to lapses of time and memory, to have such a conventional fate, as the later parts of the film will amply demonstrate.

Three Lives and Only One Death, Fairies 1

Three Lives and Only One Death, Fairies 2

In the following tale, traces of the fantastic and their accompanying experimentation with cinematic images are completely absent, as if Ruiz had worked through all this already in the first story. Instead we are presented with a story that while equally anomalous is more about social position and class than the supernatural. Georges Vickers, a professor at the Sorbonne (and this being a Ruiz film he is, of course, a professor of Negative Anthropology), suddenly turns around on the steps of this august institution and walks straight to Père Lachaise cemetery where he spends the night. Overnight he becomes a beggar and in fact is so good at it that he earns the exact equivalent of his salary at the Sorbonne. All of this is observed by his dependent mother who seems to be a prime motivation for his sudden change of role and, after initial anxieties, she is in fact perfectly happy with her son's changed occupation. In the meantime he encounters a bondage prostitute Tanya la Corse who also proves to have a double life in that she combines the roles of bondage mistress and president of a corporation. She warns him of her extremely dangerous ex-husband who will be noticeable by his white shoes, blue ring and peculiar stutter; when this character does appear and Vickers apprehends him by means of all these signs, he fails to alert Tanya thus terminating the first phase of their relationship. It is at this point that another figure of multiplicity enters the field; the name Carlos is first mentioned in the form of Carlos Castaneda, for whom Vickers has an intense loathing and cannot abide finding his works in Tanya's apartment. Eventually Carlos will also appear as a child, Carlitos, although in this story he only appears as a voice occasionally heard by Vickers, who echoes an obscure phrase written on the wall at the Sorbonne, 'I love you, Carlos', which appears to address Vickers.

This entire section seems taken up by seemingly effortless reversals of roles and fortune as Vickers becomes a beggar, then returns to being a professor on the death of his mother and then again becomes a beggar. Meanwhile it is revealed that Tanya, the prostitute with a heart of gold, also leads a double life as a ruthless businesswoman, Maria, in jail for the attempted murder of her ex-husband. While there is period of stability in which the two in their original roles attempt to form a relationship this is interrupted once again when Vickers turns around on the Sorbonne steps and becomes again a beggar, this time on behalf of the homeless and the poor, while Tanya/Maria's ex-husband reappears to re-ignite Tanya's taste for the perverse via a series of scandalous photographs, never shown to the viewer, which are so outrageous and extreme that they tempt Tanya/Maria back into a life of undisclosed perverse pleasures (this apparently being Ruiz's take on French eroticism).

However, even if the visual signs of the fantastic of the first episode are absent in the second, the story is no less filled with gaps and anomalies. First of all this is suggested in the ways the two main protagonists seem to oscillate almost effortlessly between their two socially distinct roles implying the possibilities of further metamorphoses. Certainly, there are elements of the story that are no less mysterious than the first, for example, when Vickers is especially disturbed by the combinations of the ringing of a bell and the apparition of a chestnut seller, or the intrusions of the child's voice in his head, both of which seem to call up another reality. Then there are the unspecified perversions that Tanya/Maria is being enticed into by her ex-husband that also suggest another side to her character than the two we have so far been presented with. Moments such as these can only be explained through yet another story and indeed without these and other anomalies being resolved, Bellemare introduces a third story but this time in a different way to the preceding two.

The third tale opens with Bellemare's announcement that it is based on the premise that 'extreme happiness is an extreme form of misery and excessive generosity is an excessive form of tyranny'. When Bellemare goes so far as to claim that this story is so true that it has taken place not once but several times and in a place near you, this alerts the viewer to the fact that this premise was no less operative in the preceding stories; Matteo's sudden departure from his wife being prompted by just such an excess of enclosed happiness in the first tale, a situation which also characterised the love relationship in the second tale, while the latter also explored the close relations between generosity and tyranny, or at least similar power dynamics. This already indicates that this story will only with difficulty maintain its autonomy with regard to the previous two and, indeed, it is in the course of this third tale that crossings between both the stories and the various roles played by Mastroianni start to intersect each other in unpredictable ways.

This third story is a tale deriving from Hawthorne, concerning a young couple who acquire a mysterious benefactor who gives them a mansion, inhabited only by a majordomo who turns out to be its owner. After a series of flashbacks in time in which we see a young couple desert a mansion in haste and being given its keys six months earlier we are introduced to this typical young Parisian couple, Cécile and Martin, played by Mastroianni's daughter Chiara and Ruiz's child actor-now-adolescent Melvil Poupaud. They have an all-consuming love for each other, that is difficult for anyone else to bear, especially the student Piotr, who lives next door. Immediately this story is infected by the previous ones as the couple sense their perfect happiness being observed by Mastroianni in beggar mode, shortly after which a regular weekly 'gift' of 2,000 Francs starts appearing in their mailbox. There is a darkly comic play with ideas of innocence and youthful idealism as both of them embark on affairs out of kindness and both are immediately forgiven by the other, following an almost ludicrous scene in which they seem unable to part from each other's company even for a few hours. More elements of the preceding stories become intertwined as each is pushed towards new employment; Martin decorating Maria's apartment, not knowing that she is the mother of Cécile and the latter working for Tanya/Maria as businesswoman, who is also in collusion with her ex-husband both of whom are shown attempting to entice the young couple into perverse games, a proposition which seems to be ruled out by their excess of idealism and naturalness. Meanwhile, when they take possession of the mansion they find it occupied by Mastroianni in yet another guise, as an apparently subservient majordomo; however, they soon find he is prone to hiding the bell whose ringing is the only way to attract his attention and to drugging them into sleep for days on end.

When the young couple attempt to find what is behind this, they witness a strange scene which has elements of the second tale in that, in Buñuelian fashion, the majordomo is sharing the mansion with other tramps but there are also elements that make little sense without knowing the fourth tale, since he is also referred to as 'Luc', a persona yet to make an appearance. Ultimately, after the couple has fled the mansion, the majordomo returns to claim his price, their new-born child who he leaves anonymously at Maria's door, indicating that this is the adopted child of Maria and André we see at the start of the film; nevertheless there is no sign of the latter when Matteo turns up at her door to stay, this time for good. This tale begins as even more of a fable or immortal story than the others, particularly in the way it presents the innocence of the young couple, being taken hostage by an act of extreme generosity. Nevertheless, as the story develops there are more and more gaps and anomalies, not least of which is how all these stories, which are increasingly interlocking can actually fit together. Then there is the snake which seems to accompany the young couple and is unremarked upon throughout the entire story. While it is possibly explicable as an unlikely pet, its other connotations of signalling a fall from grace are unavoidable, especially when it receives a similar emphasis to the doll in the beginning of the film. All these gaps will receive an at least partial explanation in the last story, which concerns Luc Allamand, a businessman/arms dealer who discovers that a fictional wife, sister and daughter that he has invented for dubious business reasons are about to turn up in Paris.

In the last story the various incarnations of the Mastroianni character start crossing each other at an increasingly rapid pace. The Luc Allamand story is barely sketched in when the latter becomes disturbed by a bowl of chestnuts and a note saying 'Carlos Castaneda', giving rise to a string of multi-lingual puns spoken by a child's voice based around this name: 'casta-distribution, casta-chaste, castaña-chataines (chestnuts) tañer, sonner de cloches (ringing bells)…' Spoken as this is by voice of the child associated with the name Carlos or Carlitos, this is a dense schizoid web of signification, corresponding both to the plurilinugalism of exile and to the multiplicity experienced increasingly explicitly by the string of characters Mastroianni plays in the film. Given the fact that nearly everyone speaks French in the film with a strange accent, and the depiction of a type of touristic view of Paris in this section in which the Eiffel Tower features prominently as does the Seine, Notre Dame and the Hotel de Ville, there seems to be a clear relationship between the experience of exile and these multiple personalities apparently inhabiting the same body.

From this point on there are rapid switches between personae, all following particular prompts and exhibiting habitual characteristics; soon after 'Matteo' goes home to Maria, this time forever, he soon starts acting as a tramp and talking in his sleep about his lectures on Negative Anthropology; appearing at the apartment of Tanya/Maria he responds to the ringing of a bell and begins rubbing his hands together and dusting and so on. Meanwhile all the women in his life start receiving anonymous threatening letters alluding to his multiple lives and inviting them to a rendez-vous at a café where they will all encounter both Matteo/Vickers/the majordomo/Luc and each other. Meanwhile Carlos/Carlitos materialises as a precocious child referring to Mastroianni as 'darling' and bringing him a 'toy' that is a loaded gun. Before this fatal meeting, however there are two intriguing scenes that are emblematic of the film as a whole.

In the first of these scenes, 'Luc' has returned to his office which is now in chaos and is sleeping under the desk. Diverting his attempts to metamorphose into other personalities his business associate insists that he meet a man next door who could really help him and that this will have nothing in common with psychoanalysis which Luc apparently has a loathing for. Bellemare informs us that this Luca Augusta is no ordinary psychologist but organises seminars, conducts orchestras and sits in the European parliament. Indeed this analyst speaks rather than listens and bases his analysis on case studies of actual behaviour rather than intimate confessions, possibly a trace of the encounters Ruiz had with US psychiatrists specialising in MPD. This psychologist, however, aided by images projected by a primitive overhead projector expresses only admiration for Luc's ability to manage these miraculous transformations, congratulating him especially on his invention and actualisation of non-existing relatives. In a telling exchange, telling perhaps most of all in revealing Ruiz's approach to this condition, Luca informs him that his condition is shared by all the personalities featured in the newspaper, ministers, pianists, boxers, and that far from an illness it is the price of success, the mark of being part of an elite. This is reminiscent of Ruiz's comments that MPD is perhaps the twenty-first-century disease *par excellence*, and this scene leads to the idea that rather than being a poor adaptation to contemporary life it is a kind of hyper-adaptation, a molecularisation or fractalisation of personality fitting perfectly with contemporary regimes of power which combine the necessity for self-promotion with impossible demands on any individual subject; becoming multiple being a much more flexible adaptive strategy than maintaining a single unified self.

An even more interesting scene follows shortly afterwards in which Luc recounts a recurrent bad dream to his younger wife, Hélène, who is a professional opera singer. In the dream she suddenly is unable to continue singing a familiar song and asks Luc to take her place. He is nervous and at first is unable to go on but feels the urge to sing a lullaby he remembered as a child; however when he starts singing it he needs to alter the words, presumably to translate them, and finds himself singing obscenities in French, for which he realises the price will be never being able to speak the French language again. Accepting this fate, he starts singing obscenities in Italian, thinking this will please his wife but she only smiles at him and repeats, 'you are a liar, you're nothing but a liar'. This voice is replaced by that of Carlitos asking, 'who are you' and repeating the chain of multilingual puns based on the name Castaneda. What makes the scene particularly affecting is that there is a disjunction between what we hear being recounted and what we actually see on the screen. At first we see a primitive projection, as if by the same projector of the earlier scene of a page of sheet music moving across the bedroom wall then in one of the most lyrical scenes in the whole film, Hélène gets up and moves across into the next room while in addition to the monologue an aria can be heard presumably sung by her. In the next room there are multiple statues and human figures on whom the mobile musical scores are now projected; then there are two Hélènes, one drifting as a sleepwalker in a nightgown and the other fully dressed up and actually singing the aria that can be heard. Meanwhile the dimensions of the room seem to be changing and the statues circulating while the figure of Hélène and some of the human figures have become statue-like *tableaux vivants*. This disjunction and undecidability within the image adds to the sense of multiple realities, or points of view on the same reality that in this sequence begin to cross one another more frequently, at times accompanied by similar visual effects,

Three Lives and Only One Death, the doubling of Hélène

while at the same time anticipating some of the visual techniques that Ruiz would use again in *Time Regained*.

The reason the stories making up *3 Lives and Just one Death* have been treated here in so much detail is because unlike in previous films by Ruiz in which multiple stories co-existed without any clue being given to the viewer, the multiple stories in this film are presented as part of a complex architecture that is in many ways much more accessible, even if not without its own traps, tricks and false leads. This is not so much in the way a series of supposedly individual 'case studies' revolving around the same performer, of which there are four or five rather than three, are revealed 'in fact' to be explained by the condition of MPD but rather the failure of this condition to really account for or fully explain the complexities of all these stories, its very banality pointing to a larger cultural condition of multiplicity and complexity, rather than a strictly individual pathology. After all, MPD can be understood, at least from Ruiz's perspective, as just a particular case of the production of incommensurable fictions; the scene with the psychologist, for example, serves more to pose multiplicity as a type of art of the multiple self rather than as a pathology, not without suggesting it as a symptom of a pathological culture. After all these tales of sudden reversals of fortune, prominent respected members of the community indulging in bizarre sexual games and so on are the regular fare of the tabloid media, hence justifying their presentation by Bellemare in the film. Nevertheless is is worth noting that with one exception, this is the only time that Ruiz would use such a device in his films, even if they have continued to concern themselves with multiplicity and complexity not only of identities but also of events and of cinematic images themselves. The next section will pursue further this complexity in relation to identity, focusing on the films, *Shattered Image* (1998), *Comédie de l'innocence* (*The Comedy of Innocence*, 2000) and *Love Torn in Dream* (2000).

Complicating Identities: Subjectivity as Multiplicity in Shattered Image, The Comedy of Innocence and Love Torn in Dream

After the inventiveness and originality of this initial move towards a more conventional form of cinema which was, if anything, even more the case with Ruiz's 1997 film,

Généalogies d'un crime (*Genealogies of a Crime*) which will be dealt with in the next section, *Shattered Image* aka *Jessie* can come as quite a shock. In this film, a US, Canada, and Great Britain co-production, Anne Parillaud partially reprises her role in Luc Besson's *Nikita* (1990), which by this point had not only been remade as *Point of No Return* aka *The Assassin* (Badham 1993) but was a currently screening popular international TV series *La Femme Nikita* (1997–2001) whose Canadian producers Fireworks Entertainment were also co-producers of Ruiz's film. Furthermore, far from working with a trusted and sympathetic screenwriter like Bonitzer, this was the adaptation of a decidedly B grade Hollywood script by writer Duane Poole most of whose career had been spent writing scripts for 1980s TV series like *The Love Boat* and *Hart to Hart*, not to mention *The Chipmunks* and *The Smurfs* and for whom this would be one of only two cinema credits. While not a straight to video release, *Shattered Image* was not far from it and certainly resembles in many respects the kind of mass-produced kitsch Hollywood B thrillers that were in vogue at that time in the 1990s, complete with a sub-Hitchcock mystery narrative, exotic locations and intimations of both sex and violence. Ruiz's involvement with this project most likely was via the mediation of Barbet Schroeder who had already suggested that Ruiz film a Hollywood MPD property as we saw above. Certainly it is the only Ruiz film one is likely to see screened on late night satellite TV, and not on an 'Indie' channel but one specialising in action films.

In any event, on the surface the film contains all the elements typical of its genre, leading to question what Ruiz saw in this project and why he would consent to follow a script whose dialogue and creaky plot devices seem to be expressions of everything he would reject as the worst excesses of central conflict theory. It is hard to avoid the conclusion that without attaining the unintentional weirdness of *The Black Cat*, the script of *Shattered Image* fell into the category of being so bad it ended up being unintentionally good. In other words while there is an attempt to construct a generic and cliché narrative based on suspense, mystery, betrayal and sex, all taking place against the backdrop of the exotic location of Jamaica, the script really fails to tie all its elements together, attaining in the process an involuntary Surrealism. The central premise, a kind of TV movie version of the sort of double identity explored in art films like Kièslowski's *La double vie de Véronique* (*The Double Life of Véronique*, 1991), never really holds together; is the Nikita-like contract killer Jessie just the wish fulfilment of the weak vulnerable Jessie whose husband is trying to kill her, or are these parallel realities with some strange and inexplicable connection? Certainly the script seems to intend the former but it is not difficult for Ruiz to inject undecidability and inconsistency into the equation, so that it seems that the reverse hypothesis, that the weak Jessie is the dream of the killer, is just as plausible for most of the film. Then there is the fact that both Jessies are romantically involved with a character called Brian who also seems to have little difficulty in inhabiting both realities. This is, of course, explicable as weak Jessie's desire to see the truth about the man about whom her judgement is clouded due to her romantic attachment to him. Killer Jessie can also be seen as a wish fulfilment of power and autonomy, nevertheless the film seems to undermine such a simplistic explanation of one reality in favour of another and rather tends to present them as strictly parallel but interconnecting realities. In this respect this film and, in a different way, *Three Lives and Only One Death*, parallel David Lynch's moebius strip-style films also dealing with parallel identities and realities that he was making at this time, *Lost Highway* (1997) and the later *Mulholland Dr.* (2001). In all these films what counts is not the solution to the mystery since, even if there is one, it is banal and itself a kind of red herring, but rather the problem of dual or multiple realities and identities themselves, and especially their thresholds of passage and points of intersection.

In *Shattered Image*, Ruiz seems to delight in the different possibilities for passages between the two Jessies (hereafter vulnerable bride Jessie will be referred to as Jessie 1 and contract killer Jessie as Jessie 2) and their surrounding worlds. At the beginning of the film this is simply through lapses of consciousness such as sleep with one Jessie dreaming the other before waking up and usually commenting redundantly on the scene that has just been shown. Later, however, all kinds of effects are used from thunder and lightning storm to a (non-existent) mirror shattering into a thousand pieces in order to enact passages and transitions that are barely plausible. For example, while Jessie is making love with her new husband, the scene is then shown inexplicably through a fish tank that is actually against a wall, this gives way to a whole Jessie 2 sequence which culminates in her having dominant sex with Brian in an aquarium with a backdrop of killer whales. There is then a series of dissolves between the two scenes of lovemaking framed in each case by these two aquatic environments, gold-fish and killer whales in what is a quite bizarre piece of associative editing. In another case a naïve painting in Jessie1's hotel room is used as the basis for a transformation to a similar yet modernist painting in the office of the psychiatrist that Jessie 2 is visiting, a therapeutic activity that seems quite improbable given her profession. These paintings are used for several such transitions, at times accompanied by flashbacks to Jessie's traumatic rape experience which both Jessies seem to have an identical memory of. On closer inspection, the naïve painting reveals a scene of ocean cliffs and an abandoned building from which Jessie 1 fell 'accidentally' to her near death, only to be rescued by her husband. Even stranger is the transition after Jessie 1 goes shopping and instead of buying a shell encrusted razor blade from which she recoils in horror, goes to see a voodoo priestess, Madame Isobel, who can see not only the future but also the past. The latter leads her to a kind of artificial forest of dangling sticks that she refers to as magic trees; after Jessie wanders through this forest with mounting trepidation she falls on a floor surrounded by balls from children's toys (the whole place is presented as a kind of Christmas emporium) and sees a toy car coming towards her. This cuts to a scene of her falling on the road and a real red car just stopping in front of her, after which she wakes up in terror on a bench near the waterfront.

The message communicated by all these transitions between realities is clear very early on, not least because the story is a highly familiar, even folkloric one. Brian, her protector, the one who is there to take care of her is, at the same time, the mysterious assailant who raped her thus causing her trauma, vulnerability and paranoia which, as is usual in these stories is fully justified. This somewhat Mills and Boon version of *Rebecca* (Hitchcock, 1940) is paralleled in the Jessie 2 storyline by the man Jessie meets who she fails to recognise at first as the one she is meant to kill. In both stories, Jessie's failure to recognise this leads to her killing the same wrong man, who repeats almost identical lines of dialogue and even the woman who is ordering the hit on Brian in Jessie 2's reality is the same woman at the hotel who is colluding with her husband to kill her, or at least drive her into madness in order to gain access to her money. Ultimately there is a full crossing between worlds when Jessie 2 appears in a mirror, telling Jessie 1 not to trust Brian, with the opposite effect that Jessie 1 reaffirms her love and trust in him and blames everything on her destructive other self. Jessie 1, after waking up in a psychiatric institution six months after her 'suicide attempt' that has been staged by her husband and his ex-wife, Paula, must become Jessie 2 (although how she is able to miraculously leave a psychiatric institution in which she has been placed after killing a detective, and acquire not only Jessie 2's wardrobe and hairstyle but also her gun is not explained) to have the strength to kill Brian rather than being seduced by his words. In the final scene she shoots the mirror and surprisingly (since usually in such mirror narratives this amounts to a suicidal act), finds her other self on the other side of the shattered mirror and the two smile at each other in a moment of mutual recognition and acceptance.

The lack of interest in resolving these and numerous other holes in the script point towards Ruiz's interest being precisely not to cover up either the inconsistent or kitsch elements of the film but rather to emphasise them. Each transition between worlds is used as a kind of game, in which Ruiz takes full advantage of these moments to play with what is acceptable in this type of genre cinema, as if he were following the script only for the sake of these moments of passage in which rules of continuity and narrative credibility not only can but must be broken. Furthermore, in the Jessie 2 narrative, Ruiz is clearly playing with the intertextuality around Anne Parillaud's role of the killer Nikita. Not only does she have exactly the same kind of clothing and make-up but frequently appears in the same fake noir atmosphere, all shadows and blue lighting, emphasising repeated gestures of smoking and seduction, and deliberately playing up the cliché of the cold-blooded femme fatale killer. It is as if Jessie 1 has not so much been dreaming this alter ego but rather watching her on TV since as stated above by now Nikita had already become a character of American popular culture; ironically, however, it is not Jessie 1 but Jessie 2 who watches TV, in the form of a tele-evangelist who seems to be addressing her directly about the dangers of the 'separation of the soul and spirit' and disobeying the commandment 'thou shall not kill.' This whole part of the film is visually a pastiche of the '*cinéma du look*' associated with Luc Besson and in marked contrast to the Jessie 1 storyline which for the most part closely resembles a kitsch TV movie aesthetic, despite being filmed by the renowned German cinematographer Robbie Mueller. One can't help wondering if the whole package was an elaborate kitsch joke about US TV movie style on the part of its European creative contributors. Certainly this seems to be the case with aspects of the musical score, especially when a supposedly haunting motif based on 'Silent Night' wafts through both stories, and coupled with the generic Hollywood reggae used to indicate Jamaica. It is hard not to think that either Ruiz and Arragiada had little control over the musical soundtrack or were playing an elaborate joke. Whatever the case, Ruiz's next foray into double identities, *The Comedy of Innocence* would follow a much more French/European art cinema model, closer to Haneke than Hollywood B movies, while still exploring questions of innocence and experience, in proximity to a more complex multiplication of identity.

If Ruiz's suspicion of innocence as a deceptive trap was already clearly apparent in films like *Three Lives and Only One Death*, it is in *The Comedy of Innocence* that this suspicion is given free reign. As with several of Ruiz's films from this period, this film has all the outward appearances of a bourgeois French art film, complete with its upper middle-class milieu and starry cast, in this case Isabelle Huppert, who along with appearing in Godard and Haneke films is also famous for masochistic performance of stoic female suffering, vulnerability and revenge in such Chabrol films as *Une affaire de femmes* (*Story of Women*, 1988) and *Merci pour le chocolat* (2000). As in other instances of Ruiz using well known stars like Catherine Deneuve and John Malkovich, Ruiz both capitalises on the intertextuality they bring from their other roles and attempts to subvert it; in this film the experience of Huppert's character, Ariane, is one of having her identity subverted, not by a romantic betrayal or violent attack from outside but by a 'strategy of innocence' that nevertheless opens up the bourgeois milieu to an unexpected outside. While arguably dealing with a less violent and extreme situation than she has in Haneke and Chabrol movies, *The Comedy of Innocence* still deals with a type of violence but a violence done to identity itself, coming from within the family, if still associated with an external threat.

The Comedy of Innocence is a loose adaptation of the Massimo Bontempelli novella 'Il Figlio de Due Madri' ('The Child of Two Mothers') which, like the author's other works, is a precursor to Magical Realism; as Ruiz notes its original plot which concerns great adventures, pirates and so on is remarkably similar to his films of the 1980s. However, instead of literally following either the style or the narrative of the book which concerns a child, born the day after another child dies and who ten years later starts to behave is if he were possessed by this other child, Ruiz presents a similar story in a highly naturalistic setting of a contemporary bourgeois French family. In the process, he was explicitly extracting a folkloric dimension from this story, situating it in proximity to disturbing children's stories like the Pied Piper of Hamlyn and Tom Thumb, the latter of which is explicitly referred to in the film. He also described the film as possibly being about the childhood of Don Juan and stated that despite innocent appearances, its child hero was no less monstrous than the child 'monsters' from his earlier films like *City of Pirates*.

Camille, who has just celebrated his ninth birthday, announces to his mother, who he starts referring to by her first name, Ariane, that he wishes to go to *his* home, to his real mother. He turns out not only to know the address of this other home but to be familiar with the neighbourhood, When they both meet this second mother, they behave as if they were in fact mother and son. What ensues is a strange power battle as this second mother, Isabella, insists that he is her son, Paul, despite the fact that this latter drowned two years ago. Remarkably this story ends up convincing not only Ariane but also her brother Serge, who lives with the family and is a psychiatrist. The intrusion of this other reality completely destabilises the entire family set-up; as Isabella says on being accused of being mad, 'so is everyone in this house'. While ultimately there is a return to normality and the events of the film are given some degree of explanation, there remains a type of disquiet hovering over all the familial relationships and several unresolved questions.

One of the most interesting elements in the film is the use it makes of video images shot by Camille, whose importance is underlined by the fact that they are the first thing that we see. These close-ups of shells, ash-trays, plants are rendered even more abstract by processing and frame capture indicating already that they belong to another reality. None of the adults grasp the significance of this window into Camille's world, or even the fact that these objects are not to be found in their own home; instead they adopt a mocking tone to which Camille responds by diving under the table after which the camera's viewfinder suddenly surfaces, in the manner of a submarine periscope, which is more or less its function in Camille's world. Early on we are also introduced to initially inexplicable images of water; later this is given some narrative justification in that just as Isabella's son, Paul, drowned after falling off a barge, also Camille is frequently taken to the Champs de Mars to play, an area that is both close to the Eiffel Tower and the banks of the Seine and which provides the setting for his initial encounters with Isabella. Ultimately, this aquatic perception begins increasingly to invade the spaces of the film, most notably in a scene in which Camille is being questioned, or rather interrogated by Serge. After refusing to answer questions, Camille asks 'if it is possible for a child to have two mothers' which Serge, of course denies. Camille accepts this explanation and continues in a similar vein, posing impossible questions and accepting their explanation but somehow continuing to play the same child's game, undermining the rational truths proposed by Serge. When Serge asks for a definite confirmation that Ariane is his real mother, Camille falls silent as the camera slowly tracks around behind him and stops, as if due to a blockage in the conversation. There is a sudden cut to the same scene, this time looking at Camille but with blue lighting and flickering shadows as if caused by reflections on the water. When Camille speaks in a strange 'underwater' voice he challenges Serge by saying 'come with me under the water, it's very deep, you'll like it' while at the same time getting up and running around the room, evading Serge's attempts to stop him and insisting that he is Paul, not Camille. During this time the image becomes stretched and distorted, resembling the distorted reflections in a hall of mirrors and suggesting the passage to another submarine reality. This is only one example of several scenes in which the use of distortion and other visual effects serves to destabilise the 'rational' space of the family home.

On the other hand this familial space and the people that inhabit it are already shown to be anomalous. Other than the opening scene, Camille's father is shown to be almost entirely absent, while Ariane suffers from asthma attacks and otherwise exhibits a nervous disposition. Serge, the 'rational' character, is prone to bouts of irrational anger such as when he discovers that Camille is playing with his model car, while Ariane is no less furious to discover that their maid, Hélène is playing with her dolls, which are supposedly important for her work as a set designer. In fact everyone in the house has their own fetish objects, which includes both the classical statues in the family home and the African ones in Isabella's apartment. In fact the house itself takes on the role of a character in which the arrangements of objects seem to have magical effects. For example, at a certain point, Ariane turns one of the statues to face a drawing of the Judgement of Solomon, the classical story of two mothers fighting over who is the real mother of a child that was also repeated in Brecht's *Caucasian Chalk Circle*. Close-ups of various aspects of this drawing are shown in several successive shots and later on Serge criticises Ariane for this seemingly unconscious gesture, describing it as too pertinent to the situation. Later, when the situation is approaching a resolution, Ariane returns the statue to its previous orientation; however, in both gestures she seems more to be led by the décor rather than the other way round as if it was the statue that was in control of these gestures rather than the reverse. Another scene that reinforces the animism of the house is one near the end when Ariane is supposed to be looking for Camille. Instead of the camera following Ariane from room to room, it keeps escaping from her moving to a neighbouring room and then when Ariane enters the frame, departing again to a different room, as if playing hide and seek. Ariane has just got off the phone to Serge who tells her she should look for Camille who he has just dropped off at the house. After a few moments the camera tracks left, along the hallway to the dining room, the one full of statues; shortly after Ariane enters the frame the shot tracks a little to the right, along the line of statues leading to the drawing of the Judgement of Solomon. When Ariane moves into the frame it pauses for a moment then tracks right again to the first room and this pattern is repeated again until Ariane, visibly disoriented sits down on the couch, at which point the camera resumes its focus on her by slowly circling and tracking towards her. At this point a door or gate can be heard closing followed by footsteps and Camille's camera appears outside the window; ultimately Ariane joins him in the garden. The point of view in this sequence does not correspond to any character and although it is suggested it could be that of Camille, he seems to enter the scene from the outside. Instead the impression is of an animism of the house itself in which its objects and décor have taken precedence over its human inhabitants, reversing the usual relations and functions of *mise-en-scène*.

This of course mirrors the question of who is responsible for the intrusion of the second mother and second reality, which goes through several phases: that of possession, in which Camille seems mysteriously taken over by the dead child, Paul; that of manipulation in which the grieving madwoman Isabelle has imposed her deranged reality on Camille; and finally that of reverse manipulation in which Camille, as monster, seems to have manipulated the whole situation in order to generate a great adventure, or at least an escape from an oppressive family situation. All of this gives rise to a complex series of doubles, not only the second mother, and the second child Paul but also another child double, Alexandre, who Ariane had taken to be Camille's imaginary friend. Despite this imaginary status, Alexandre actually appears at a crucial moment of the film, when 'Camille' has been abducted and Ariane realises that the key to understanding the situation lies in the videos Camille has made; however, these cassettes are nowhere to be found. The sound of piano playing alerts Ariane to Alexandre's presence and he gives her a bag of these cassettes, supposedly following Camille's instructions, even though his presence seems highly spectral throughout, reinforced by his exit via a window. Of course he could be explained as a secret neighbourhood friend but this does not seem too convincing. Interestingly while Ariane's first viewing of these tapes seems to reinforce the hypothesis of manipulation and abduction by Isabelle as madwoman, a conclusion she and Serge have already come to, since they concocted a plan to take her to the mental asylum where the latter works, a second viewing confirms the opposite interpretation, espoused by Isabella, that it was all Camille's doing and that he is the one who manipulated her into his plan to choose another mother. In the end the truth does not really matter since it 'didn't work out' between them anyway, thereby deflating the abduction drama that the film seemed to be turning into.

Some commentators seem to have been misled by the apparently naturalistic surface of a lot of *Comedy of Innocence* which is nevertheless one of Ruiz's most subversive films. Even while adopting the veneer and production values of the French art movie, in fact precisely through adopting this veneer, it subtly undermines it by introducing passages of the fantastic and the impossible that are all the more effective for being grounded in a familiar cinematic setting. Just when we think we are in a drama by Chabrol or perhaps Haneke, in which the evils of the bourgeois family unit are going to be the subject of attack, or themselves generative of tragic violence, something else take places which partakes of the comic and the fantastic but is in its own way no less violent. This violence is that of the irruption of a completely other reality within the normative reality of the family through the introduction of another origin which, however unbelievable, starts to exert an occult influence over all the characters. As such despite its apparent realism, this is a deeply surrealist film not only for its insertion of a dream world within the everyday but also for its particular way of attacking the bourgeois family. The downfall of this bourgeois unit is shown to be made possible precisely through being excessively reasonable and therefore paradoxically open to subversion by the 'irrational' claim of another origin. This is mirrored in the behaviour of a minor but significant character, Laurence, played by Edith Scob, famous for her roles in films by Georges Franju, an important point of reference for this and other films by Ruiz. Laurence is the attentive and impeccably behaved neighbour who greets Ariane and Camille when they first arrive at Isabella's flat and who nevertheless invites these strangers into Isabella's flat despite the fact that their connections to her seems vague and ambiguous, and reveals key personal information about Isabella. At one point she says that she has a discretion that can seem very much like its opposite and this very much sums up not only her behaviour but that of Camille's family; an absent workaholic father, a neurotic mother who has a semi-incestuous relationship with her brother, a psychoanalyst uncle prone to attacks of rage who has secret rendez-vous with the family's teenage maid. At the same time the childhood innocence around which the family is organised, that of Camille, is shown to also pass into its opposite, a form of monstrosity. In other words it is the projection of an image of bourgeois normality as full of anomalies and violence as that shown in Buñuel's *Le charme discret de la bourgeoisie* (*The Discreet Charm of the Bourgeoisie*).

Nevertheless, this reading might be too narrow in that the film is really more interested in multiplicity and complexity than any reduction to a stable explanation in terms of a surrealist impulse to *épater les bourgeois*. This interest in complexity is expressed in another minor scene in which the maid, Hélène, is throwing dice as part of her studies in the field of probability. Every time she throws the dice the same numbers keep coming up, two threes and a one, which she says has been happening for quite a while. In a later scene she reassures Ariane that probabilities are susceptible to sudden inversions, which is supposed to reassure her that Camille will come back to her, which in fact does shortly happen. At the risk of over-stretching the significance of this in the film, it does seem to indicate that the whole story of alternative origins is an unlikely but still possible probability that reigns for a certain period in a metastable disequilibrium before dissolving again into a previous pattern. In other words it suggests the way in which, for Ruiz, narrative cinema is always a type of combinatory practice in which a certain number of elements, not only characters but also décors and objects come to influence each other and form particular patterns that need not correspond to the dictates of linear narrative or believable verisimilitude, or at least not all the time. This combinatory approach to narrative and identity was, however, taken on in a far more extreme way in Ruiz's previous production, *Love Torn in Dream*, which is perhaps one of Ruiz's boldest experiments in the combinatory multiplication of identities and cinematic worlds.

While many of Ruiz's films of the late 1990s can be seen in relation to the ideas of cinematic complexity expressed in *Poetics of Cinema,* the most direct and radical actualisation of these ideas is undoubtedly *Love Torn in Dream.* One of the key reference points for Ruiz's idea of cinema as a combinatory rather than linear system is the work of the Medieval philosopher Ramón Lull, despite the fact that he is only mentioned by name in the preface (Ruiz 1995: 7). Lull was a philosopher and mystic whose work was sometimes seen as devout and sometimes heretical and who was a major influence on fields as diverse as hermetic mysticism, alchemy, Leibnizian calculus and information theory. In fact it was the rationalist philosopher Leibniz who ascribed to Lull and other mystical precursors to his own thought the term '*ars combinatoria*' and this term is now generally applied as a summation of Lull's work (Yates 1966: 383). As Frances Yates puts it in her study of this tradition, *The Art of Memory*: 'Ramón Lull believed that his Art, with its letter notations and revolving geometric figures, could be applied to all the subjects of the encyclopedia … Giordarno Bruno, putting the images in movement on the Lullian combinatory wheels had travelled all over Europe with his fantastic arts of memory. Leibniz is the seventeenth-century heir to this tradition' (ibid.). The reference to movement is essential here, since Lull's innovation in his *ars combinatoria* was in fact to put the reigning schemas of Medieval Christian cosmology into motion, by this gesture opening established hierarchies to systemic variations. To do this he developed a nine part notation system using the alphabetic letters B, C, D, E, F, G, H, I and K representing the divine qualities or 'dignities' of God such as *Bonitas* (goodness), *Magnitudo* (greatness), *Eternitas* (eternity) and so on and placed these on a wheel. According to Yates, all of this was derived straight from Neoplatonist philosophies like those of Pseudo Dionysus and Scotus Erigenes and also reflected Cabbalistic practices which were similarly based on divine names and levels of creation organised within a complex system. However, Lull's innovation was to place these attributes in a series of mobile concentric circles so that with a twist of the inner wheels different combinations of these attributes would be generated. In other words, despite the supposedly proselytising function of these devices, which were intended to convert Jews and Muslims to Christianity, they also function as a type of calculating machinery or even computer, producing novel combinations of different qualities and elements. As different versions of this apparatus included not only divine attributes but also the nine levels of creation from inanimate objects via man to God, or the four elements, or virtually any phenomena Lull turned his attention towards, the *ars combinatoria* have a tendency towards universality, abstraction and complexity at odds with the Medieval world-view and very much in tune with the more adventurous spirit of scientific creativity and invention of the Renaissance. Yates considers Lull's *ars combinatoria* as a key bridge between Classical and Renaissance arts of memory which are mnemotechnical systems, usually operating through arrangements of images whether in paintings, architecture or other forms. One of the effects of this abstraction is that, in distinction to picture-based Classical arts of memory, Lull's system of artificial memory dispenses with images altogether: 'The Lullian Art works with abstractions, reducing even the names of God to B to K. It is more like a mystical and cosmological geometry and algebra than it is like the *Divine Comedy* or the frescoes of Giotto' (1966: 185). This is not to say that Lull's art dispenses with the visual altogether but rather that it enacts a passage from the image as icon to the diagram or schema, in which lies its surprising modernity.

The appeal to Ruiz of Lull's art is clear; not only does he have a similar fascination with complex or 'baroque' systems but he is especially interested in mnemotechnical ones as we saw in the case of *Memory of Appearances,* which was already a highly Lullian film. The problem, of course is to rework the geometric non-imagistic nature of Lull's system in cinematic terms; nevertheless, bearing in mind that Lull's system was based on abstraction in order to put existing theological and philosophical categories into movement, Lullism is arguably already cinematic and Ruiz clearly believed it was

Raymond Lull,
'*Ars Brevis*'

possible to substitute cinematic sequences for Lull's geometric algebra. Ruiz expresses his attraction towards Lull's *ars combinatoria* as a method of cinematic construction in *Poetics of Cinema;* Lull may not be mentioned by name but it is clearly his art that Ruiz has in mind:

> Insofar as story structure is concerned, I should like to propose an open structure based on *ars combinatoria*. A system of multiple stories, overlapping according to certain established rules. This process is capable of generating new stories. For instance ten themes ... story lines which are both dramas and vectors. These themes can be considered either as 'bridges' or schemas. They may be simple stories, fables, or sequences from everyday life, numbered from zero to nine. At first they are exposed in order, then combined in pairs ... this is not just a way of writing but a way of filming. (1995: 88)

While this combinatorial approach to cinematic construction can be seen as a tendency of several of Ruiz's films and especially those from this period like *Three Lives and Only One Death*, in *Love Torn in Dream* this combinatorial art is applied literally and explicitly, even including an explanation of how it will be applied to construct the film in a humorous black and white prologue. In this prologue a representative of the Portuguese minister of culture (played by regular Ruizian Portuguese actor Duarte de Almeida) announces to assembled guests the way the film will use Lull's system to combine no less than nine stories. The reference to Lull and his times are not limited to the use of this system, however, since it is stated in the prologue that the director is absent since he is in Rome to obtain permission from the Pope for the film, a clear reference to the troubled fate of Lull's ideas which were at various times decreed by the church to be a dangerous heresy. Furthermore the content of the individual stories directly play out the intersection between philosophy and theology that constituted Lull's own endeavours, for example, in the story of the theology student who loses his faith from reading Descartes' meditations. Other stories recapitulate obsessive Ruizian themes such as pirates and lost treasure, paintings with animistic qualities and the power to heal or to curse, or the proximity of the sacred and eroticism to the extent that it is almost a meta-cinematic reflection on Ruiz's own work. Finally, in this film the shift from a baroque approach to one drawing more on Arabic modes of storytelling like the *One Thousand and One Nights* (2011) can clearly be seen not only due to the multiple stories and their interferences but also the fact that within these stories, characters tell yet other stories. In this respect the cinematic work it is closest to would be Wojciech Has's deliriously complex film *The Saragossa Manuscript* (1965) from which several elements are borrowed and Ruiz has expressed his enthusiasm both for Has and for the Polish writer Jan Potocki, on whose multiply imbricated stories Has's film was based.

After the exposition in the prologue of the Lullian schema presented in the form of a chart of successive combinations of pairs of letters on a blackboard, the film at first presents each story individually via a simple image accompanied by a voice-over (switching from a male to a female voice during the exposition of the third story).

Following the first story of the theology student losing faith from reading Descartes' meditations (B), there is the tale of a thief who steals a mirror that makes all it reflects disappear (C), the various emotions surrounding the different owners of a magical painting, 'The Sultan's Pearl' (D), a tale of twenty two rings and a Maltese cross that when combined permit their possessor to live in several worlds simultaneously (E), the dispute between two brothers, a theology student and his heretic brother who argue day and night over predestination and free will (F), the story of two phantom pirates in search of a treasure too well hidden two centuries earlier (G), a story set in the present day about a young student whose life is foretold on an Internet site twenty four hours in advance (H), the story of two lovers who meet every night in a dream (I) and finally the story of a young devout Catholic who learns on the day his father is taken away by two men that he is in fact, Jewish (K). Matters are complicated immediately by the fact that the young man or men in each story is played by Melvil Poupaud, and there are reflections of other characters in multiple stories as well, so that the woman in the painting in D also appears in the mirror in C and is the nun with lubricious dreams in E, as well as the nymph that she dreams of in story I and will meet Paul, the student in H. The men who take away the father in K are also the pirates in G and are also seeking the twenty two rings in E and so on. Nevertheless in the first half an hour of the film we pass from one story to another in the correct order, even if there already seem to be considerable interferences between the stories caused by the fact that the same characters seem to pass from one story to another, even if their identities shift in the process.

After a title stating 'the first ring', a direct reference to Lull's schema, we enter into combinations between the stories, starting with that between the first two of the student reading Descartes and the thief who steals the mirror; the student seems happy to be rid of it, considering it an 'evil demon' in true Cartesian fashion. However, after the thief has left the entire contents of the room have disappeared. Next there is a combination between the second and third stories of the ring and the painting as the thief is trying to sell to a collector the painting, from which the pearl, that of the seductive princess, is missing. By flashing the mirror over the painting the thief is able to restore the pearl, stating that theft is like a river whose direction can be reversed. Already it is beyond the capacities of any but the most attentive viewer to keep track of the individual stories and their combinations even if, at least for the rest of this section they do more or less follow the order set out in the original schema.

What is clear is that Ruiz is making a direct connection between the alchemical properties of Lull's art and the art of cinema, something that is referred to more and more explicitly as the multiple stories that make up the film continue to intersect in ever more complex patterns. In the process there are several themes or series of figures or objects that pass through the film. For example there is the collection of the twenty two rings that when gathered together in conjunction with the Maltese cross, a sword, a lamp and various other symbolic objects permit the passage between stories. At one point when the two phantom pirates/travelling companions meet in an inn they initiate an almost parodic sequence of displaying one object after another followed by a display of gestures accompanied by names; for example, the first man moves two fingers of his right eye and says 'the bridge', while the second rubs his chin and says 'the shipwreck.' The exchange of these talismanic objects and signs will later repeat itself across different stories, up to and including the one set in the present.

Another key story is the one of the pirate colony, the brotherhood of the black scarf, set up by twenty two men, each with a ring who were escaping their imprisonment during the inquisition. Here we learn that one of these men, an ancestor of the student was an artist who had learnt the art of hermetic painting and was responsible for painting both 'The Sultan's Pearl' and another painting of the pirates themselves, which contained the key to where treasure was buried. This painting was painted by numbers since the painter was going blind and it is in fact these numbers that indicate the geographical location of the treasure. One place that this painting resurfaces is in fact on the computer screen of the contemporary story, somehow associated with the site that predicts the student's future. A third obsessive theme of the film is the relationship between devout faith, heresy and erotic love; this is expressed not only in the dispute between the two brothers, the second of whom, perhaps a student of Lull himself maintains, that faith is a fantasy and fantasy the visible aspect of eroticism but also in the devout sister who dreams she is a courtesan, Lucrezia, indulging in sensual orgies in a sisterhood of nymphs and that she meets in this dream a young man that she strongly desires. Of course she is recounting this to exactly the same young man, this time as a theology student pretending to be a priest who has also met her in the same dream.

Finally there is a transposition of the Lullian art's stated purpose, that is the conversion of Muslims and Jews to Christianity. In fact this purpose is highly disputed and the strong parallels between Lull's system and Cabbalism could lead to the opposite conclusion and interpretation that Lull was merely using Christian discourse to disguise a deeply heretical and esoteric art with non-Christian sources. In the film this is expressed beyond the problematics of heresy and crises of faith with both the Jewish and Islamic aspects of the stories. The former is especially expressed in the final story of the youth who discovers that his father and many others are in fact Jews with 'secret names', a direct reference to the Inquisition and Jewish persecution in the Iberian peninsula. At the same time, there are Islamic touches as well ranging from the name and appearance of the first painting of the two sisters to the very structure of the whole film which directly and indirectly makes reference to the *One Thousand and One Nights*. It is here that there is also the strongest allusion to Has's film which also involved a plethora of imbricated stories, featuring two Muslim sisters who are also possibly demons that bewitch the central character. At one moment in the film the main character wakes up lying in the lap of his beloved Lucrezia, while her sister explains 'correspondence' and 'representation' in the following terms: 'If you make love to me and think of my sister that is correspondence and if you make love to my sister and think of me that is representation.' As absurd as this is, it seems to follow the unconscious logic of the film which is one of interlocking worlds linked by multiple correspondences between images, words and events.

By the second circle elements from all the stories are well and truly mixed up and the film seems to take place in a limbo space in which maybe more than one or two characters are phantoms or the living dead. For example that man Paul kills in the contemporary story who is a fashion stylist turns up in the Inquisition period session and has a hilarious conversation with the theology student, based on the incompatibility between theological and modern languages; this also seems to indicate that this man's living dead status might equally apply to all the characters and hence the entire film could be unrolling in a bardo state like the ship of the dead in *Three Crowns of a Sailor*; after all we first see Paul in the contemporary story after a motorcycle crash, an event that is frequently returned to. At this level there is an awakening of sorts as Paul, now after the murder, meets a girl, Jessica, (the same one from the other stories of course) in a nightclub who seems obsessed by stories, and describes her approach to life as 'hyper-romanesque'. One of the stories she alludes to is *Love Torn in Dream* itself, which turns out to be an esoteric work that she happens to have in her apartment and that contains, in both words and pictures, all the adventures that constitute the film. Again this is a direct reference to *The Saragossa Manuscript* and like that film raises questions about pre-determination since 'everything is already written'. That this is a question that applies as much to cinematic stories as to theology is confirmed by Paul's increasing tendency to look straight at the camera, as well as Jessica's explanation that this is the book of an oneiric cult who convert movie theatres into 'dream places' where hypnotherapy sessions take place, an idea Ruiz had already explored in the short film, *The Film to Come* (1997). By this point it is as if Ruiz were adding a delirious cinematic coda to Yates' *Art of Memory*, in which cinema would be the direct inheritor of the alchemical tradition of Lull, Giordarno Bruno and others.

One way to account for the convoluted labyrinth that makes up this film is simply to see it as one of Ruiz's most radical attempts to resist central conflict theory by multiplying narrative worlds as much as possible and constructing as many non-linear connections between them. After all, this was hardly the first time Ruiz had based a film on passages between multiple stories or made use of mnemotechnical architectures, the closest comparison in his oeuvre being *Memory of Appearances*. This seems to be how critics such as Guy Scarpetta have read the film as being 'among the most amusing, vertiginous, insolent, outlandish, delirious films imaginable. And perhaps, as well, the freest that Ruiz has ever made' (Scarpetta 2004). This sense of the film as expressing Ruiz's cinematic virtuosity and making the ultimate statement against narrative linearity is indisputably one key aspect of this film. Another is certainly a reflection or rather refraction of his previous works including the pirate films of the 1980s, the use of mnemotechnical systems and the incorporation of *tableaux vivants* that populate films ranging from *The Hypothesis of the Stolen Painting* to *Dark at Noon* and as we shall see shortly, *Genealogies of a Crime* and the more recent *Klimt*.

Nevertheless the question remains as to why Ruiz wanted to create this almost monstrous labyrinth which, in contrast to most of the other films he was making at this time, is virtually impenetrable on a first or even second viewing and can only be fully taken in by resorting to the reconstruction of a Lullian schema capable of mapping the complex relations between overlapping stories and worlds. Might the film not itself be an expression or emanation of a type of Lullian alchemy, operating at an unconscious level whose very operations are designed to perform a type of magical effect on the spectator. Such a hypothesis may be disallowed in a rational field such as film studies and yet everything in the film points to either of two explanations; either the film is a huge joke, playing with the most elaborate narrative schemas Ruiz was able to draw on, both from his own work and from that of other baroque/alchemical directors like Has, merely for the sake of complexity itself, or it is the genuine attempt to construct not only a highly poetic but also a shamanic cinematic work capable of or at least pointing towards cinema as a form of contemporary alchemy. A third hypothesis is that this film is, like other works of Ruiz, both these things. At the very least, through a type of serious play, it suggests the ways that we are possessed and inhabited by stories, rather than merely consuming them. If this is the case then more complex, open and interconnected cinematic works, like *Love Torn in Dream,* might at least give us the relative freedom of a passage between multiple stories, that are already mysterious and anomalous in themselves, rather than being shunted along the single track of central conflict. As such this film offers a very different and richer form of subjective multiplicity than the rather toxic one presented in *Three Lives and Only One Death* and for this reason alone deserves to be considered as one of the key expressions of Ruizian aesthetics across his entire career.

In this section we have passed from a case of merely double identity in *Shattered Image,* via an eruption of doubling within a familial context into a perhaps ultimate expression of multiplicity through the much more esoteric and partly for this reason far less seen film *Love Torn in Dream.* In the next section we will follow a slightly different approach to multiplicity in a different series of films focusing less on complicating identities than on complicating events, via a particular relation to crime films, beginning with 1997's *Genealogies of a Crime.*

Complicating Events: Crimes and Genealogies in Genealogies of a Crime, Savage Souls and That Day

If *Genealogies of a Crime* continues the engagement with abnormal psychology that was evident in *Three Lives and Only One Death,* it does so in relation to a markedly different field to that of multiple personality disorder and its cognitive treatment, namely that of classical psychoanalysis. The film has a basis in the strange but true tale of Hermine Hug-Hellmuth, a Viennese psychotherapist in Freud's inner circle who was murdered by her nephew who she was treating at the time. She was mainly known for advocating the use of psychoanalysis with children using techniques based on play, a direction later pursued by Anna Freud and Melanie Klein; prior to her sensational murder she was associated with a minor scandal, namely the publication under the pseudonym, Grete Lainer, of a supposed adolescent coming of age memoir, *A Young Girl's Diary* (1921), which Freud had written an admiring preface for and which was later exposed as being a fraudulent account written by Hug-Hellmuth herself, perhaps in order to legitimate the then relatively new practice of psychoanalysis.[3] It is hardly surprising that a story such as hers would have appealed to Ruiz, who was particularly taken by her conviction that the fatal and pathological character of her nephew had already been decided by the age of five, while at the same time attempting to help him via psychoanalytic treatment. In Ruiz's account, Hug-Hellmuth even wrote of a dream, shortly before her death in which her nephew was strangling her which is indeed what happened (Ruiz, Jousse and Lalanne 1997: 57). This according to Ruiz, 'raises a suspicion. It is perhaps she who, right to the end, manipulated this man so he would kill her exactly as she dreamed it' (1997: 57). At any rate this *'fait divers'* transcends the everyday in the direction of a quotidian Surrealism and seems to at once evoke the key paradoxes of psychoanalytic transference and constitute a type of Ruizian immortal story that has a good deal in common with the more theological than psychological themes of free will and predestination.

In the film version, this story is complicated by another layer in which a lawyer Solange (played by Catherine Deneuve) is charged with defending the teenage murderer, René (played once more by Melvil Poupaud) and in doing so ends up fully identifying with his psychoanalyst aunt Jeanne (also played by Deneuve). More accurately, however, it is rather the character Solange, who plays the role of the psychoanalyst, Jeanne, a point that Ruiz subtly reinforces via the *mise-en-scène*; when we see the paintings that adorn the walls of Jeanne's house, in which she has had her own face superimposed on the pictures which were formerly of courtesans at first this face is of another woman. However, after Solange has read Jeanne's diary the face on the paintings is her own, showing how far the 'transference' between her and Jeanne has advanced. However this exchange of roles is by no means limited to a direct one between the two women but also facilitated by their engagement with René, who denies his culpability in the crime and insists it is the fault of the 'Franco-Belgian psychoanalytic society'. It turns out that Jeanne was using an unusual therapeutic technique, namely of switching identities, 'I'll be you and you'll be me', a 'game' that René also insists on using with Solange with both comic and disturbing results. This we are told has nothing to do with Moreno's psychodrama and finds its ultimate expression in a psychoanalytic use of the *tableau vivant* which will be addressed shortly.

Before coming to this it is worth noting that the film has another framing story that both begins and ends the film and places these tales of law and psychoanalysis in a more folkloric and universal context. After a credit sequence that shows René disposing of a bloody knife, during a nocturnal storm, we see various configurations of the black and white pieces of the Japanese board game, Go, a game of strategy that has been seen as an oriental equivalent of chess, and hear the following Chinese story: a man, who has been predestined to commit murder, killed a woman of the Liu Bao family. A solitary woman agrees to shelter him but in reality she is the murdered woman's ghost. The man falls in love with the ghost who in time reveals her true identity and that she is only there to seek revenge. This tale is not merely a Ruizian flourish but adds another, allegorical level to the interconnected stories of pre-determination that the film presents. Within this framing, the film presents one tale, the 'true' one of a psychoanalyst who attempts to save a murderer from his destiny as a killer only to become his victim, and a second tale in which a lawyer, in her efforts to defend a wrongly accused killer, ends up killing him, although this fate is only fully revealed at the end. Much of the film maintains a phantom-like quality through its use of *mise-en-scène*, particularly the use of foregrounding of objects with no particular place in the narrative in close-up or extreme close-up. This technique which was more common in Ruiz's film of the 1980s has the effect of derealising the human figures by emphasising their place in a simulacral and fetishised *mise-en-scène*. After the Chinese legend, justified as being the book that Solange's son was reading, we have an interrogation scene, in which Solange recounts everything that happened in the time between the first crime and the second. Since this includes her investigation of the first crime and even her reading of the journal Jeanne kept about her treatment of René, the result is a complexly interconnected but highly structured double fabulation, operating at times like a classic suspense story and at others as a cerebral comedy at the expense of the two professions involved, psychoanalysis and law.

In terms of the latter it is not coincidental that Solange is a lawyer famous for losing every case, since she only defends lost causes; she herself comes across as somewhat unstable, especially in her lack of reaction to the accidental death of her son. This is particularly apparent in interactions with her mother, including a memorable scene in which she is shown to have difficulties in choosing between different objects, for example whether to pick up a glass of water or a glass of wine, an affliction she apparently shares with the murderer. We also learn she had a childhood habit of defenestrating cats. Later in the same scene she approaches a sideboard and places her hands close to a porcelain vase which seems to move telekinetically from its place and smash on the floor. Apart from expressing the unconscious hostility between mother and daughter, this also indicates that the world of the film is as much a phantom or magical one as it is a psychoanalytic one, or rather that the latter is presented as an instance of the former. Other members of her profession seem equally eccentric, especially the judge who keeps having multiple heart attacks despite his supposedly strong disposition. In fact the legal profession is represented as not being that far removed from psychoanalysis in its use of a range of intuitive techniques to attempt to construct meaningful narratives out of seemingly chaotic and random events. As one character puts it in the film, behind psychoanalysis there is the law and behind the law, fairy tales.

However, it is really psychoanalysis that Ruiz is playing with in this film. First of all there is the Franco-Belgian psychoanalytic society represented by Michel Piccoli's character Georges Didier, who exhibits all kinds of tics and signs of a disturbed and guilty personality and also has to carry a notebook with photos of people's faces in order to remember them. From the beginning his inappropriate behaviour such as haranguing Solange at her son's funeral seems to implicate him in criminal or at least dubious practices and his psychoanalytic society is indeed under investigation for fraud. There is also his arch-rival and member of the Île de France psychoanalytic society Christian Corail (Andrzej Seweryn), who seems to believe in a literary version of Jungian archetypes or narrative therapy and who maintains that everyone is possessed by fictions and these fictions are what determine their actions rather than the reverse, even going so far as to ascribe to various characters particular novels whose spell they are under. The conflict between these two analysts is played for comic effect and is very much a parody of the conflictual relations surrounding such psychoanalytic groupings as the École Freudienne de Paris, which was notorious for its breaks with individuals and groups that did not follow the correct Lacanian line (without there being any allusion to Lacanian psychoanalysis in the film). For Ruiz, psychoanalysts seem to be only a step away from being both sorcerers and charlatans as is revealed in the scene of Solange's mother Louise's session with Didier, in which she makes the shocking admission that she is thinking of changing analysts and going to Corail since the latter's sessions are cheaper. While she is recounting a dream in which she cuts up and cooks her daughter, as if she was a chicken, and whose double then arrives and starts eating her other self, the camera, which has framed her from above on the couch, does a half circle down her body up the opposite wall across the roof and arrives on Didier who is now framed upside down, shortly after the words, 'a hen pursuing a fox, that's the world upside down'. After a few seconds of Didier scratching his face, the camera then rapidly returns on the same half circle indicating therapy as being a similarly upside down world of the unconscious, which is also a conventional way of indicating sorcery. It is after this that she indicates that not only is she considering seeing another therapist but that the therapist is his enemy Corail. While Didier laughs this off at first, telling Louise in good Freudian style, 'if you want to indulge in masturbatory fantasies go ahead', when he hears that the other therapist is Corail he starts engaging in threatening behaviour precipitating Louise into a fit that proves to be fatal. Without making it into a polemical point, these and other depictions of psychoanalysis in the film show it as a technology of power, whose capacity to elicit trust and simulation of intimate relations make it all the more a form of dangerous complicity.

This dangerous complicity is played out in Jeanne's relations with René which will be replicated later by Solange. From the beginning René is considered a 'monster', a monstrosity that begins to be played out via petty crime and demands for money as he matures. This intensifies after he reads his own case study that predicts he is fated to be a killer, a fate that increasingly seems to have been constructed via the therapeutic games deployed by his aunt as treatment techniques. However, it ultimately becomes apparent that this treatment goes beyond mere role reversal; eventually Solange is invited by Didier to witness a therapeutic scene, the same one that preceded and even perhaps constituted Jeanne's murder. While Solange watches through a one-way mirror, the various members of the psychoanalytic society enact a *tableau vivant* of the scenes just before Jeanne's murder; the idea being that the simulation of this event will pre-empt it by giving the killer the chance to reflect on the consequences of the fatal event and the opportunity to alter its course. The focus on the isolation of the protagonist is emphasised first by blindfolding everyone except him, then by reversing the situation and having only the protagonist blindfolded and finally by leaving the killer alone with his potential victim. Another layer is added by having the subject observe the scene via a one-way mirror from the next room and having his role played by a double. Of course, the consequence of this practice is revealed to have been the opposite, namely the setting up of the perfect conditions for the crime rather than its prevention. This poses the question, already posed in the real life tale of to what extent the crime is actually the result, not of any innate murderous disposition but of the therapeutic *dispositif*, the series of relations that produced the conditions in which the murder of Jeanne seemed to be the predetermined outcome.

The use of the *tableau vivant* also connects this film to other works in the Ruizian filmography most notably *The Hypothesis of the Stolen Painting*. As in this earlier film, the *tableau vivant* partakes both of simulation and dissimulation, both revealing knowledge according to a rational paradigm, whether of art history or psychoanalysis but also of conveying a more occult meaning connected with ritual and sacrifice. Just as in the earlier film where the series of paintings reconstituted as *tableaux vivants* constituted 'the ceremony', or the sacrifice of a youth according to the rite of the Baphomet, in *Genealogies of a Crime,* the *tableau vivant* of the moment before the crime seems to partake of an equally esoteric subject, enacted by a group which is more like a cult than a therapeutic gathering (a point emphasised by the mass suicide performed by the group at Solange's office party on the acquittal of René). On another level the use of the *tableau vivant* constitutes a type of meta-cinema in which all the elements of the cinematic apparatus are recreated in such a manner as to become the objects themselves of attention. As Valentine Robert puts it, 'It is certainly not by chance if the tableau vivant, which allows for the satisfaction of this [scopic] drive, is staged here in such a way as to reflect all the components of cinema: spectator, screen, projection (in a 'double' character and time), a director, performers, role plays, a cyclic spectacle' (Robert 2009: 47). As such the tableau vivant extends the psychoanalytic *dispositif* into a cinematic one, while simultaneously relating both to an erotic one; after all the house with its one-way mirrors and the practice of *tableaux vivants* are explicitly associated in the film with brothels. Finally the *tableau vivant* as reconstruction of the scene of the crime is evoking policing *dispositifs* such as the practice of forensics which aims to reconstruct the exact nature of a scene based on physical evidence. As such, despite its brief appearance in the film, the *tableau vivant* of the 'moment before the crime' acquires an incredible density which is a reflection of multiple fields of knowledge and experience, namely psychoanalysis, policing, cinema and esoteric practices. It is in relation to all these practices that this scene and the film as a whole problematises 'the will to knowledge, will to power and dissimulated logic of manipulation' (Jousse 1997: 55) not only of psychoanalysis but of all these fields.

In the film, the idea that the crime itself is produced via this therapeutic assemblage is presented so convincingly that René is acquitted and a relationship is formed between him and Solange, very much resembling that between him and his aunt. After a brief

The 'moment before the crime' in *Genealogies of a Crime*

period he starts exhibiting the same destructive behaviour towards Solange, leading eventually to the situation in which she kills him. While it is more difficult to link this second murder to predetermination, it is still the result of a chain of transference operating not only through the psychoanalytic relationship but also the legal one. In the end it is as if Solange has become the phantom from the Chinese legend, whose role is merely to exact revenge on Jeanne's behalf. As such it seems to confirm Corail's hypotheses that everyone is possessed by stories, only in the case of René and Solange it was a compulsion to repeat with a twist a story of murder that had already been played out with Jeanne. The film is very much about the idea of causality or genealogies, the idea that events are predetermined to repeat themselves according to the narrative lines and apparatuses they are inscribed in. As such while there is certainly a complicating of identities, especially in the direct and indirect transference between Jeanne and Solange, it is much more about the power of chains of events to repeat themselves, to form patterns independent of the wills of individual subjects. It is perhaps for this reason that the crime film, as a fictional mode based around the crystallisation of chains of events and their causalities, proved to be a particularly fertile territory for Ruiz in several other films of this period.

One film that would seem to be in this vein is the 2001 film *Les âmes fortes* (*Savage Souls*). This was an adaptation of the novel of the same name by the 'Provençal Stendhal', Jean Giono, whose stories had famously been adapted by the filmmaker and writer Marcel Pagnol in the 1930s. Pagnol in turn was also famous for the novels, *Jean de Florette* and *Manon des Sources,* which played a key role in the early 1980s return of the once reviled French 'cinema of quality'. Ruiz would seem to not fit too comfortably into this 'cine-literary' Provençal tradition and indeed this does seem to be a project that he had relatively little control over. The script had already been developed by no less a figure than Alexandre Astruc and Ruiz was constrained to a fidelity to this script that was hardly typical of his other literary adaptations. The film certainly has the high production values of the quality cinema tradition, but is a good deal stranger and more elliptical than films like *Jean de Florette* (1986), even if relatively linear for a Ruiz film.

In the film, four women in mourning at a funeral remember the past of one of them, Thérèse, whose late-nineteenth-century life was accompanied by scandals and dramatic turns of events. She is shown eloping with her new husband, Firmin, both fleeing at night across a mountain scene. The young, poor couple arrive at the town of Châtillon. Soon there is a mutual fascination between Thérèse and the wealthy Madame Numance the most elegant and generous woman in the town; these two women are the savage or 'strong souls' referred to in the title. However, Firmin can only see in this wealthy benefactor the opportunity for extortion and blackmail, a plan which results in the disappearance of Madame Numance and unleashes perverse and criminal tendencies in Thérèse, leading to the betrayal and murder of her husband. All of this is interrupted by the grieving women at the funeral who act as a kind of Greek chorus speculating about events and their motives. As such the film is not that far removed from *Genealogies of a Crime* in that it shows an inevitable passage from one crime to another and yet, despite the interruptions of the course this is done in a far more linear manner than before.

The lyrical cinematography, especially of stunning natural scenery, as well as the period realism seems counter to Ruiz's usual insistence on cinematic artifice and in the end the film is one of the least recognisably Ruizian in his entire career, even more so than B movies like *Shattered Image*. Nevertheless, some critics like Christine Buci-Glucksmann have seen in this film a continuation of Ruiz's obsessive interest in the perverted and undecidable relations between the real, the unreal, and the dream. For Buci-Glucksmann, this film maintains, as *Genealogies of a Crime* did before it, that this perversion is in the soul: 'Between Thérèse and her other, who is strong, who is perverse? It's the creation of a "disturbing strangeness", of an ambiguity so that one is constantly and without solution between love and murder' (Buci-Glucksmann 2003: 57). In other words despite the apparent realism of this film it is still a question of undecidable doublings of both characters and events so that a tale of love is susceptible at any moment to become one of murder and a normal or even strong character to become unspeakably perverse. These dynamics were, however, given a much more delirious expression in Ruiz's 2003 film, *Ce jour-là* (*That Day*), with which this section will conclude.

That Day apparently began as Ruiz's take on the American film noir; he wanted to make a film about a woman who experiences a great deal of tragedy during one day but it nevertheless turns out to be the best day of her life, since everyone who dies wanted to kill her. However, as he was writing the script he felt it was a story that 'Dürrenmatt would have appreciated' (Ruiz in Lozachmeur 2003), and that the story could have happened in Switzerland which indeed became its setting. In Erwin Lozachmeur's excellent film about the making of *That Day*, Ruiz explains what appeals to him about Dürrenmatt who, in a similar way to Ruiz, crossed between avant-garde and modernist critical work and engagement with popular genres like the detective genre. In fact Dürrenmatt wrote several novels that could be considered meta-detective novels in that they consisted in deflating the usual heroics surrounding the genre, insisting on the role of luck and chance in criminal investigations.[4] According to Ruiz the surprising behaviour of the detectives in *That Day* who spend their entire time in a local café is pure Dürrenmatt and this debt is acknowledged via a direct reference to the writer at the end of the film. Ruiz also said that the only way he knew to make the film seem Swiss was via literature and making the actors speak French in a German manner, and indeed all the representatives of both the police and the state have German names. This influence is not limited to a pastiche of Dürrenmatt's low-key detective style but also includes the writer's critique of both the Swiss state and market capitalism, even if this comes across also as pastiche. It would be hard to argue that this film is a political one but certainly it has elements of social critique in its portrait of the members of a wealthy family arranged around a table as corpses, a scenario Ruiz suggests is also taken from the Swiss writer.

The film concerns a day in the life of a Swiss heiress Livia (Elsa Zylberstein), who is also slightly crazy; she is shown at the beginning seeing a falling leaf and calling it her sister and she believes that anyone who falls is an angel. She believes, based on a reading of runes, tarot cards and the I Ching that this will be the best day of her life whereas in fact it is the day that her family have decided to kill her with the help of local psychopath Emil Pointpoirot (Bernard Giraudeau), resident of the local asylum owned, like everything else in the town by her father, M. Harald (Michel Piccoli). After he is let out from the asylum by his 'friend' who turns out to be acting on behalf of the Swiss state, which is also part of the conspiracy, the local police start to investigate by pursuing a strategy of 'doing nothing'; not just doing very little and pretending to do something as usual but actively giving the impression of doing nothing by spending all day at the local café. When an earnest policeman comes by asking when they will go and make investigations they point out politely that they are busy having breakfast, after which they will be reading the newspapers, then it will be lunchtime and so on. Nevertheless this is the ideal way to pursue their investigation since several of the key protagonists come to the café at various points of the day. The film is also concerned with the subject of the tabloid media, the café proprietor being able to fill them in by reading from *Gala*. Meanwhile Pointpoirot turns up at the house and proceeds to massacre everyone else who arrives there including several of Livia's family who are all in on the conspiracy and a few 'innocent' bystanders, resulting in a macabre reconstitution of the family dinner scene that opens the film in the form of a dining room tableau of corpses that are assembled gradually as they arrive at the house to check on Livia's killing.

Several commentators have commented on the complete lack of suspense usually associated with the crime genre which Ruiz deflates in several ways; not only through the low key investigation but through several comic scenes surrounding Emil. First of all when he arrives instead of getting on with the killing he stops in front of the window and shaves, which is the situation in which Livia first sees him. Then, he delays the killing further by checking his blood sugar level, since he is a diabetic, an act that is foregrounded throughout the film. When killings do actually take place they are also done in a humorous way; the first victim, Luc, is killed by a hammer wielded by Livia, one of the characters, Hubus, dies of a heart attack and another, Leone, runs out onto the road and is run over. Her brother Ronald and Emil have an almost slapstick shoot-out appearing and disappearing through various doorways and after Emil finally kills him he goes immediately to take his blood sugar level. Meanwhile, amidst the carnage Emil and Livia get to know each other and start to fall in love. It is therefore surprising that Michael Richardson should dismiss this film as taking us 'into a realm in which reality is not so much brought into question as annulled [since] if you eliminate conflict … at the same time you also eliminate motivation and desire' (Richardson 2006: 159). This is surprising since this is one of the most classically surrealist instances of '*amour fou*' in a Ruiz film, even accompanied by a return of some of the most surreal of Ruiz's cinematic techniques from *City of Pirates* in the subtraction of key scenes from the film and the insertion of shots with the extreme magnification of foregrounded objects at the expense of human figures, especially in the (non) investigation scenes in the café. This is not at all a succumbing to commercial pressures but rather a more subtle way of subverting them; throughout the film there is a clear narrative conflict between Livia's desire for a perfect day and her family's plot to kill her, between her assassin's desire and her desire to live and so on but these conflicts are both deflated and dispersed in a larger web that takes in both business and the state, as well as the killer's medical condition, Livia's theological world-view and the love that develops between them. As Giraudeau describes it, the world of the film is shown from a psychotic perspective, which it could be argued is an intensification of a highly surrealist mad love, hence justifying the film's apparent unreality as one of Ruiz's more surrealist creations.

One key factor reinforcing the madness of the film is its particular use of music. Not only is there a relatively dissonant score throughout the film but it is punctuated by Livia's singing, usually of high pitched dissonant tones, autonomous from the background music. This dissonant singing is present from the beginning of the film and when Livia is first left alone in the house, she goes from room to room emitting these tones as if testing the specific reverberations of different spaces in the house. In contrast, Emil is shown several times playing the piano but always only Ave Maria, since this is the only tune that he knows. Both of these musical pieces come into relation with one another when Livia sings along to Emil's playing and this musical conjunction is one of the strongest expressions of their encounter in a space of madness. It is interesting to note that most of the scenes in the house, apart from the initial pursuit of Livia by Emil, is presented without visual distortions, which instead characterise the scenes taking place in the café with its seemingly gratuitous extreme close ups of food, objects and speaking lips. In this regard it is interesting to note that whereas Ruiz was initially planning to include various scenes presenting Livia's perception of the world directly, for example by showing the angels that she sees, these scenes were all cut from the final film, even if they still produce effect as absences. One of the scenes that was cut was of Livia calling in to her favourite TV show and in which she maintains that she suffers from a condition where, when she hears a disturbing sound her vision changes. Instead of this synaesthesia what we have in the film is a separation between the sonic and the visual so that while Emil and Livia's relationship develops in sonic terms, this is only possible by a visual denial of not really 'seeing' the corpses that are accumulating around the dining room table. Meanwhile the distortions of the visual field in the 'normal' space of the café may imply either the neurosis surrounding normal social relations, or the investigative technique of seeing things clearly by not doing anything, or more exactly by focusing on seemingly irrelevant things like having

The dinner table with corpses in *That Day*

lunch, playing pool, reading the paper or chatting to the proprietor, rather than investigating the crime.

Another key factor in the film is the association of madness with the divine, which as Ruiz points out was a commonly held belief up until quite recently. In the film's portrayal of madness there is no attempt to give an anti-psychiatric perspective although the film does pursue similar questions about the modern categorisation and exclusion of the mad. Both Emil and Livia perceive the world in theological terms whether in Emil's idea that he is following the will of God (which turns out to be the will of the state) or Livia's belief in everything from the runes to angels to the wisdom dispensed in her favourite TV show. In contrast most of the other characters, especially Livia's family members, are uniformly cynical and all seem prepared to sacrifice her life in the interest of corporate profits. This does not mean that there is no reaction on Livia's part to the macabre piling up of corpses around her and at times she does reproach Emil for going too far but she is able to interpret what happens within a larger framework of divine justice, based initially on her belief that since this is the best day in her life, anything that happens in it must be good.

From another perspective this film also pursues questions of causality and genealogy in the way it shows crime as a kind of logic related to a network of events, rather than the product of individual wills. This is firstly in the way that Livia's murder is overdetermined in the narrative with several co-existing plans to carry it out, none of which work out as planned. This is contrasted with Emil's actions, since Emil is presented as a kind of killing machine who just needs to be pointed at a target, provided his blood sugar level is under control. However, the ultimate force or will behind the conspiracy to murder Livia is soon revealed to be that of the state, 'the coldest of all cold monsters', as Nietzsche put it, and it is indeed a representative of the state who releases Emil on a killing spree, apparently not for the first time.[5] In other words, the question of who is willing Livia's murder, while initially seeming to be a collection of greedy individuals, ultimately turns out to be the state itself since Livia's inheritance is so vast as to compromise the state's integrity. While it is hard to take much of this seriously in terms of a political critique of the co-implication of the market and the state, it does point to the ways that both the market and the state operate as artificial automatisms that overdetermine the desires and wills of individuals. On the other hand, it is probably more fruitful to read these critical aspects of the film more in terms of being a Dürrenmatt pastiche so that when Monsieur Harald ends up sitting with the other corpses and shooting himself in the head, it is as much about constructing a macabre tableau worthy of the Swiss writer than it is about making any profound point about justice. Nevertheless even in this pastiche there is an ironic reflection on the contemporary corporatisation of the public sphere, since at the very end of the film we are informed that the new corporate state has awarded Dürrenmatt a posthumous award.

Complicating Images: Cartographies of Memory and Perception in Time Regained and Klimt

In several of the films already discussed in this chapter, we have seen how in apparently more conventionally realist productions, Ruiz has been able to nevertheless insert the same destabilising and disorienting effects that characterised his earlier work, in the process developing more subtle and arguably more subversive means of doing so. Nowhere is this more apparent than in his lavish adaptation of Marcel Proust's *Le temps retrouvé* (*Time Regained*), the final instalment of the latter's lifetime *magnum opus*, *Á la recherche du temps perdu* (*In Search of Lost Time*). The high stature of Proust as one of France's most important and most philosophical modern writers, who is central not only to French literary criticism but also has been commented upon by prominent contemporary philosophers like Julia Kristeva and Gilles Deleuze means that any attempt to adapt his work cinematically is bound to meet with intense critical scrutiny. This is all the more so since Proust inherited Bergson's profound distrust of cinema to do anything other than reveal the empirical surfaces of the world, a point he emphasises several times in the very volume Ruiz chose to adapt. Indeed the criticism usually levelled at Proust adaptations, not without reason, is that they merely attempt to reconstitute the décors, characters and incidents recounted in Proust's work and altogether miss the philosophical aims of Proust's *Recherche*, which is the attempt to capture lost time itself, however this is understood.

Ruiz's *Time Regained* has also been criticised in these terms, for example, by Alessia Ricciardi who compared Ruiz's film negatively with Godard's *Histoire(s) du Cinéma* project. Partly this was in the following terms which would seem to apply to any attempt to actually adapt the *Recherche,* rather than just be partially inspired by it: 'a literal-minded fidelity to his narrative model and a concern for décor d'époque, a concern which unfortunately conveys the impression of a Merchant-Ivory period piece, or perhaps a minor Visconti costume drama' (Ricciardi 2001: 643). More serious though is the accusation that Ruiz's film is a failure due to its use of *mise-en-scène* and more specifically multiple superimposed images within a single shot rather than montage to cinematically transpose the dynamics of Proustian involuntary memory: 'the Chilean director's insistence on a surrealist manipulation of the image within a single frame (for example the scenes carpeted with upturned hats or populated by multiple Marcels) rather than on the organizing work of montage mistakenly results in an adaptation that reduces the *Recherche* – a novel whose very title suggests an operation of some epistemological importance – to a trivial dramaturgical puzzle' (2001: 643–4). There is certainly nothing wrong with the hypothesis that a radical practice of montage, such as Godard's in the *Historie(s) du Cinéma* project, is one way of cinematically reconstituting Proustian involuntary memory but it is problematic to insist that this is the only way. In fact, one reason Ruiz may have avoided a too-obvious reliance on montage is because this is almost the standard cliché for imagining multiple temporalities and was heavily featured, for example, in the Harold Pinter script that was to form the basis of Joseph Losey's never realised adaptation. Furthermore, to construct such a total distinction between *mise-en-scène* and montage also goes against Godard's own understanding of montage; as early as the 1956 essay 'Montage, my Fine Care' (Godard 1986: 39–41), he rejected the Bazinian opposition between montage and *mise-en-scène*, pointing out the ways in which montage is perfectly possible within a single shot and also demonstrated this numerous times in his cinema from the 1960s. Also, with regard to Proust's writing, both superimposition and montage are used both in the *Recherche* and, as Ricciardi later acknowledges, within Godard's film. Ruiz's emphasis on the former also in no way precluded the supplementary use of montage but rather rejected its use as an indirect presentation of time in favour of constructing images in which time is directly perceptible, following Ruiz's 'dimensional' reading of Proustian temporality. As such, in Ruiz's film no less than in Godard's project, (with which the comparison should not be taken too far since one is an audiovisual poetic essay on the history of cinema and the other is, despite everything, a form of literary adaptation), it is also a question of 'a reinterpretation through which the very temporal ground of interpretation would reveal itself allegorically' (2001: 644).

The treatment of the film here will concentrate on this allegorical aspect of Ruiz's *Time Regained*, without sustained comparison to the other partial or complete cinematographic adaptations of Proust's work that have been detailed in Beugnet and Schmid's *Proust at the Movies* (2005), which deals with, in addition to *Time Regained*, Von Schlöndorf's *Un amour de Swann* (*Swann in Love*, 1984), Akerman's *La Captive* (*The Captive*, 2000), the Visconti and Pinter/Losey unrealised adaptations of the entire novel, and several films including Godard's that are less adaptations of Proust than inspired by his work. However, it is first necessary to say something about Ruiz's particular take on Proustian temporality, in the light of the major philosophical readings of Proust by Benjamin, Deleuze, Kristeva and others. In a 1999 interview, Ruiz distinguished between the Kantian idea of time as a transcendental category and time as duration, which Ruiz presents as both an oriental and Bergsonian conception, and the idea of time as a dimension that should, in principle, be perceptible. Referring to a statement of Gödel's about Einstein, Ruiz proposes, clearly with Proust's project in mind, that 'in particular moments, certainly mysterious, it seems that one arrives at having the perception of time as a totality. Not that one would be outside of time, as if the latter no longer existed, but on the contrary one is taken over by time as such as a dimension' (Ruiz 1999: 76).[6] This kind of Einsteinian/Gödelian conception of time was already at work in some of Ruiz's earlier projects like *Manoel's Destinies* but it is especially apparent in *Time Regained* in which a supreme effort is made to construct just such moments, corresponding to their literary elaboration in the final volume of the *Recherche*. As indicated above, for Ruiz, as for several key philosophical readers of Proust like Kristeva and Benjamin, the influence of Bergson on Proustian temporality has been overestimated and Deleuze's Bergsonist reading of Proust is clearly an object of critique here. In *Proust and the Sense of Time,* Kristeva argues that Proust's philosophical formation was far more indebted to Schopenhauer and interestingly the sociologist Gabriel Tarde, and above all she rejects reading Proust in Platonic terms as Deleuze did in *Proust and Signs* (Kristeva 1993: 85–86). However, there is a quite different reading of Proust, albeit still in proximity to Bergson, in Deleuze's *Cinema 2,* in which Proust is seen as a fabricator of crystalline images of time, or direct presentations of time as such: 'In the novel it is Proust who says that time is not internal to us but that we are internal to time, which divides itself in two, which loses itself and discovers itself in itself' (Deleuze 1989: 82). This reading of time in terms of a bifurcation into virtual and actual series departs from Deleuze's earlier 'idealist' readings of both Bergson and

Proust and comes close to Ruiz's conception of time as a cinematically perceptible dimension of virtuality.

However, the closest philosophical guide to Ruiz's Proust is undoubtedly Benjamin, paradoxically a key reference point in Ricciardi's critical essay. There are several points of connection here, for example, in Benjamin's emphasis on the socially critical aspects of Proust's project as that of an outsider posing as an insider to high society, all the better to mercilessly critique it. Benjamin writes in 'The Image of Proust' that 'The upper ten thousand were to him a clan of criminals, a band of conspirators beyond compare [...] Proust's analysis of snobbery, which is far more important than his apotheosis of art, constitutes the apogee of his criticism of society' (Benjamin 1999: 205). This has clear echoes in Ruiz's statement that in distinction to Henry James, whose fictions are dependent on an upper class social milieu, 'Proust's novel is a way of seeing things. I have difficulty in imagining a Jamesian Patagonian, but no difficulty in imagining Proustian Papuans, Pygmies or even Chileans' (Ruiz 1999: 79). More important is Benjamin's account of Proust's writing as a kind of web of memory and forgetting that enables a sense of eternity 'that is by no means a Platonic or utopian one; it is rapturous [...] The eternity that Proust opens to view is convoluted time, not boundless time' (Benjamin 1999: 206). This is as accurate a description as possible of the experience of Ruiz's film that, perhaps more than any of his other films, allows for a type of rapturous spectatorial pleasure, derived not from the specific content, the narrative, characters and décor, lavish as they are, but from the cinematic passage of time itself. Benjamin's account of the experience of reading Proust very much captures what Ruiz is attempting in *Time Regained* via the transposition of the experience of involuntary memory into a series of complex cinematic images: 'anyone who wishes to surrender knowingly to the innermost overtones in this work must place himself in a special stratum – the bottommost – of this involuntary memory, one in which the materials of memory no longer appear singly, as images, but tell us about a whole, amorphously and formlessly, indefinitely and weightily' (1999: 209–210). This dense, 'materialist' description of reading Proust, gives some idea of why Ruiz's film, instead of juxtaposing single images or representations of the present and the past via montage, prefers to construct complex temporal images, or multi-temporal images, as a way of grasping this material weight of the past in the present, which Benjamin compares to the weight a fisherman senses in his net. It is therefore possible to argue that even if this film enabled Ruiz to acknowledge to what extent much of his earlier cinema was already Proustian, it is in this film that Ruiz's cinema reaches a type of apotheosis of artificial memory, 'between Proust and Benjamin' and therefore must be counted as one of the more successful cinematic engagements with Proust's work, whether voluntary or involuntary.

One of the key ways that Ruiz transposes Proust's novel into cinematic terms is via populating it with all kinds of optical devices and techniques ranging from photography, magic lanterns and stereoscope apparatuses to cinematic projections. While some of these find justifications in Proust's text, their presence in *Time Regained* is certainly in excess of the importance given to them by the author and instead is a sign of Ruiz's cinematic interpretation of Proust. For Ruiz, Proust's project, along with both photography and cinema partake of a longer history of arts of artificial memory, arts which Proust and the cinema were rediscovering simultaneously, even if Proust's actual experience of and interest in cinema was very limited.[7] The first example of the presence of photography in the film comes at the very beginning of the film when Proust (the writer rather than the character Marcel) is examining a series of portrait photos presumably in order to stimulate the memories evoked by each face, which he names in turn. However, as Alain Freudiger has pointed out, this series does not serve the expected function of introducing us to the key characters of the film since several of the photographed subjects are not featured or barely feature in the film, like Marcel's father, while important characters like Morel or Charlus do not appear in the photographs (Freudiger 2009: 69). There is even one photo of a character to whom Proust's reaction is to say 'what's he doing here?' demonstrating the inadequacy of the photos as a full and complete record of the past. Instead the photographs operate as memory triggers for the writer-narrator who, confined to his bed, must make use of what means he can to gain access to lost time. The fact that he is doing so via a magnifying glass only increases the cinematic aspect of this series of photos which finish on a photo of himself as a child. While we are seeing this series of photos we hear what will become a familiar musical refrain and voices, as at a ball announcing the appearance of various figures, only partially corresponding to the series of photos; when finally this mnemotechnical procedure evokes a fully formed memory, it also departs from the actual series of photographs. Instead of a childhood memory, we see a party of the Verdurins during the war, during which Morel is playing waltzes by Beethoven and it is only shortly *afterwards* that we see Marcel as a child. This indicates that if the cinema is to be used as an equivalent of involuntary memory, this is only if it is used in a non-linear way in which there a gaps and leaps between different segments of the past, the latter often indicated by the opening of adjacent spaces that nevertheless open onto different times.

An example of this comes straight after the party scene; as Odette is storming out of the party, she opens a door behind which there is bright white light that spills out into the space of the party. She then, in what seems to have become another time leads the guests into a room where Marcel is projecting images onto the wall by means of a magic lantern, a scene that is indeed recounted in Proust's novel. However, at this point something very strange happens; the room is suddenly twice as large and the curious guests have been transformed into statues on which the magic lantern images are then projected. It is as if two different moments from the past have been superimposed and while one becomes clear the other is frozen into the virtual form of statues; nevertheless these 'statues', like *tableaux vivants*, exhibit faint traces of movement and indeed as they are illuminated by the colours of the magic lantern they seem more like actual people made up as statues and start moving as if animated by the magic lantern. At the same time Marcel's mother has materialised and is calling him, while the legend of Geneviève de Brabant that the magic lantern images illustrate is heard on the soundtrack. At a certain point Marcel puts down the lantern and looking straight at the camera asks, 'am I disturbing you, should I stop?' and meanwhile the statues have become human beings again, the original party guests. When this shift has barely taken effect Marcel walks towards a door, where the guests should be but are no longer which opens by itself onto an ante-room, the floor of which is covered by symmetrically arranged top hats and gloves. At the far end of the room, after playing hopscotch amongst these hats the child Marcel meets an adult Robert de St Loup, in military uniform, who is looking at an image through a stereoscope. Despite St Loup's warning, the narrator looks at the image, a tortured *moving* image of a horse in agony. Looking up there is no St Loup and no hats and when Marcel goes to a window to look out, we see him in a reverse shot, wearing different clothes and then inexplicably floating down from the first floor, while raising his hat, to have his key childhood meeting with Gilberte during which she made an obscene gesture that he was too naïve and shy to correctly interpret.

The recounting of these transformations from one layer of the past to another, gives some idea of the ways in which the flow of memories in the book is condensed and re-articulated in spatial, cartographic terms by Ruiz. This goes against the accusations of reducing Proust to a mere parade of décors and characters; instead the latter give the bare coordinates for the elaboration of complex cinematic images and passages between them that are less a literal adaptation of Proust than the attempt to find a cinematic equivalent for the operations of involuntary memory. After all, it is no accident that Ruiz chose to adapt 'Time Regained' the most non-linear part of the *Recherche* and the one given over to the least adaptable passages of philosophical speculation on time and memory. This is the part of the *Recherche* that is most abstracted from any specific content and instead aims to present the processes of memory as such, including all their unexpected associations, sudden leaps and non-rational connections. This is nowhere more evident than in the scene just introduced that passes from the scene of the child Marcel meeting the child Gilberte in a rose garden to the image of an adult Gilberte picking roses and hearing Marcel's adult account of this incident, the camera ultimately tracking left to reveal the adult Marcel in the frame. Meanwhile in what seems to be another time in the background a group of people including Saint-Loup are preparing to be photographed and call Gilberte and Marcel to join them; the camera cuts back to the young Marcel and then as Gilberte and adult Marcel join the group we see the young Marcel who has come to watch the scene which starts to go in and out of focus. We then cut back to the young Marcel spinning around with his eyes closed and arms outstretched like an aeroplane which also echoes his adult gesture in the photo pose; when we cut back it is to the actual photograph which the ageing Proust is examining in his room, thus taking us back full circle to the scene with which the film began.

This dizzying superimposition of different layers of the past slows down somewhat as we then enter the scene of Marcel's stay with Gilberte at Tansonville with which the book begins. Nevertheless this opening sequence sets the tone for the whole film where it is always a case of different layers of memory opening onto one another in a non-linear and fractal way. As far as fidelity goes, it should be clear that while most of the elements are drawn from the book they are subject to processes of re-ordering and condensation, and also being accompanied by purely Ruizian inventions such as the photographs and the spatial adjacency of different scenes and times. In many ways while the film seems more like a respectful adaptation, this is more in spirit than in a

From literature to cinema in *Time Regained*

literal sense, since the film is, necessarily, no less a pastiche than his earlier engagements with literature.

A final example of the incorporation of cinema into Proust's work is the scene in which Gilberte is recounting her war-time experiences at Tansonville in a letter. While hearing a more or less faithful version of the letter in Gilberte's voice, the camera circles around a café in which Marcel is reading the letter, while on the back wall cinematic newsreel images of the war are being projected. At a certain moment Marcel, still reading the letter, starts moving in relation to the room at first horizontally then rising up so he is against the projected cinema images, with the shadow of his chair on the left of the screen. At this point a camera projector, wielded by the young Marcel as he had done with the magic lantern comes into view from the right. For a while both Marcels are visible against the cinematic image, the reading adult and the projecting, filming child, indicating a type of double assemblage of writing and filming, literature and cinema, before both float away from the screen, return once more in close-up only to depart leaving a silent cinematic image of bombs being dropped on the French countryside. Unlike the previous incursions of optical apparatuses within the space of the novel, this one has no justification in terms of adaptation but is pure invention, showing Ruiz's appropriation of the 'apparatus' of the search for lost time to the cinematic apparatus indicated by both the projected archival footage and the behaviour of the young Marcel as filming/projecting double.

A key example of how Ruiz transforms and condenses the novel into cinematic form is given in the passage in which Marcel reads the Goncourt journal and reflects on the strange experience of reading a literary account of a social occasion at which he himself was present but would never have described or remembered it in the same way. In the novel the Goncourt journal occupies some ten pages (Proust 1992: 23–32) and the narrator's reflections on reading it and on literature in general almost as many (1992: 32–39). In the film this is all rendered in five minutes through the use of several devices for condensation; first of all selected parts of the journal are recounted first in Marcel's voice, then by another narrator, presumably Goncourt, then in the voices of the characters themselves who constituted the scene. As Marcel introduces the scene of a dinner at the Verdurin's, there is already visual disorientation as an aerial shot of the table tilts downwards to frame the carpet while servants cross the frame bringing dishes and continues up the wall to a tapestry which appears in

Marcel's X-ray vision in *Time Regained*

the frame inverted ninety degrees. However, as soon as we hear Goncourt describing the elegance of the plates, on which the lavish dinner was served, the image is fractured into multiple images, resembling a type of insect vision, for which no reason is immediately apparent. The filming then returns to relatively normal style as the guests discuss a range of topics and the camera mixes a slow circling from right to left with cuts to various members of the dinner party including Marcel. At a certain point while the camera is framing Marcel, the lights go dark and as the camera pans up the wall, we start to hear his troubled reflections on reading about this scene. Suddenly we see multiple superimpositions of the characters within the same shot followed by a difficult to describe shot in which superimposed images of rows of these characters and their servants move across each other, no longer limited to the original scenes but including other spaces as well, while the head of Marcel is visible again in a foregrounded but distorted image. As the voice-over repeats the words from the novel about not seeing the charm of the guests but 'when I thought I was looking at them, I was in in fact examining them with X-rays' (Proust 1992: 34), we realise that what we have been seeing, even at the beginning of this sequence is this kind of x-ray vision, made possible not only via Proust's focus on the essences rather than the external features of his personages but also by the cinematic techniques employed by Ruiz. This is quite a remarkable feat since this x-ray vision is precisely what Proust ascribes to literature at its best and claims is lacking in both bad writing and cinematography which only describes the surfaces of objects and fails to grasp their inner and temporal connections.

Of course, not all the visual techniques Ruiz employs are so dramatic; some of them are as subtle as using two different sized rooms for Proust's room, thus subtly destabilising the spectator's sense of where they are, or the superimposition of St Loup's supposed lover Rachel and Gilberte's faces when the latter dresses up as the former in order to capture her husband's attention. While the latter is a 'superimposition' that also takes place in the book, cinema enables it to be rendered in quite a different way as there is a dissolve back and forwards between close-ups of Gilberte as Rachel and Rachel herself. This doubling is emphasised by Ruiz via a shot in which Gilberte as Rachel descends a staircase twice, indicating the doubling of her identity as well as perhaps her double betrayal, since St Loup's affair with Rachel is just a mask, as much for himself as for Gilberte, for his real love for the pianist, Morel.

However, the densest and most difficult transformation is enacted in Ruiz's presentation of the moment when Marcel trips on a paving stone, thereby unleashing the joyous evocation of lost time, of the places such as Venice, Combray and Balbec that the narrator had just before been only able to evoke in a sterile way, like looking at pictures from a boring album. In the novel, Proust recounts this experience:

> The emotion was the same; the difference, purely material, lay in the images evoked: a profound azure intoxicated my eyes, impressions of coolness, of dazzling light, swirled around me and in my desire to seize them – as afraid to move as I had been on the earlier occasion when I had occasion to savour the taste of the madeleine while I tried to draw into my consciousness whatever it was that it recalled to me ... and almost at once I recognised the vision: it was Venice, of which my efforts to describe it and the supposed snapshots taken by my memory had never told me anything, but which the sensation which I had once experienced as I stood on two uneven stones in the baptistery of St Mark's had, recurring a moment ago, restored to me complete with all the other sensations linked on that day to that particular sensation, all of which had been waiting in their place. (Proust 1992: 217–18)

This absolutely key passage detailing the distinct difference of involuntary memory from everyday memory evokes earlier similar experiences such as those provoked by eating the famed madeleine and by the Vinteuil sonata and will be extended into the impressions caused by the sighting of a book from the narrator's childhood, *François le Champi,* in the Guermantes' library. This is the rapturous discovery of time past that will then sustain a train of thought for around fifty pages concerning the power of literature, dreams and simple accidental experiences to regain lost time, that is the absolute core of the volume and indeed of the entire *Recherche* since it is the moment that Marcel brings together, with a feeling of ecstatic happiness, the various modes by which the past can be regained. What is surprising in Ruiz's treatment of all this is that, at least in the initial incident of the tripping on the paving stones, he follows the book quite literally, providing the chains of images that the trigger of involuntary memory evokes: we see Marcel trip, then the other paving stone in Venice, followed by Venice itself and the various images associated with this initial involuntary recol-

Marcel in the throes of involuntary memory, *Time Regained*

lection. Then in a similar manner to the way Proust describes maintaining the same awkward posture and staggering with his feet on paving stones at different levels, we see something very similar in the film. When he is shown into the Guermantes library, we then see several other examples of involuntary memory that are recounted in the novel, the sound of a spoon against a glass recalling a railway journey in a forest, the stiffness of a napkin directly evoking a stiff towel at Balbec as he gazed out the window at the sea as an adolescent. Finally a very condensed version of Marcel's train of thought about these extra-temporal experiences follows in voice-over, including the final example of *François le Champi* evoking a childhood scene with his mother. This whole sequence, which lasts no more than a few minutes, of course can in no way match the detail of Proust's reflections on regaining lost time but nevertheless, through the carefully chosen and timed articulation of cinematic images, a cinematic equivalent of involuntary memory is nevertheless effectively constituted that does as much justice to the book as is cinematically possible.

It is also necessary to say something about the performances in *Time Regained* which incarnate a series of phantoms whose existence is indexed to Proust's attempts to recapture the past. One of the more noted aspects of the film was the use of international stars but this is done in often unexpected ways. Emannuelle Béart as Gilberte, for example, performs less as an object of male desire than with a moving feminine melancholy, while Catherine Deneuve incarnates a type of ageless grace, ideal for her role as Odette. Most remarkable, however, and most remarked on, is John Malkovich's performance as the Baron de Charlus. This was a difficult character to play since Charlus is at once slightly mad, condescending and politically reactionary and yet treated with a good deal of sympathy. Malkovich's not quite natural French, delivered in his syncopated manner and accompanied by a high-pitched manic laugh was an ideal way of incarnating Charlus and expressing his difference and self-generated isolation from many of the other characters. Both these and the minor characters, whether played by Ruiz regulars like Elsa Zylberstein and Melvil Poupaud or more unlikely casting choices like Alain Robbe-Grillet as the bad writer, Goncourt, are less rounded psychological characters than circulating ghosts, characterised by particular tics of gesture, voice and movement that reveal, as in Proust's writing, their essences rather than their personality and are all the more haunting for that. Since Ruiz usually treats cinematic figures as phantoms, this is another way in which Ruiz emphasises the cinematic dimensions of Proust's *Recherche*.

While the above only gives a bare indication of the rich ways in which Ruiz's film works over Proust's text, what should be apparent is that this is in no way a mere adaptation of the narrative contents or settings of the *Recherche*. On the contrary, via the various means discussed above, Ruiz sets out to constitute a cinematic equivalent of the *Recherche,* that adds another, cinematic layer to Proust's original project of recapturing lost time. Of course, by transposing Proust into cinematic terms, his project inevitably take on different qualities, for example, the scene of writing of the *Recherche* as well as its World War I time period and aristocratic milieu, is now also a form of lost time, far more distant from our present than the lost time Proust was originally evoking. Nevertheless, this does not make it a heritage piece whose only aim would be to objectively capture the time of a vanished era, or a '*zeitgeist*' or 'funeral parade', as Cyrile Béghine has argued (2004). Rather than seeing this film in such morbid terms, I would argue that it is one of Ruiz's most rapturous works and one that expresses the idea taken from both Proust and Benjamin that the past can be regained or even redeemed via processes of involuntary memory and in doing so add new dimensions to the present. This is, of course, provided that cinema is regarded as a privileged, 'untimely' art of memory in a line that would extend backwards via modern projects like Proust's to the alchemical arts of memory of figures like Ramón Lull or the Chinese painter Shih Tao.

This understanding of *Time Regained* places it in proximity with Ruiz's more recent film, *Klimt,* that in addition to being set in a similar period and also prominently featuring John Malkovich, this time in the role of the Viennese artist, is also very much concerned with fabricating complex cinematic images in relation to earlier media forms, in this instance painting rather than literature. As such this continues an already quite developed interest on Ruiz's part in the relations between cinema and painting ranging from its pseudo-documentary treatment in *The Hypothesis of the Stolen Painting* to the prominent role of the carnivorous painting in *Dark at Noon*, to the exploration of the work of the painter Jean Miotte, *Miotte by Ruiz* (2001). However, considering that Ruiz's film, as is stated in its subtitle, aims to present Klimt in the manner of a fantasy by Arthur Schnitzler, whose works the performers were encouraged to read as preparation for their roles, this film is also not without literary antecedents. In addition, since Schnitzler's *fin-de-siècle* writings have already inspired several films most notably Max Ophuls' *La Ronde* (1950) and Stanley Kubrick's *Eyes Wide Shut* (1999), in different ways these films constitute cinematic antecedents for Ruiz's film, despite their clear differences.

In part these reference points of not only Klimt but also Egon Schiele, Schnitzler and the Viennese author and parodist Karl Kraus, are gateways for Ruiz to an evocation of 'Vienna circa 1900', the Vienna synonymous with the fading of the Austro-Hungarian empire, the Viennese secession in which these artists took part and the period in which Vienna was at the forefront of culture in the spheres of visual arts, music, literature, theatre, architecture, philosophy and psychoanalysis. This is an already highly museumified history and one can see 'Vienna 1900' permanently displayed at cultural sites like the Leopold Museum in Vienna and indeed all around the world. This has rendered this period and its surrounding atmosphere of nostalgia the height of kitsch, a quality that Ruiz was well aware of in undertaking this project. In fact it was the very crossing between modernism and popular culture, high art and kitsch that characterises Vienna 1900 as a whole and Klimt in particular that appealed to Ruiz. Ruiz has stated in several interviews that he feels an artistic affinity with Klimt, an artist indifferent to particular schools and movements, who was criticised for over-emphasising the detail and the ornament over the whole and whose work took place somewhere between the popular and high art, at times becoming, along with the artist, the object of scandal.

As Ruiz has stated the film is far from being a biopic and he has described it as being more a phantasmagoria, a fresco or even a waltz, showing Vienna 1900 as Klimt might have seen it. In Ruiz's statement accompanying the release of the film, which he signed as being written by himself, with the posthumous collaboration of Karl Kraus, he described the film in the following terms: 'The film will be a reverie: exuberance of colours, distortion of space, extreme complexity of camera movements' (Ruiz 2006), and indeed this is an accurate formal description of the filmic techniques deployed. In terms of the structure of the film, this is where the reference to Schnitzler comes in since Ruiz deliberately avoided a linear or even multi-linear structure in favour of the structure *'en ronde'* deployed in Schnitzler's writing. This is particularly evident in the early theatrical work of Schnitzler, especially *Roundelay* or *The Round Dance*, which was the basis for Ophuls' film *La Ronde*. In this play the episodic love stories that constitute it follow each other in a circular pattern explicitly compared to a carousel, with no over-arching narrative line, principal idea or moral message. One of the effects of this is to emphasise theatrical artifice, an aspect taken up in the beginning of Ophuls' film in which the master of ceremonies who conducts the carousel, asks, 'but where are we now? On a stage? In a film studio, who can tell? ... We're in Vienna, 1900'. Beyond this, Ruiz refers to Schnitzler's work as a 'mixture of the real and dream, the everyday and madness, games of mirrors, merry-go-round, carousel' (Ruiz 2006). It is more this structure and lack of overarching moral judgement, than the play's admittedly frank sexual content, that was shocking at the time and meant that it was not until twenty years later that it was actually performed and even then it 'aroused vociferous and violent opposition on the grounds of gross indecency' (Skrine 1989: 131). Schnitzler's interest in sexuality, desire and dream was clearly related to the burgeoning movement of psychoanalysis and there was a mutual respect and acknowledgement between Schnitzler and Freud. Nevertheless, the playwright questioned the categorical certainties of Freud and his followers, writing in a letter to Theodor Reik that 'there are more paths into the dark depths of the soul [...] than the psychoanalysts permit themselves to dream of' (Letter to Theodor Reik cited in Loewenberg 2006: 259).

This rejection of the psychoanalytic domestication of unconscious dreams and desires was no doubt behind the explorations of sexual fantasies in his *Dream Story* that was the basis for *Eyes Wide Shut*. Nevertheless, for different reasons, neither Ophuls nor Kubrick's films fully capture Schnitzler's explorations of these depths of the soul, the former due to a surfeit of nostalgia and tact, perhaps made necessary due to the reigning tendencies in film censorship and the latter due to the desire to at best universalise Schnitzler's work and at worst accommodate it to contemporary Hollywood norms.[8] While some critics like Laleen Jayamanne have shown that elements of Schnitzler's world are maintained in the latter film, especially via the use of colour, the presence of symbolist paintings and modes of performance, especially that of Nicole Kidman (Jayamanne 2002), it is nevertheless the case that the link to both the original time and place and also the ethnic specificity of the Jewish main character were completely erased. More than this, the film introduces a moral judgement of the characters in relation to consumer culture, which is not at all present in the book at the same time removing any dynamism from the erotic fantasies the couple explore. While this can be argued as a strength of the film, it certainly does not present the same level of complexity and ambiguity between dream and waking life, fantasy and desire that characterised the original story; in this respect, Ruiz's film could be seen as a response to Kubrick's, a counter-argument on the ways that the modernity of Schnitzler's writings can be brought to the screen, even if in Ruiz's case this is pure pastiche since *Klimt* was not based on any specific work by Schnitzler.[9]

However, perhaps a more fruitful way of approaching *Klimt* is as directly following on from *Time Regained* despite the temporal gap between the two films. This is not merely because the film continues and extends many of the cinematic devices in the earlier film or because of the artificial resemblances in terms of period, décor or performances. More importantly, *Klimt* can be seen as Ruiz's most complex evocation of the complicated temporality explored in *Time Regained,* now liberated from any adherence to a prior model such as Proust's. The fact that the time period in question is one that Ruiz only knows through art, literature and philosophy in no way discounts this hypothesis, since it is via all these forms of aesthetic articulation that the director is able to constitute a space of involuntary memory, a memory of a world that has only been dreamed rather than lived. At the same time, elements of the film are very much connected to Ruiz's own past such as the tableaus he presents of the different intellectual circles in Viennese cafés which recapitulate similar café scenes he wrote about in Santiago de Chile in *Poetics of Cinema* (1995: 27–28), or the pressure to situate a creative practice in relation to both political demands and the state, an experience he lived in different ways both in Chile and in the years of exile.[10] Behind or rather alongside the aesthetically rich portrait of the artist presented in this film, which is another continuity with *Time Regained,* there is also a profoundly political dimension of showing the will to create as inevitably in conflict or at least tension with existing political forms, whether these forms are the micropolitical ones of dominant aesthetic practices or the macropolitical ones of the reliance of artists on the state or the Empire.

As Ruiz has stated, *Klimt* can be compared to an onion, made up of 'very fine leaves, skins that form a spherical figure' (Ruiz 2006). The film begins with Schiele visiting Klimt, who is stretched out in a water-bed, on the verge of death and we enter into the latter's hallucinations of his past life. In deference to the ornamental style of Klimt's works, Ruiz emphasises a detail of Klimt's life, namely his (supposed) affair with the dancer Cléo de Mérode, at the time that Klimt was awarded a Gold Medal at the 1900 Exposition Universelle in Paris for his controversial faculty painting, Philosophy. While Klimt is supposed to have had numerous affairs and fathered many children to his models, he was also scrupulously discrete, leaving behind not a single love letter or other direct evidence of romances, so in a sense Ruiz had free rein to invent what might have been with the dancer, although he was obliged to change her name to Léa de Castro. Certainly the two met and given the fascination exerted by the dancer not only on other artists but also King Leopold of Belgium whose mistress she may have been, it is certainly possible that they had an affair. In the film, however, all of this is presented in relation to simulacra and connected with the beginnings of cinema; Klimt first sees Léa, or rather the 'fake Léa', in a projection of the pioneer filmmaker/magician Méliès, whose cinema projection opens a pathway leading the artist through a hall of mirrors in which it is impossible to distinguish the true from the fake and indeed suggests they may well be indiscernible. The focus on this time period also allows Ruiz to deal with a key moment in Klimt's artistic career, namely the scandal surrounding the faculty paintings commissioned for the University of Vienna. While Philosophy won the medal in Paris it was the subject of critical debate in Vienna, with University professors declaring that they rejected it because it was 'ugly art' not because it was free or naked art. The critical reaction to the second painting, Medicine (a rotating image of which the film starts with), reached a parliamentary level with ministers asking whether the Austrian state was ready to support this direction in the arts. Ultimately the paintings were rejected for the University and an outraged Klimt withdrew from the whole commission, choosing to effectively 'buy back' the paintings, rather than being further embroiled in political debate. In fact after this point, Klimt would never accept another public commission and some critics believe these works, which have since been destroyed, were his most radical and accomplished works.[11] Certainly as at once highly aestheticised and at the same time political allegories, it is unsurprising that they would exercise a fascination on Ruiz, especially since the scandal surrounding them expresses very clearly the troubled relations between the artist and the state. In the film these relations are, in addition to their direct presentation, also shown by means of an allegorical civil servant, a third under-secretary, who constantly pops up in Klimt's world. This is a way of showing the relations between 'mystery and ministry' that Ruiz discussed in *Poetics of Cinema* (91–106) but also functions as an allegory for the issue of the political status of art and artists in the context of hierarchies and cultural certainties.

As with *Time Regained,* Ruiz uses numerous devices to pass from one layer of the past to another, for example, the smashing mirror that transports the scene from the Café Central to Klimt in his water-bed and then smashes again to a scene in Paris which is where the mirror actually smashed. This is accompanied by echoes and repetition of dialogue and in general sonic elements are used far more than in *Time Regained* to indicate passages between different layers of memory or hallucination. For example, in various scenes we hear the sounds of water or Klimt's laboured breathing which are sometimes used as a passage back to the hospital and sometimes just provide a sonic and temporal counterpoint to the scene that is visible. One of the key elements is the way Klimt is led, following the Méliès projection, to pursue Léa. Partly this projection is a way of relating Klimt to the origins of cinema and in addition to the forms of spectacle which include what looks like a display of a Muybridge style moving image of a galloping horse and the display of real cannibals in cages. This echoes the way that Proust's perception of the world was shown in relation to both early cinema and various cinematic techniques. Certainly in part this is to underline the affinities between Klimt's perception of the world and early cinema, at least in its more magical variants, but as with *Time Regained* this cinematic perception goes well beyond actual projections. In fact, Klimt in his fascination activated by the cinematic projection of Léa is led into a meta-cinematic apparatus of perversion, albeit based on more archaic technologies.

When Klimt meets the 'real' Léa, played by Saffron Burrows, at first the scene plays in an uncomplicated way but as the seduction continues, we soon realise that it is being observed via a one-way mirror by a shadowy figure, Duke Octave and the naked legs of another woman are visible on his lap. At what seems to be a prearranged signal, the first Léa leaves Klimt and the other woman takes her place, surprising Klimt not because she is dressed differently but because in the place of her free flowing hair it is now arranged in a complicated hairdo. They too begin to make love while the Duke comments 'the little whore, the bitch'. The Duke has already been introduced as a character who likes to keep a discrete distance, except in relation to works of art and toward the end of the film this hall of mirrors is revealed as a complex apparatus set up so that the Duke can observe a number of erotic scenes simultaneously, all via one-way mirrors. This is a type of erotic meta-cinema, a trap into which Klimt's erotic desires have led him to become entangled for the Duke's amusement. Every time Klimt meets Léa she claims to be the real one and to have never met Klimt before and by the end of the film it is suggested that Klimt may never have met the real Léa at all.

Furthermore, when Klimt is finally able to confront the Duke, the animator of this simulacral apparatus, the latter describes himself as a collector, 'once of weapons, works of art, even of castles' and now of Léas. This is a strange panoptic device not only for observing but also for generating erotic scenes, another respect in which it resembles the cinematographic apparatus which at once represents and activates erotic desire. This is, however, not the only such hall of mirrors into which Klimt falls. At one point in the film his long-term but Platonic companion Emilie Flöge tells him of a dream in which she has an aged husband who locks her in a room and obliges her to have sexual relations with a different man every night. Later on leaving the café with 'the professor' who is in fact, in Krausian fashion, a retired waiter, Klimt finds himself embroiled in this fantasy, since, shown into what is supposed to be the professor's room, he encounters a veiled woman, in an exact repetition of Emilie's supposed dream. This scenario, at once reminiscent of Klossowski and even more of Schnitzler's *Dream Story*, shows that *Klimt* is not limited to the desires and fantasies of Klimt but also allows for those of others like Emilie and also Schiele, which complicate further the spiralling phantasmagoria that the film presents. It is also a way of showing Klimt as open to the dreams and desires of others.

There are, however, further kinds of alterity in *Klimt* beyond the artistic and the erotic. In particular the role of ethnic otherness in Klimt's life is emphasised in the film, even if several of these scenes were removed from the shorter version of the film that originally circulated in cinemas. In one of the rare scenes of his home life with his mother and sister, Klimt's mother is shown distressed not only that her son has had numerous, seemingly uncountable children but that his liaisons have all been with Jewesses and comes out with an anti-Semitic chorus that his sister chimes in on before they both descend into fits of hysteria. Later Klimt is shown visiting Mizzi, his model/mistress who is once again pregnant. She is asking him not for more money but to bring up their son in the Jewish religion; despite Klimt's objections to religion in general he does not oppose this but instead becomes angry when he sees Mizzi scolding their son for playing with his Chinese neighbours. Holding the boy on his lap he says, 'you know, your father is a Chink ... except when I'm a black'. This coupled with earlier scenes such as the exhibition of the cannibals and even the scene with the Minister in the African room of a brothel, show Klimt as going against the prevailing racism of his era, not out of any political idealism but because he prefers a complex world in which it is possible to be open to the life and creativity of others rather than categorising different ethnic groups according to racialised hierarchies of value. This is especially demonstrated when Klimt visits the neighbouring Chinese household and the arts of traditional painting are demonstrated both by the boy and his grandfather. Later in the café, Klimt says to Schiele that for him these paintings are not lacking in dimension but multi-dimensional and this is shown in the film to directly inspire his 'golden period' and most famous paintings like *The Kiss*. While this comment is addressed to a question of artistic style, Ruiz seems to be emphasising that being multi-dimensional is at once an aesthetic, ethical and political issue and that in the case of Klimt these spheres were intimately connected.

Klimt's connections to the wider society and politics are shown largely through two types of public space, art exhibitions and the Viennese café and it is in the latter that relations between artists, philosophers and politicians are played out. These public and political aspects of Klimt's work are especially played out in relation to the Faculty paintings mentioned above but the role of actual public figures ranging from Ministers to Klimt's patrons and allies like Serena Lederer are doubled by the shadowy figure of the Secretary (Stephen Dillane), whose obsequious and slippery behaviour is an allegorical embodiment of bureaucracy as such. This figure is no less of a phantom than Léa and in fact is shown on several occasions to be perceived only by Klimt. As such he is a kind of shadowy double of Klimt, his political side, expressing the way that even though Klimt only wanted the freedom to be an artist, he and his work were frequently embroiled in political debates and scandals. As such this secretary is a kind of necessary mediation between Klimt and the public world, at once purporting to be supportive of his interests while at the same time actively undermining them, a mode of behaviour also evidenced by several of the actual government officials Klimt deals with. Through this intermediary Ruiz shows how Klimt, like all artists, does not exist in a utopian world of art but a pragmatic one in which complex tactics are needed in order to maintain enough autonomy to allow for creative freedom, always in a context which is indifferent or even hostile to art; as one politician remarks in the film, 'too much beauty is far worse than too little'.

However, the most important aspect of the film is not its presentation of real or fictional events in Klimt's life or its presentation of the relations of art and politics but its representation of Klimt's mode of perception of the world via cinematic means. This is done as much through the transitions between different layers of Klimt's hallucinations but there are several scenes which attempt a direct presentation of Klimt's vision of the world and as such are uniquely beautiful shots expressive of the intimate link between cinema and painting in the film. In one scene, Klimt is shown working during his gold period, in an argument with Emilie. As the latter continues talking against the backdrop of an out-of-focus gold painting, elements of the background start to be superimposed on her face and then actual gold leaf is seen on her lips, neck and shoulders. Meanwhile the background keeps changing from gold leaf to a floral pattern at

Emilie Flöge and Gustav Klimt in the latter's golden period in *Klimt*

times superimposed on Emilie's face. These shots alternate with inverted shots of Klimt stroking a black cat against a detail of one of his gold paintings and this sequence is accompanied by eerie minimalist music as the two discuss Klimt's financial problems caused by his insistence on taking back his Faculty paintings. When Emilie leaves she deliberately slams the door resulting in a 'rain' of gold leaf which continues into the next scene as the secretary appears with Klimt's cat; it is as if Klimt was perceiving everything in this period via a type of golden wash. This scene is echoed in another beautiful scene at the end of the film in which, in blue lighting, it is snowing inside Klimt's studio as he encounters, standing in different doorways the key figures in the film, Emilie, Léa and the secretary, as a type of mobile allegory of Klimt's life. Into this painterly image a young girl, Sophia, appears, who 'just like Klimt', likes to get lost. After they leave the room from which the other figures have disappeared the scene cuts to the hospital, where Klimt has died, observed by Schiele and a nurse. Here it is also snowing and Schiele has been talking to Klimt about flowers. In a mirror on the wall both the images of the nurse and Schiele, the actual inhabitants of the room and Klimt and the little girl can be seen as Klimt recites the poem, 'Drowning Swimmer's Dream', that has been heard earlier in the film, recited in German. Midway through the poem the image changes from this actual virtual tableau of four characters to an image of Klimt in profile against a rain of gold, reminiscent of the rain of gold leaf in Klimt's studio. The combination of the poem with the image and also the transcendent music that has been building during this final scene constructs a complex image of memory and passage from one realm to another, a passage summed up in the final lines of the poem that are equally applicable to the film as a whole: 'I see again, as in a drowning swimmer's dream/All the strange sights I ever saw/And even stranger sights no man has ever seen.'[12]

Ruiz's Late Projects, from Cofralandes to A Closed Book and Mysteries of Lisbon

Despite some favourable reviews, *Klimt* did not obtain the same level of critical and commercial success as some of its predecessors. In fact, it was denounced by some critics as a type of Euro-pudding, despite the narrative and visual complexity of the film and its clear developments of Ruiz's aesthetic concerns. This may have been partly attributable to the awkwardness of the English dialogue, written by Gilbert Adair which seems incapable of being fully adequate to the visual dimensions of the film, as well as the atmosphere of kitsch that inevitably attaches itself to Klimt; whatever the case this film was the last highly visible Ruiz project for a number of years. In fact it would be perfectly possible to imagine, in English speaking countries at least, that Ruiz had been relatively inactive since the production of *Klimt,* since this was the last film by Ruiz to be given a widespread international distribution up until the 2010 release of *Mysteries of Lisbon*. This was far, however, from being the case and in this last section and the interview that follows, some of these later, twenty-first century projects will be discussed.

One of the reasons that some of Ruiz's later work has been less visible is that a good deal of it took place in Chile, much of it for Chilean TV, very little of which has been accessible outside of this context. These projects began with the folkloric 'documentary', *Cofralandes* (2002), qualified by the alternative subtitles *Chilean Rhapsody* and *Impressions of Chile* and the two fictional mini-series, *La Recta Provincia* (2007) and *Littoral: Cuentos del Mar* (2008). These works for Chilean television are complemented by two feature films Ruiz made in Chile, *Dias de Campo* (*Days in the Countryside,* 2004) and *La maison Nucingen* (*Nucingen House,* 2008) and it is only the latter that received much in the way of international distribution, and in most countries this was limited to the film festival circuit. The key to all these projects was a new engagement with folklore which Ruiz described in the following terms, in a statement accompanying the release of *La Recta Provincia*: 'I wanted to approach folklore theoretically [...] I believe folklores are ruins, something that existed before in a more complete manner of which elements persist, like a town that has been destroyed and which several aspects remain: a wall, a mural, and that beginning from these fragments, one can construct other things' (Ruiz 2007 cited in *Le Cinéma de Raoul Ruiz*). It is not that Ruiz did not engage previously with folklore, in fact most of his cinema has this folkloric dimension of fabulation. However, even in his most delirious tales there was also a certain caution with regard to the subject, whether out of the desire not to be assimilated into Latin American Magical Realism, or simply as an effect of the experience of exile. However, the experience of returning to Chile for these projects enabled Ruiz to approach folklore much more directly and engage with the tales he had both heard in his childhood and through reading, where he 'noticed that these stories could be found in many places, in Europe, Arab countries and Spain. And curiously in Germany and Nordic countries' (Ruiz 2007). This is not so much a belief in the universality of folk tales as in Propp, although Ruiz is interested in these ideas, so much as an idea that different cultures, for different reasons, come up with related narratives, as if the human brain keeps generating similar stories, even if these are situated in very different contexts.

This folkloric dimension is especially apparent in *Cofralandes,* whose title refers to a popular Chilean utopia of a land of plenty in which even the houses can be eaten. Loosely based around the impressions three foreigners (a French writer, a German artist and an English journalist) have of Chile to whose foreign impressions are added Ruiz's own as an exile returning after many years, *Cofralandes* presents a dizzying stream of heterogeneous images and sounds that problematise any clear cut distinction between documentary and fiction, as Alejandra Rodiriguez-Remedi has argued (2009: 89). Instead what emerges is a multi-faceted vision of Chile in which first impressions are conjugated with stories, legends and historical events to present a type of unfamiliar dream Chile or perhaps in Ruizian terms, its optical unconscious. In Rodriguez-Remedi's words, 'The heterogeneous images interlaced with this nominal narrative are charged with multitudinous contents and referents from memory and dream, and therefore rarely correspond to linear reason. Examples include militaristic Father Christmases and blind men evoking the 1973 military coup in the height of summer (in the first part), a sleeping dog's political dream (second part), the Museum of the Sandwich (third part) and a diabolical hen (fourth part)' (2009: 91).

The film's opening sequence gives some idea of how this complexity functions. After a credit sequence over an image of the sun setting over the ocean, there is a voice-over by Ruiz, describing not being able to sleep due to an earthquake and thinking of a country house he remembered from childhood. As the camera tracks around this house, a voice recites a Chilean poem typically memorised in school. As the camera tracks back to a previously deserted courtyard, it is now seen populated with Father Christmases. The poem and melancholic music on the soundtrack now give way to a clandestine recording from the day of the Allende coup describing the unfolding military operations surrounding the attack on the presidential palace. This in turn is replaced by the military-style training of the Father Christmases who repeat 'I swear to defend my beard' and other absurdities. As the camera tracks past them they are revealed to be both male and female and made up of a variety of social types, and as the camera moves increasingly rapidly across these figures, bells and religious music are heard, to be replaced in turn by the sounds of a group of male waiters that has appeared in front of the house and banging large pans. Inside the house there are human bodies covered in newspapers while outside the waiters peer in from one side and the Father Christmases from the other. Suddenly the atmosphere changes and we see a group of female Father Christmases dancing in a circle and singing what appears to be a nursery rhyme and laughing while the waiters watch holding placards as a form of protest. Despite the heterogeneity and apparent absurdity of these images, their relations with recent Chilean history are clear; it is as if Ruiz was attempting to devise a type of folklore adequate to the recent traumatic past of Chile, a cinematic fabulation able to perform for contemporary Chile what traditional story telling did in earlier times. As Rodriguez-Remedi has pointed out there is a clear pedagogical dimension to *Cofralandes* and it was hardly accidental that this project was funded by the Chilean Ministry of Education. As she puts it, *Cofralandes* is an 'anthology or compilation of miscellanea, poetic texts and lessons (*aprendizajes*) about Chilean history, stories, culture, language, landscapes and national identity' (2009: 93). At the same time its functioning is not so different from the combinatory methods used in several of Ruiz's recent feature films and it shares the Proustian aims of recapturing lost time, only now in a specific national context.

Many of these folkloric aspects of *Cofralandes* are also evident in the feature films Ruiz made in Chile, which also share the aim of re-imagining Chile, albeit in a less pedagogical context. *Days in the Country,* for example, is very much concerned with questions of return after exile. Adapting stories by Federico Gana that Ruiz remembered from childhood, this film recounts the evocation of memories on the part of Don Federico, a writer who is talking with another old man in a Santiagan bar but there are doubts as to both the truth of these memories and the place in which they are being told which may in fact be in the after-life. In this way the story recapitulates the experience of exile in which the eventual return to the native country inevitably partakes of the spectral.

Similarly, in *Nucingen House*, Chile is presented as a site of spectral memory in the figure of a haunted or possessed house. In this film, which despite its title bears no relation to the Balzac story of the same name, the improbably named William Henry James III, wins a house in Patagonia through gambling and takes his young wife to see it. The house, based apparently on a real house in Chile, is inhabited by German-speaking characters who nevertheless observe a strange rule of only speaking French within the house. Despite the death of his wife, the man remains in the house, only to re-encounter her several years later and resume his relationship with this spectre, apparently a reworking of a Medieval tale. Once again Chilean history and folklore are combined, this time via a filter of gothic literature and B movies, all shown through the experimental use of digital video, a first in Ruiz's feature filmography. So while the idea of the haunted house populated by numerous spirits, or the return of the dead wife are classic tropes of the Gothic, their re-location to Patagonia directly connects up this spectrality with the political. As Garin Dowd puts it, 'The film features a *revenant* but also the ghosts of the dispossessed peasantry stand in the background observing the activity in the foreground [...] this continues and adapts a long-standing Ruizian fascination with the *tableau vivant*, but here the explicitly political reference points return us to the direct political engagement of early films' (2009: 4). This reading of the film was also echoed by Vera Adolfo, who stated in an incisive article that the film displays, in addition to its more conventional forms of spectrality a '*political* effect of spectrality as anachronistic force: is not Chile, a country where, precisely, after so much blood spilt in the streets, after so many disappeared becoming literally spectres returning to haunt us [...] a land of phantoms and vampires?' (Adolfo 2010: 6). This political spectrality is not only the continuation then of Ruiz's already spectral filmography but also the continuation of the pedagogical project in *Cofralandes* of generating a new imaginary cartography of Chile, one that would also include its historical spectres.

Ruiz's activities in his final years were not, however, limited to these Chilean projects but also included a range of other films in various European locations. Ranging from what Ruiz referred to as 'guerilla' projects to fully developed feature films, many of these projects were even further below the radar than his work in earlier decades. Ruiz produced, for example, several projects in collaboration with students such as *Vertige de la page blanche* (*Vertigo of the Blank Page*, 2003) in collaboration with Marie-Luce Bonfanti and students of CIFAS, and *Agathopedia* (2008) which was produced with students at the University of Calabria. This reflected Ruiz's increasing engagement with pedagogical institutions, including his position as visiting professor of film and modern thought at the University of Aberdeen. Other feature films like *Une place parmi les vivants* (*A Place Among the Living*, 2003) or *Le domaine perdu* (*The Lost Domain*, 2005) simply did not find international distribution despite being every bit as interesting as Ruiz's cinema of the 1990s. The former in particular, with its noirish story of a deal struck between a writer and a serial killer in the Paris of 1950s existentialism seems like a story that would have been capable of reaching a wider audience and yet this film, like several others from this period, was barely seen outside France.

A case in point of this invisibility was the film he completed in England, *A Closed Book* (2010). This film came even closer to being a straight-to-DVD release than *Shattered Image* and received almost unanimously poor reviews, that made little or no reference to Ruiz's previous filmography. This was in part due to the presentation of the film which was released as a cheap thriller with no highlighting in the credits of Ruiz's involvement; even *Shattered Image* had been presented as a Raúl Ruiz film but it seems almost as though the producers of *A Closed Book* considered Ruiz's involvement more of a liability than an asset. The one notable exception to this negative press was Catherine Wheatley's review in *Sight and Sound*, which provided a generous reading of the film in relation to Ruiz's filmography, arguing that it was closer to films like *Comedy of Innocence* than his more well-known films like *Three Crowns of the Sailor* or *Time Regained*. In fact the film is closer to Ruiz's B movie projects like the abovementioned *Shattered Image* or even *The Territory* without, however, the kitsch or baroque excesses of these films being allowed in this British production. Yet even this review struggles to come up with a positive response to the film; referring to Holbein's painting, *The Ambassadors*, a jigsaw puzzle of which appears in the film, Wheatley argues that the film provides a similarly anamorphic perspective on reality and that 'It's this final skewing of events that lifts Ruiz's work from the level of the Sunday-night thriller to a horrible, haunting tragedy' (Wheatley 2010: 51).

Despite this negative reception, the project seems like one that could have been quite promising, at least as a Ruizian B movie. The film is based on a rather vicious and suspenseful Gilbert Adair novel of the same name, in which a man, John Ryder, becomes the secretary of a blind writer who, it turns out, had sexually abused him as a child. Ryder plays a complex power game with the writer, destabilising his controlled environment and ultimately exacting revenge. In the treatment that Ruiz was working with the gender of the secretary had already been changed, as well as the directness of their common history; Jane Ryder is now a woman whose husband had committed suicide, essentially due to a bad review on the part of the writer who had accused him of paedophilia. This more indirect and improbable version of the narrative actually appealed to Ruiz, since the original version risked being too much like an issue of the week film. Given Ruiz's long-term association with Adair, and the use of, if not major stars, then the type of minor star that Ruiz often prefers, namely Tom Conti and Darryl Hannah, the production would seem to have had some potential. Furthermore, Ruiz's obsessive interests in visual perception, which have led frequently in the past to the presentation of blind figures, coupled with the ludic nature of the scenario, taking place almost entirely in the claustrophobic environment of a semi-occupied country house, would seem to be ideal material for a Ruizian treatment. That this was not in fact the case is largely due to production and editing decisions that are detailed by Ruiz in the interview which follows. Of course there are still some flashes of Ruizian inventiveness in the *mise-en-scène* ranging from circular tracking and rotating aerial shots to games with the differences in the protagonists' perceptions to play on the theme of anamorphosis, but all these flourishes are very constrained within a scenario that at times borders on the banal. In an already cited interview with Benoît Peeter, Ruiz has discussed his desire to 'annihilate the script'; it seems that *A Closed Book* was, in fact, a case of the reverse, the film being annihilated by the script.

Fortunately, Ruiz was not a filmmaker to be easily discouraged and as will be made clear in the interview which follows, continued his work in both film and other areas at his usual frenetic pace right up to his untimely death, and arguably beyond it with the completion of *Linhas de Wellington* (*Lines of Wellington*, 2012), directed by his wife and frequent collaborator Valeria Sarmiento, according to Ruiz's shooting script. Key among these projects is the 2010 film and TV series *Mysteries of Lisbon* which won several awards, and was shown at several prestigious film festivals such as São Paulo, San Sebastián and London and was hailed by many critics as the culmination of Ruiz's career. This project, which like *Manöel's Destinies* involved simultaneously filmed but distinct film and TV versions, was the adaptation of the work of the nineteenth-century Portuguese novelist, Camilo Castelo Branco. While not made on the same budget and lacking the well-known international stars of *Time Regained,* it was nevertheless a major project and one that fully overcame the esoteric tendencies of Ruiz's other recent work to gain a much wider international cinematic release than had been the case recently, especially in the UK and the US.

As with most of the more complex Ruiz films since the 1990s, *Mysteries of Lisbon* involved multiple narratives, this time embedded in a labyrinthine neo-baroque structure whose only point of cinematic comparison might be Wojciech Has's *Sarragossa Manuscript,* or the more delirious films from Ruiz's own filmography like *Love Torn in Dream*. Nevertheless unlike the latter's arbitrary and aleatory scheme for combining distinct worlds and stories, in *Mysteries of Lisbon* the stories revolve around several key points, represented by the key characters João/Pedro da Silva (João Arrais and José Afonso Pimentel), Father Dinis (Adriano Luz), and Anotonio de Magalhaes (Ricardo Pereira). Instead of a story based around a central conflict, it uses these multiple centres to narrate

João's anamorphic reverie, *Mysteries of Lisbon*

multiple stories which nevertheless all have a bearing, however remote, on the destiny or destinies of the main character, introduced in the beginning as the parentless João. However, even if he is the point at which all the stories converge, the film constantly emphasises that rather than being a causal agent of these stories he is rather just an accumulation of their effects, effects which ultimately overwhelm him and lead him inexorably towards an early death. Furthermore, all of these seemingly stable subjective points are revealed to be so many disguises and metamorphoses, so that the pirate/assassin 'Knife-Eater' becomes the Byronic aristocrat de Magalhaes, João becomes the lost love child of Dom Pedro da Silva and Ângela de Lima, and Father Dinis does God's work by passing through disguises too numerous to mention. In a key scene, João enters the forbidden room where Father Dinis's costumes are all kept: solider, gypsy, young aristocrat and so on, as the camera completes a 360 degree pan of this eerie room seemingly only occupied by João and these empty disguises and ultimately comes to rest on Father Dinis himself who seems to have entered the room without opening any door. This gives the impression that his identity as the philanthropic priest Father Dinis is only yet another of this series of disguises, an impression that renders his identity, along with that of other other key characters, strictly undecidable.

While shot in a distinctive style, with constantly gliding, circling, almost dancing camerawork, there are only a few scenes in the film that radically distinguish the film from European art cinema aesthetics. Some of these, such as shots from under glass tables during the scene set at the Paris Opera, seem almost like gratuitous Ruizian flourishes, as if the filmmaker was tiring of this European standard and wanting to remind the viewer of the purely fictive nature of the events being presented. More essentially, in the period in which João is entering into a delirium following what appears as a kind of epileptic fit, the image distorts into a sort of anamorphosis, rendering the figures surrounding his bed, one of whom may or may not be his mother, as floating distorted fragments.

This is when a typically Ruizian device appears, a type of puppet cut-out theatre that from this point on punctuates the rest of the film, as if all the events that transpire are the product of play with this simple representational device.[13] This is emphasised by the fact that during a scene whose outcome João does not like – his mother leaving to visit the deathbed of the man who kept her a virtual prisoner of years – he flicks all the personages to the floor of the theatre. All the multiple imbricated tales of doomed loves, sexual exploitation, romantic obsession, betrayal and sacrifice, heroic rescues

João's puppet theatre in *Mysteries of Lisbon*

and multiple disguises would then be so many disguises called up by this impoverished visual device as a machine which, analagous to the cinema itself, generates multiple worlds, characters, events and stories. This corresponds closely with the ultimate undecidability of the film, namely, whether all the events recounted and specifically those involving Pedro da Silva's short life and ultimate death in Brazil, actually took place, or whether this was the delirial wish fulfilment of an orphaned child, without a story, fabulating ancestors, conflicts, rivals and benefactors, and ultimately a phantasmagoric if doomed identity for himself, to fill in the void of his existence, and those surrounding him like Father Dinis. The anamorphosis coupled with the puppet theatre suggest that this question is unanswerable since history is only the product of incommensurable stories and fabulations, as is suggested in the very opening scene of the film in which entirely contradictory versions of 'current affairs' in the form of a reputed invasion of Portugal, are presented orally and without resolution.

Given all these typically Ruizian elements of multiple imbricated stories, characters subject to metamorphoses, mnemotechnical and fabulating machineries, and stories told from the point of a delirium between life and death, not to mention the relatively unbroken use of a high art European style, it is hardly surprising that several critics saw the film as both the culmination of Ruiz's career and a disguised autobiography. Jonathan Romney, for example, in his *Sight and Sound* review of the film stated:

> While *Mysteries of Lisbon* was not in fact Ruiz's very last film, it could be seen as a valedictory *summum* of his oeuvre – his fabulously omnivorous contemplation of imagination and history. The film flickers with echoes of Ruiz's work

[...] One could [also] see *Mysteries* as a disguised autobiography, 'Ruiz' almost rhyming with 'Dinis' – for the Chilean was himself a disguise artist as well as a manipulator of story, masquerading variously as a French, a Portuguese, even an American filmmaker. (Romney 2012: 61)

While such an account is plausible, it is overstating the case to see this film as summing up and embodying Ruiz's work or life as a whole. Ruiz himself preferred to describe both as a kind of pendulum, and *Mysteries of Lisbon* would only account for one swing of a pendulum that also, as this book has hopefully shown, encompassed many other styles, themes and importantly many modes of filmmaking of which high budget European costume dramas were only one variant. Certainly there is a lot of Ruiz in this film, not least in his engagement with Portugal as a type of memory bridge to Chile and Latin America, of which this *does* constitute a kind of ultimate statement, as well as being a film that will inevitably be read as a meditation on death and mortality. Ruiz's last major film, *The Night Across the Street*, would indicate a quite different, and darker summation of his work, more in common with his recent Chilean projects, before the pendulum swung back to the high budget, 'European' Lines of *Wellington* that Ruiz was not able to complete before his death. But many of Ruiz's concerns and stylistic tendencies escape this 'summation', however vast and encompassing it might be. Nevertheless, it certainly remains a key Ruiz film and one that will continue to remind twenty-first-century audiences of the significance of this most paradoxical of cinematic auteurs.

Notes

1   This article was originally written in Spanish and the French version was published in *Cahiers du Cinéma* in 1978.
2   See Walter Benjamin (1999 [1968]), 'The Work of Art in the Age of Mechanical Reproduction,' in *Illuminations*, London: Pimlico, 230: 'The camera introduces us to unconscious optics as does psychoanalysis to unconscious impulses.'
3   See Grete Lainer 1921.
4   See especially Inspector Barlach novels such as 'The Judge and his Hangman' and 'The Quarry' in which the ill health and unconventionally old-fashioned and low-key detection style of the main protagonist is very much in keeping with that portrayed in Ruiz's film, especially in the question and answer between the inspector and his colleague, 'Cramp? Cramp!' See Dürrenmatt 1985: 7–177.
5   See Nietzsche 1967: 104–5.
6   Gödel's mathematical ideas such as strange loops and recursion were presented in relation with the music of Bach and the art of Escher by Douglas Hofstadter in the 'spirit of Lewis Carroll' in the extraordinary book *Gödel, Escher, Bach* (Hofstadter 1979), a work that would no doubt appeal to Ruiz.
7   Most accounts limit Proust's experience of cinema to one 'Cinema Guignol' screening in 1908 and apparently the writer regretted never having set foot in a cinema. See Martine Beugnet and Marion Schmid 2005: 11.

8   In this regard, it is worth noting the scene close to the end of Ophuls' *La Ronde*, in which one of the erotic encounters is interrupted by the MC, still dressed in top hat and tails, who is menacing a film roll with a pair of scissors and appears to be cutting out the scene we have just witnessed while singing, 'censorship'!
9   There is some basis, however, for Ruiz's pastiche in Schnitzler's late play, *The Comedy of Seduction*, in which he also bases a character on Klimt.
10 Interestingly, Ruiz contextualises this description of the different conversations at the café tables in Santiago as concerning so many utopias, political, philosophical and cinematic all of which were swept away by the 'four horsemen of the apocalypse' (Ruiz 1995: 28) an image he also used to describe the fate of Klimt's world.
11 The originals of these works which had been acquired by a friend of Klimt's, August Lederer, were destroyed in a fire in 1945 in Immendorf Castle, see Sternthal 2006: 74–75.
12 This poem, 'Drowning Swimmer's Dream' has no attributed author and as it sounds very much like a pastiche of Dante may well have been written by Ruiz for the film.
13 These effects, which had also been used in earlier Ruiz films like *Time Regained*, were obtained by the use of archaic lenses that, according to Adrian Martin, Ruiz liked to collect, in this case one known as 'The Mesmeriser'.

CONCLUSION

Ruizian Cartography from Chile to the Cosmos via the Littoral, or The Film to Come

This book has attempted to follow Ruiz's complex trajectory from Chile in the context of the New Latin American cinema of the 1960s, via the vicissitudes of exile, to his latest complex modes of cinematic production and other forms of creative work in the new millennium. Rather than providing a linear history, it has sketched a number of successive cartographies of Ruiz's work, in line with its own concerns with cartography and passage. In the Chilean period of the 1960s and early 1970s this was done primarily in relation to political cartographies of gesture and behaviour that constituted a subversive micropolitics in relation to the wider political and cultural transformations that were taking place in Chile prior to and during the Allende period. Nevertheless, even in this period the sobriety in relation to political certainties resulted in a distinctive aesthetic style in Ruiz's cinema, albeit a very different one from that which would be later developed in exile. In the first period of exile in the 1970s the cartography was more of genres and formats of image production ranging from films to art and political documentaries to 'photo-romans' and other forms that defy categorisation. In this period, Ruiz was experimenting with visual and narrative techniques that would be more fully deployed later on but at the same time producing singular works in which the cartography of cinematic, televisual and other images was privileged resulting in a distinctive combination of political and aesthetic concerns; in other words, during this period Ruiz was interested in exploring and destabilising both aesthetic and political rhetorics and especially in rejecting the certainties and truth claims of political documentary cinema in favour of ambivalent and multiple fictions and simulations.

In the 1980s, Ruizian cinematic cartography was much more expansive both geographically and stylistically. In part this was a re-invention of Ruiz's early interest in the surreal and the baroque, while at the same time it was an opening up of spaces of fabulation, through the elaboration of wild fictions. At the same time it was a rediscovery of cinema, after years of television and other commissioned small projects, as a wider canvas on which to develop the experimentation with both images and storytelling that in the 1970s had only been able to exist as sketches. Finally it was a period of cartography in the geographical sense that Ruiz was making most of his films outside of France and especially in Portugal, which began to function as a kind of bridge towards Chilean memories and imagination and thereby allowed for a new type of mapping. In particular this involved the explorations of the related themes of the sea, maritime tales, pirates and piracy in all its senses, and childhood and children's stories to be explored. Later in the decade these journeys took on more spectral dimensions but continued the cartographic impulses of Ruiz's cinema of piracy, even in films taking place in specific regions of Paris, as in *The Sleepwalker of the Alma Bridge*. At the same time these journeys allowed for the full elaboration of a unique neo-baroque aesthetics reaching its peak in films like *City of Pirates* or *Memories of Appearances*. Finally in the period of Ruiz's filmmaking from the mid-1990s there was a focus on complex cartographies of cinematic images, whether this complexity has been primarily in terms of subjective identity, events, nationality or cinematic images themselves. While this period has been seen by some commentators as Ruiz adapting to art movie conventions or even commercial norms of well-made films, even in his most expensive projects there remains subversive dimensions in the complication and rendering undecidable of cinematic images, which is sometimes at its most radical precisely in bigger budget films such as *Time Regained* and *Mysteries of Lisbon*.

The task of producing an adequate cartography of Ruiz's entire cinematic career is no less an impossible one than the most delirious cartographies presented within Ruiz's films. As Adrian Martin has commented, Ruiz's cinema presents challenges to film criticism not only because of its dispersal or the tendency of one film to be many films and conversely for themes and characters to drift across several films but also because of the complexity of Ruiz's specific practices of *mise-en-scène*: 'There is a challenge to film criticism in Ruiz's work – especially to *mise-en-scène* criticism, which would have to transform itself utterly to grasp what is going on here, picking up the road it very rarely took when modernist filmmakers began radically reshaping *mise-en-scène* in the 1960s' (Martin 2004: 51). Needless to say, the challenges addressed to film criticism, theory and even film history are more than can be addressed in a single work. In addition to Martin's call for in-depth critical engagement with Ruiz's film-work as a director in terms of *mise-en-scène*, I would also propose several other areas of further research. Firstly, Ruiz's work is one that merits examination in relation to both film theory and the emergent field of 'film philosophy' to which it could make substantial contributions. This is not merely in Ruiz's own written articulations of theory in *Poetics of Cinema* and elsewhere although these are uniquely valuable contributions to any film philosophy worthy of the name; more than this Ruiz's cinema itself is a uniquely rich and multiple example of a thinking by means of cinematic images, a cine-thinking whose analysis has a lot to reveal about the existing and potential relations between cinema and not only philosophy but also theology. At this point one could add the clear resonances between Ruiz's work in cinema and contemporary and classical philosophers including Leibniz, Foucault, Benjamin and Deleuze that this book has only been able to allude to.

A further challenge that Ruiz's work presents is a rethinking of cinema and politics. This should not be sought necessarily in Ruiz's more seemingly political cinema, in themes of political transformation, nor be limited to questions of exile and disapora. Instead, Ruiz's practice or rather practices, as a filmmaker but also a writer, teacher, producer and ally should be seen as contributions toward a micropolitics of contemporary image production aiming to maximise both its aesthetic and critical potential via a range of tactics for escaping from the dominant modes of production that Ruiz names as central conflict theory. This critical dimension of Ruiz's work is not at all a case of advocating any normative type of political cinema but instead supports the idea that creativity is always already political, precisely through its indifference to dominant norms whether these are the norms of commercial production or those of official resistance. These further engagements with Ruiz's work 'to come', which have only been barely sketched out here, are precisely what this book aims to encourage.

To finish on a more poetic note it is worth examining a short film by Ruiz from 1997, *The Film to Come*, which crystallised some of the issues raised by the director's cinematic work with which this book has been engaged. In this film there is a secret society, the 'Philokinetes' who devote their energy and money to promoting and studying a single fragment of film called 'The Film to Come'. There is nothing extraordinary about this looped film fragment which lasts twenty three seconds, except when watched in a form of 'enlightened viewing' meaning the hypnotic state that repeated viewings of the fragment itself provokes. The philokinetes apparently believe that cinema is in fact an autonomous form of existence, 'the primeval soup of a new life form'. The narrator, some kind of investigator, is attempting to find his daughter who has disappeared after being implicated in the disappearance of the film fragment. Visiting the headquarters of the cult, he is present at the hypnotic reading of the book, which doubles the film fragment and is composed, like the book in *Love Torn in Dream* or Has's *Saragossa Manuscript,* of heterogeneous diagrams, occult symbols and other 'mumbo jumbo'. As the cult's adepts who have taken a 'vow of illiteracy' turn the pages of the book this generates a type of film which ultimately engulfs the narrator who ultimately realises that he, like his daughter, has become a virtual being, a part of the film fragment, 'The Film to Come'. In the eight minutes of this black and white film, Ruiz is able to play with and condense many of his most cherished elements ranging from aberrant and artificial behaviour of bodies in hypnotic states, to the combination of modern and archaic elements, to passages from 'reality' to a type of virtual cinematic existence associated with strange, archaic rituals. There is even a diasporic multi-cultural dimension to the film since the fragment at one point is rediscovered in the back of a Muslim photographic studio, not to mention a good deal of play with images, objects and shadows. More than this the film condenses the key Ruizian idea that cinema itself is a new and autonomous form of life whose mysterious existence among us is worthy of the greatest respect and whose life should be encouraged rather than being reduced to pre-existing political or aesthetic schemas. In this way film was, for Ruiz, even in the digital era, always still 'to come' or, in other words, to be re-invented.

APPENDIX

Raúl Ruiz Interview, Paris, November 2009

This interview was conducted with Raúl Ruiz in 2009, since when many of the projects discussed as being in the future have been completed and, of course, Ruiz's death a year later renders the tense of many of the statements both anachronistic and poignant. Nevertheless, it has been kept in the present tense precisely to preserve the untimely quality of presentness of both Ruiz's cinema and his discourse, in accordance with the concept of 'crytpesthesia' elaborated by Ruiz within the interview.

MG: I thought one place to start might be with [your] recent projects, the films that are in production or that I haven't got to see yet. Maybe we can talk about the film you are about to make in Lisbon, based on Camilo Castelo Branco's, *Misteriós de Lisboa* (*Mysteries of Lisbon*).[1] What drew you to this project?

RR: Well as you know I am a pendulum, I move between films that are not mainstream but made to a European standard and films that are pure bricolage for many reasons. For myself because I can find much more liberty there, more freedom, and I still try to invent or discover through these films which are tests, but not only tests, since sometimes I discover there is much more cinema there than in the other [more standard] ones. So now I am moving to the other part with *Mysteries of Lisbon* which is a film with a quite normal budget – for Portugal it's a lot, about four million Euros but it's a co-production with France – and it's a film that has to be shown in film theatres in Portugal, not Spain, not elsewhere and on television in France, Greece and several other countries.

MG: So the TV version and the film version will be made at the same time?

RR: Well it's really complicated because the film version has to be different because its produced by the film institute and the television version by the television, and for the film institute the producer, Paulo Branco, signed a contract where he has to make a different film, so at least three or four scenes or more have to be made just for cinema and not to be shown on TV; and it's three times one and a half hours for Portugal on TV but for France it's two times 100 minutes for *Arte*. The other countries, well, they are not still there; it's officially a co-production with Brazil but Brazil has a very strange reputation, you never know, they may be there or not. The contract is signed … sometimes you have to talk because it's part of the nature of the film and sometimes a condition of the production.

MG: Was this a film you wanted to do for a long time?

RR: No, it was a proposition of Paulo Branco, what I wanted to do for a long time before I had this proposition is to make a kind of soap opera, a natural one, that means a kind of nineteenth-century so-called *feuilleton* like the *Mysteries of Paris* by Eugène Sue, there are thousands of examples of this kind of literature but it was the basis of the Latin American so-called soap operas.

MG: *Telenovelas*?

RR: Exactly. And I started working on these, my first professional work was on *telenovelas* in Mexico, making the ends of chapters as a scriptwriter and what I like in novellas is first that the fate, the destiny of characters if you want, does not depend on the structure, it depends like in life [on chance]; curiously they are more realistic because they are completely unbelievable somewhere.

MG: *Colloque des Chiens* would be an example of this in your work…

RR: Well this is another aspect, this is the ironical one, in Camilo Castelo Branco there is also a lot of irony … In most of these novellas, not the *telenovelas* but the old nineteenth-century *feuilletons*, it is impossible to know what will happen because the writers do not know, because there is the contamination with high level literature, high culture; sometimes it's very hard to make the distinction, from that point of view between Charles Dickens, for instance, and a bad writer.

MG: Dickens was also publishing his novels in newspapers.

RR: Yes, because of the economic determinations, because of the industry, but also to keep a sort of freedom, freedom is essential as you know in this game where freedom is not very welcome, in cinema. John Malkovich once said, there is a distinction in Hollywood, they say there are two kinds of directors, the dreamers and the screamers, normally the directors are screamers, bad humoured, nervous and totally fractious … and the dreamers are very peaceful, because they are 'wandering and wondering', walking around and thinking … and they are not welcome in the Hollywood system, the dreamers, because you never know what the film will be. You know there will be some level of narrative but maybe not enough.

MG: This is maybe why David Lynch is now working independently on digital video.

RR: This is really funny, I met him and we stayed together for ten days, when we were part of a jury in Cannes Film Festival, he believed that his films were commercial; his films are *popular*, it's not the same. The level of the production and the level of the money which comes back, is not enough by American standards. You can say that David Lynch is European, you could say even a bit Franco.

MG: I think lately David Lynch has become slightly Polish, he's become an honorary citizen of Łódź, there's even a David Lynch suite in one of the hotels.

RR: David Lynch is very important with young people, on the Net he's very important, he's very popular but the amount of people that go to the theatre to see his films is not enough. Well this film, to go back to the *Mysteries of Lisbon* is very curious; as usual in this kind of work there are many characters, thirty nine principal ones. So I said we'll divide it into three galaxies; [galaxy] one is the story of someone who is dying, a young man. Thesis: tuberculosis. He goes to Brazil in order to die and to write his memories and the memories are the book. But inside that there is the history, which is another galaxy – I say galaxy because they are structured like galaxies, there is no narrative arrow, no conflict.

MG: So it's more of a spiral?

RR: Yes it's baroque in *that* sense, of a spiral, the structure of a spiral and with points of attraction and finally that gives the classic model which is the *Arabian Nights*. Well the second galaxy is around the popular, a woman who is a fish-seller, she sells *bacalhau*, cod, the national Portuguese fish, she poisons people, she's a terrible person but will become a saint at the end because with Castelo Branco you never know. And there's this third [character], who is the connection between all these stories, who is a priest like Father Brown, who is a kind of a mixture of Father Brown and Robin Hood, he's a saint but also an adventurer, he's a maverick who is many characters and officially he's a priest who tries to help people, with the humour of Father Brown. So these three frames, this is the structure of the film, but for me there is something very deep, it's deeply Lusitanian-Portuguese, that is that all the characters pass through three stages. In the first one there is a *coup de foudre*, they fall in love suddenly, always it's a young man who falls in love with the wife of his best friend, it's impossible love. The second is treason. Of course it's treason, because it's betrayal of the best friend or of the woman. The third part is redemption. Castelo Branco was Catholic. So redemption, like in Father Brown, they go to the church and they become priests or, redemption means simply to be alone and live with the fate they have. And this redemption is normally in a *feuilleton*, in this structure which is called in France the structure of *plan incliné*.[2] So you are like balls running down very fast, going to hell, it is tragedy and there is, of course, some miracle. This is [also] the structure of soap operas in Latin America

MG: And this film will be made in Portuguese?

RR: All in Portuguese, it happened in the romantic period. Castelo Branco's a romantic writer; there's something of Balzac and a lot of Stendhal, Stendhal liked a lot of narrative uncertainty, a narrative which goes nowhere and this is [also] what I like in the script. It's not written by me but by a Portuguese writer, because I can't do it in Portuguese, I can talk and communicate in Portuguese but not write. Portuguese by the way is a very difficult language because it is very close to Spanish but was made against Spain, it's made not to be understood by the Spanish, the enemy, because as you know Portugal was built against Spain. And the Portuguese character is the opposite of the classic Castillian or Andalusian character, or the Basque one, this is one aspect. And the other aspect that interested me is that I started about five years ago to become seriously interested in folklore, so in popular culture, moving from there to the low level popular culture. I found that well formulated by Antonio Gramsci, the

Marxist Italian writer who said you have to take bad literature seriously, the so called low level, the low level is one aspect but there is another aspect that is very serious.

MG: So this understanding of folklore is part of the projects you did for Chilean TV like *La Recta Provincia*?

RR: *Le Recta Provincia* is folklore, let's say, so folklore is universal. The first thing you discover when dealing with folklore is that it's not local culture because the stories I found in *La Recta Provincia,* even the stories I invented, or the stories my grandmother told me, you can find them in Scotland, or in the Germanic tradition and it's not necessarily only because there is communication, because the Spanish *were* Germanic, you know, Visigoths, it's not because of that, it is because of that but there are many other hypotheses which are very strange. That everywhere we re-invent the same stories because if it was only in Germanic stories and popular stories in Chile, you can say it's normal but [if it is also] in China it's not normal.

MG: Wasn't it Propp who talked about the morphologies in the folk tale as maybe having very much to do with perception, or the brain, that certain particular functions were necessary.

RR: It's Frazer. *Folklore in the Old Testament.* In the beginning it's just the connection between folklore and the Old Testament. Then you find the same stories in Oceania, in North America, the native people of North America, in China, in Africa, so it becomes tricky, why? And you go back to the old dilemma [surrounding folklore in] anthropology [as expressed by] Julio Caro Baroja [the nephew of the famous writer Pio Baroja].[3] Caro Baroja says that folkloric phenomena like carnivals, popular feasts and stories, arrive [either] by genealogy, by generations that come from far away, a long time ago, or by irruption and this irruption comes from both outside and inside by contamination: abruptly the story appears. The story is really invented literally. You have, of course, the explanation of the structuralists, of Levi-Strauss that we have the same kind of brain, so we have a basic structure, it seems to me much more complicated than that. I'm not enough of a theoretician and a lot of theories have been written on that but reading is one thing but [sic] reality is elusive in the field of the human sciences, very elusive. So I was working with that for *La Recta Provincia* but then I moved to the stories that my father used to tell, my father was a ship captain, a merchant captain, they are stories that are supposed to happen in Chile but also happen in other countries, all the sailors tell them. You remember in the Orson Welles film of the novella by Isak Dinesen [Karen Blixen], *The Immortal Story*, all the sailors pretend that they have lived that story; this story happens to one [of them] and he says 'how useless because no-one will believe me' because everybody tells that [story] everywhere in the world, it is this aspect which has been making me produce in my brain several fictions. I use it in *The Littoral,* and now this [latest film] is a continuation of that but now with this idea of Gramsci's. As you know Gramsci wrote his ideas in letters when he was in jail, he was in jail a long time, a good part of his intellectual activity took place there, so he said that [folklore is] not a theoretical, philosophical development. You know that Italy is a very extraordinary country able to invent everything and forget it immediately afterwards. Italy, that is modern Italy, moves always between Gramsci and Bernadetto Croce: one is right wing or conservative and the other is revolutionary and sometimes you don't know who is who. Suddenly Croce, in writings about popular culture is much more materialistic than Gramsci who becomes suddenly very spiritual, when you read it now you notice that [although] at the time it was not evident. As you know I was talking about that in Aberdeen, the presumption that theory is not dangerous for creativity and this is a very strong superstition that if you know, you will not be able to invent, you invent from zero and if you know that forty people before you thought the same thing you would lose your energy. So I believe that it's not dangerous for me and I know perfectly [well] that many of my last films start from theory before moving to action, to the filming and the film becomes the origin for new theoretical speculations and developments.

MG: But even that seems to go back quite a long time, even *Hypothesis of a Stolen Painting* was a film that was testing a certain kind of theory or a certain conception of the image or the *tableau vivant* and seeing what happens when you actually make that in cinema.

RR: Well yes, of course. I started in 'hot places' with logic, in taverns where in Chile at the time (I'm talking at the end of the 1950s so I was a so-called teenager), there were many of the people who used to work in philosophy, it was analytic philosophy but in popular bars and taverns not in the University, which was dominated as now by Heidegger or by Ortega Y Gasset, or the Catholic [University] by Thomism, St Thomas. And the analytic philosophy which was supposed to be not a philosophy as the analytics say the others [continental philosophers] are not philosophers, (you know this polemic is still continuing now in England), and I was interested in that [and] slowly I became interested in cinema because of just that connection, the very simple distinction by Wittgenstein, which is obvious but you have to think about it. This is the 'Columbus egg'. You have to make a distinction: either you show it or you talk about it and cinema is made of the combination of these two attitudes.

MG: It seems to me some of your writings, too, in the *Poetics of Cinema* volumes and 'Six functions of the shot', seem to follow this Wittgensteinian model, because there are certain logical propositions about the relations between objects or about the shot and what it might be or do, and there are various thought experiments to see how that might work in practice. So you have this kind of relay that seems more similar to Wittgenstein's genre of writing than it is to anything else and certainly to any kind of normal film criticism or most reflections on film. Would you agree with that?

RR: Sure, because we were talking about this project of Castelo Branco, the *Mysteries of Lisbon*. It was in trying to find a way to shoot that I was reading about autism and Asperger's syndrome and I found this test to know if [a child has autism] because there are children who are simply melancholic who don't like to talk with others. In Germany, in England, in all the Anglo-Saxon countries there are people who are just simply melancholic, who like to be alone, the main character of the Castelo Branco [novel] is like that. But the test for autism is you show a letter 'e' and the 'e' has small points made with an 'f', and you ask the autistic child what letter it is and he will say an 'f', because the priority is the detail, the small detail and then he builds a reality, and I feel this has many things to do with cinema. In a moment I realised that we could make an autistic film and I realised that many films I made before were, from that point of view, autistic because the detail is amplified and you have to build the space behind the detail, the space is not evident. In fact in *Time Regained,* for Proust's room I used two spaces, one was normal, a normal sized Parisian room standing in Proust's house, the room where he lay and the other was two and a half times bigger, so everything was bigger but not Proust! So there was an *Alice in Wonderland* device if you like. Moving from one to the other very fast you feel a type of insubstantiality of the space; where are we? This was, you remember, one of the functions of the shot. I called it critical, which is not a good name but the idea is: did I see what I just saw?

MG: So it poses a question or a doubt?

RR: Yes. A film can be built like that. Let's assume that a character is autistic, this is a detail, it's not important because the word will not be pronounced, but we can say that in the *mise-en-scène* of the film this will be the visual priority, to force the audience, the spectator to say 'where are we?' Starting always by a funny place, by a strange place, by the unusual, and starting by the detail.

MG: This seems to me like it's almost the principle of your films, in a sense. How is it possible to free the detail or, another way of putting it might be to liberate, at least to a relative extent, the shot from the whole set of the film.

RR: Yes I am trying to kill the realistic space, because reality is not realistic as you know. So for me I know now how we will make the film and why, I know that I will be more moderate, that it will not be exhausting to see it, that could be the good part of this starting by [sic] the idea and moving to testing, to the filmmaking and back to theory.

MG: So filmmaking can almost become a kind of philosophical or aesthetic form of research?

RR: Last year in Aberdeen I made a commentary on Eisenstein, *The Film Sense,* which is a late text of Eisenstein, it's the first chapter mainly, where he says that there was a time when editing was everything, and people believed that simply [by] connecting images you can create something like the equivalent of language but only with images. You can call that a principle, the principle of continuity. In opposition to this principle of continuity is 'one shot is one film', separate from the others. So if you shoot, trying to move in that sense, you will create such a discontinuity that the film may become many films at the same time, which is not such a bad thing because you force the spectator to invent the film and the principle of continuity is more abstract. You take many pieces of film and put them in any order and they will always make sense. What sense? That will be always different if you change the order of the images. Sometimes it will be nothing but sometimes it will be one kind of film and if you move the editing (all the editors know that), the sense will shift not inside the images but outside.

MG: Because in a sense narrative is not something that exists in films, it exists in the brain, whatever images people perceive they will try to make some sense out of?

RR: But that can become evident and stimulating if you play [with] that in a very radical way. I am trying not to move outside fiction, I don't want to move to video art, although I like it and have done some work like that, I try to stay in fiction because I like popular cinema too and to use elements of popular cinema, popular in the sense of Gramsci. So I try to develop ideas around this principle of continuity and discontinuity and this year it was a little bit different, it was *more*, it was the principle of extension; to develop the detail and to go outside the detail which becomes bigger. So this extension is the third principle and the other is synaesthesia, using this word in the sense of neurologists, this curious disorder. I listened for the first time, I saw it on television. You know Oliver Messiaen the French musician, he had a friend with synaesthesia and he said, I would like to have this disorder; for this friend when there was a sunset, there was a music that came with it or the music provoked sunsets, so there was a connection which was fixed: a noise provokes an image or an image provokes a noise. But sometimes fried eggs provoke a colour and the vowels, like the poem by Rimbaud, the 'Sonnet of the Vowel', are connected with colour. That was examined for a long time by child psychologists, mainly one of the student followers of Freud at the beginning but there seems to be another thing, as usual psychoanalysis tells a part of the truth but there is another part. If you play that as a function, function is not the word but as a principle in cinema of synaesthesia, you can provoke this state and this emotion, which is a specifically cinematographic emotion, simply playing systematically on the connections between the sound and the image and then playing on the disconnection of that. In *City of Pirates* for instance, I used music that was like a Wagnerian *leitmotif*, and then I mixed it, I put the music in the wrong place so a landscape with the music of a crime becomes a landscape in which there was a crime or there is a potential crime, or the landscape is criminal. This is the fourth principle I was developing and the fifth, which is more recent, is from these interviews, the transcription of a meeting of mediums.

MG: A séance?

RR: A séance or a conversation with spirits, *spiritism*. In this book which is incredibly funny, the séance is half of the book, which was done in 1920 during the summer, in London and Oscar Wilde came, the book is a really good pastiche of Oscar Wilde, sometimes too much because Oscar Wilde wrote like that but talking is slightly different.[4] He was known to talk normally. Then there is somebody who developed the theory of 'cryptesthesia'. So after synaesthesia, cryptesthesia. He believed, this is not scientific as it has not been tested, that there are some mediums [who have this experience], like the people who didn't know how to play piano, who suddenly start playing piano in some conditions, or people who start talking Danish and they are Portuguese or Spanish, and then suddenly they start. There is a kind of expansion of their capacities and it's a kind of sceptical way of explaining something like this pastiche of Oscar Wilde. So what happens with the medium is divided in two. One is the medium who talks to other people and the other part is [composed of] the dead people who the same medium has this capacity to become, God knows how. This is pure fiction but I am using it like a fiction and fictions sometimes are right.

MG: It seems also that cinema begins at the same point where there is this fascination with spiritualism and séances and all these kinds of phenomena.

RR: Of course, it's about ecstasy, it's about fascination. Here it works until the point where the medium starts talking about things she didn't know, she couldn't know, the fact that Oscar Wilde wrote his book, one of his very last books, *The Opinions of*

Sebastian Melmoth, and then the medium used another name, Sebastian Mismoth, so she was wrong. And then she was not wrong because in a letter of Oscar Wilde, a letter that she could not know, Oscar Wilde tells a friend that maybe the character will be called this, so this is the tricky part, this is the amusing part of it. So moving to film theory, cryptesthesia could be this capacity to create situations in such a way that they will push you outside of your own capabilities by creating difficulties, in the way of creating enigmas, making the film cryptic: cryptesthesia. I have been doing that for a while but suddenly this year, it seems to me that playing with these five principles, I could organise better and curiously in a more moderate way. It is 'other' but it is not pushing, the film is not beating you. Sometimes I feel that my films were beating the spectator too much which was good but then the spectator was tired.

MG: But I think that also leads to a misunderstanding of your films of the 1980s. Certain people see the more recent films that seem to be more mainstream like the adaptation of Proust or *Three Lives and only One Death* as if these are suddenly very normal films, whereas there is just as much going on, even if they are not attacking the spectator in quite the same way.

RR: I saw recently, a couple of years ago, *Hypothesis of the Stolen Painting,* and of course I can understand all the implications, but I was exhausted by my own film, because all the implications, if you know and you can go [along with them] and you can, everything comes at the same time and maybe if you do it in another way, you will see one film in the first viewing and then [another], through implicit memory. I believe, we have to believe, it is proved that it exists, this is an idea of Daniel Schacter.[5] Daniel Schacter started studying why the amnesiac remembers so many things if they are amnesic, and then he realised that there were two memories, actually there are many, but two systems which are the totality of the brain's cortex, which are implicit and explicit according to the region where the memory works. That was important because one researcher at MIT wanted to go to [work in] another place and he had to sign that everything that belongs to MIT I will not use. But this discovery of implicit memory means, you will not be able to forget. It will be there and you will not be able *not* to use it because it's the totality of your brain that works when you are inventing or suggesting a new experiment, your brain will move in a direction that implies you are using what you have used at MIT. Consequence: you are a slave of MIT because you can't leave; by the simple fact of moving to another company you are stealing material that belonged to MIT. So there was a legal discussion.

MG: Of the problem of copyright and intellectual property?

RR: It's a problem of copyright, of course, so MIT have *your* copyright (I'm joking). So in relation to film, if you make it in such a way that there may arise inside of you, elements that do not have a narrative function in the film but which have in another way wider effects; let's look at a narrative element. Let's say you have several narrative arrows and the explicit narrative arrow is more separate from the others, you will have everything and you will not be exhausted and it will move through emotions and this point is interesting because apparently the film is simpler, so you have lost something since the film is not so complex as the others.

MG: But you can find those other arrows?

RR: Yes, by the principle of extension, you will see a detail that will be expanded and become bigger than the film, this is synecdoche.

MG: Perhaps we can also talk about *Nucingen House* because this film was also populated by spectres or shadows?

RR: There are some shadows, of course, because they are a parodic element. But I would say there are narrative shadows there, suspended fictions.

MG: It was also made in Chile?

RR: You can call it a story of colonisation, of recent colonisation. I met people like that, they are Austrian, or German, or French, who live in a kind of oasis or limbo. And they talk in their own language and they are strangers in the country where they live. They are not Chilean, their descendants will become Chilean but they are not. This is one aspect. The other aspect is the ghost story which is written by the character who is there, another is the conspiracy of the family and yet another is maybe the reality of ghosts. Because behind all that is a quite well known Germanic legend of the knight who loses his wife because her body is kidnapped by the fairies (it's a very Scottish story, somehow), and then he found her dancing near the forest. He says 'Hello, I miss you ... so come back to home', 'OK' and she has three children and the story becomes a normal story but in the middle there is something incoherent. It is incoherent because she was supposed to be dead. And when the husband found her, he is not even surprised. So he lived in a special world. So this is the hidden part of the story. All these stories give shadows to the the other story and that makes it a film of shadows but narrative shadows. The house exists, it's called *Schule Haus*, the house where I shot it, the real one.

MG: This is where in Chile?

RR: This is a hundred kilometres south of Santiago, not very far. But it's completely incoherent to have found this house there. A house connected from the seventeenth century, it was a Jesuit mission, then a Spanish government house of the region, then a Chilean house, then French, and then German and they added new parts so the house became a house without style, became 'intemporal'. You could say I built the story, starting from the house. It's not completely true because I wrote the script before but there was this connection which was unexpected.

MG: So the place is very important in relation to cinematic emotion, a lot of which is a feeling about particular spaces?

RR: Yes, the house has some ghosts, by reputation they have many ghosts and I perceived something which was not, of course, a ghost but there is some magnetic field, this can be a room; with all these hyper-natural, surrealist or ghost impressions you will never know because it's always between, you always have a known interpretation with a spiritualist one. What does it mean to say, 'That may be a ghost'? That it may be you with some kind of presence. I have never had a real supernatural [experience] but of course I have to accept that cats see people you will not see, other animals have perceptions that you don't have and there are some electro-magnetic fields that are a reality so if you cross a door, you cross a magnetic field but that may be anything.

MG: Maybe we can come to another film, a recent film. I wonder if you can situate this film you recently completed, *A Closed Book,* based on the book by Gilbert Adair?

RR: I had some problems with that film that maybe you know; it's that the way that films are produced in England is radically different from how films are produced in many other countries. In England, the filmmaker is a technician, this is different to a director, and I had a very funny letter at the beginning of the shooting, 'remember that this is not a film of an *auteur*, (using the French word), we don't want that, we want a normal feature'. So I followed the script, you know the sermon, 'I serve to make the script, only the script and nothing but the script', but then the script changed every day, it was changed by the actors, by the producer, by money problems, so I was following something that was not very clear, it was quite cloudy, and then I made a version and they started working with this version, I always try to make a film in such a way that you can edit it only in one way, or sometimes in two but not more, and because the film had to be made in three weeks and something and so was fast, I have my alibi. I can do only that, I have no time for many cuts. So I have no close-ups, no shot-reverse shots, there were some, of course, but in a different way. So they could not finish that and they started changing the shots; [they changed] one shot for another and suddenly the film became weaker and weaker and lost all the energy. I saw the film, I have the original and I have this one and it's a sort of deception, it's the only film where I had this experience.

MG: So it's more difficult to make a film in England than in Hollywood?

RR: I have made films in Hollywood and it's not a problem, Hollywood's another world. It has many other problems, it's much more violent.

MG: Is the film going to have a wide distribution?[6]

RR: Well it seems they have a distributor for this year or next year, I don't know.

MG: But you're not happy at all with the version coming out? It's a shame because it's a Gilbert Adair novel isn't it?

RR: It's not, because it's a woman and a man and in the book it's a gay relationship. The script was very interesting because at the beginning there was an American producer who decided to change everything, and this was not for worse in the film as it was shot … And its more or less the same [as the released version] which is curious because it's completely other *and* it's the same. The same order, the same situation, everything is there. They changed the music, but something is completely wrong there. But what's interesting is you are thinking all the time about rape, it's about a paedophile, something like that, and you're thinking about that and then at the end it's completely different, so from that point of view it's a British film; it's not at all that, but it is about that, it's about creating a painter to be a paedophile; the painter was the husband of the woman, he committed suicide. Well, this is the TV comedy aspect, but the way it was played by Tom Conti and the actress [Daryl Hannah], there were two different kinds of acting which we were trying to put together because as you can see from the films I have, I am fascinated by American cinema, the old one and some of the new but something wrong happened there … this was roughly what happened. I had [experienced] something like that but not to the same point with *Les Âmes Fortes*, *Savage Souls* in English but it was never sold there, never shown.

It's a case to study because they cut very few things, they cut something like five minutes and they completely destroyed the film. The version on the DVD is the wrong

one. They put the music very low, as in American movies and so it became furniture music. Simply by this balancing, the film can be destroyed. Producers always forget; the dialogues are important and the images are important but not the sounds and not the music, so that film had almost that problem. And when I say my version, it's not that I was right and the others were wrong, because what I'm calling 'my version' is the result of much conversation and discussion at the editing table, there is a collaboration there, the other version is a version of panic. After they see the film, a producer who is nervous, even if the money does not come from him because in Europe and in the UK, the money comes from public money, and in America it's money coming from the bank, so the idea is that the producer risks; of course, he risks many things, he risks his reputation and some money but not so much, so there is a kind of panic of reputation. The problem with English producers, with an Anglo-Saxon production, is that everything is about blame and panic. And this is quite true.

MG: Was there any similar story with *Klimt* because you mentioned there is more than one version of the film?

RR: For me there are *really* two different versions. On DVD you can find the director's cut. In Vienna, I was shown both versions at the same time, in different theatres but at the same time, which multiplied the audience; well, *Klimt* is important in Austria. I won't say they doubled the audience but there were many more spectators than if the producer had shown only one version. It was about reification: I prefer this, I prefer that. In *Klimt* they used one of the best editors to do that who always takes care.

MG: So you are happy with both versions?

RR: I accept the short version. The only thing which is a pity is that they cut all the 'inferior races'. I said, you've got only white people there. You cut the Jews, the Chilean Indians and the Chinese. There was a big chapter concerning the Chinese ... and I am sure it was not on purpose, it was because they are peripheral people in the story but that exists in the life of Klimt, the connection with Oriental Chinese and Japanese painting, that exists.

MG: Did *Klimt* come out of a biography about Klimt or was it more a pastiche of different sources?

RR: The main problem in *Klimt* is that Klimt is not exactly a hero and not an anti-hero, not a traitor, he is someone who does his job. This was a way that I made my emotional connection with the character, through this aspect. You have to do your job and then to think about it, of course. But Klimt is described by people of his time as a sad, unfriendly character: *triste*.

MG: Melancholic?

RR: Yes. He has something similar to *Alice in Wonderland*, who is always fascinated by things, and he followed everybody and said, 'I want to show you something', he would never say what. He always has time.

MG: Did he really meet with Méliès as in the film, or is this just someone he could have met?

RR: Yes, that could happen because [they were there] at the same time. You know Méliès made a fake newsreel, actualities, he filmed the news with actors. So that is historically true. And the fact that Klimt won the golden medal is true so you can connect that, he *could* be a character and then the film is shown like a fantasy in the manner of Schnitzler and he used Klimt as a character in a comedy, *The Comedy of Seduction*. There was something else in the case of this film, it was curious because the two films [ended up with] more or less the same duration, all of the situations are there and then something wrong happened by dubbing the actor. As you know it's one of the points that Jacques Rivette is completely right about, if you dub then you have lost at least half of the quality of acting, you have lost it always, except if you move the film to an artificial level, which is the case of most of the so-called well made English serials and English TV movies. They are very well made and sometimes there is a sort of virtuosity but there is something you feel that is the fault of the King Arthur who went to the Holy Land and when he came back the parliament was there and everything became parliamentarian. Now if you make a film with a parliament, everybody has an idea or point of view, the solution is by voting.

MG: Everything works by committee, also in the universities.

RR: I know it's like that because I have many friends I ask who say it's always like that but they were not bad with me, not particularly bad with me. The only problem is there is a waste of energy and a waste of film quality. Film quality, it is very difficult to know *where* it is. It's not good photography, it's not good acting, it's something around these things.

MG: One of the other things I wanted to talk with you about was places, because one of the films that almost seemed like a key film to me was this short film *Le Jeu de l'oie (Zig-Zag)*, with Pascal Bonitzer.

RR: That was advertising! ... It was advertising for an exhibition in the Beauborg about maps. I do not remember it too well. It was well-known Parisian intellectuals playing those characters. About mapping, it's curious because the mapping function is very important in visual perception, the idea that you always have when you walk in the street a mapping function, you have a version of yourself looking from up to down.

MG: It's like proprioception?

RR: Yes, one of the thirty-something functions of vision is that one.

MG: I was wondering also about cartography because there is cartography of images, of faces but also of particular places. We talked already about Portugal because you seem to have a particular relationship with that place ... I wondered is there a connection for you between Portugal and Chile?

RR: As a bridge. Because for a long time I was divided between Chilean memories and nostalgias and all that and reality which was Europe, France. And Portugal was between. I started making a bridge there with *City of Pirates*. It was made at Baleal, on the coast. At Sintra I made *The Territory* and *Love Torn in Dream*. Portugal has that idea of the secret which I always connect with cinema, in cinema you have a secret film inside a film, and you have to keep that secret. This is about cryptesthesia. How to keep a secret somewhere is the motor of film emotion. It's very easy to talk about emotion in cinema but between the emotion – if you take a story and somebody lost his wife, or his daughter, or he's endangered, different kinds of emotion, and [there is also] the emotion which is very special and very difficult to translate, the cinematographic emotion which is connected with [affect]; you have to use this expression from Spinoza, *affectus,* which is a mixture of emotions and rationality.

MG: An impersonal kind of emotion?

RR: Because emotion, as the famous Damasio claims, but there are many others who say the same thing, pure emotion disappears very soon in the history of man; then you have emotions, consciousness, reason, 're-emotion' and then emotions little by little become something connected with reflection, with *intellectus.*[7] And there begins *affectus,* which is connected with the idea of friendship with ideas. One of my colleagues, Chris Fynsk,[8] said to me 'you always move from theology to the French revolution, but it seems to me they are very different. Why?' For me it's hard to say why because I believe that the connection between a question and an answer is not so evident. But I said maybe because you can't understand why after all this time and given the actual level of technology and production, still we have poor people and we have misery and that's the French revolution. And then, 'what the hell are we doing here?' And this is theology. Well that's an extreme simplification of the situation that we do not know what we are doing here but what is tricky is not that we don't know, the tricky thing is we start knowing more and more and it's becoming more and more complicated and fascinating. But what is not fascinating is why misery is developing with new technology

We were talking about emotion in cinema. That can explain the reason why I do not want to forget about narrative cinema. Because narrative, much more than narrative cinema, is at least human. Games are before humanity, the termite plays, the animal plays, and the particles play funny games but narrative is human. Narrative is connected with this. You know Frobenius,[9] Frobenius 'discovered' African civilisation; his most famous book is called *African Civilisation,* which proved that Africans have their own civilisation which is not an excrescence or product of the Arab civilisation, they are not primitive. It is very strange for a Nazi to support such a thesis. He discovered a pre-Arab version of the *One Thousand and One Nights* in which Sheherezade is a man. And it is from the first years, not centuries but years of the great Islamic revolutions, so in the seventh century, at that time the region of Sudan, Kordofan, was a region in which Africans were living and they had a theocratic system of astronomers.[10] And the political game is to take a young man, a boy sometimes, who will become a king, via all kinds of astrological games. They take the guy, he will never see the world, he's a prisoner. And at the age of puberty he is forced to make love with his mother, and/or sisters with a witness, many witnesses. And then at the time of the coronation the witness comes into the street and proclaims that he committed the crime of making love with his mother and he's killed. He goes to heaven, he will become a galaxy and from there he will be the king, with the interpretation of the astrologers. Well this is the story of the people of Kordofan and then there arrives 'Sheherezade'. Sheherezade is a man, who will be the friend and counsellor of this young man who is waiting to be killed. He is a story-teller, he tells stories to the young man, and suddenly the victim has the idea to push him to tell stories to everybody. He starts telling stories and one night, in the legend, all the people of the kingdom, which must be a village, gather and he tells stories the whole night. And in the morning, all the astrologers commit suicide; you have to understand they were killed. And then the idea, the message if you want, is what happens in the stars is important but much more important is what happens with men, in everyday life. This is what I argue with myself when I try to explain why I stay in narrative and in popular narrative as the basis of all my work of experimentation.

Notes

1. Camilo Castelo Branco (1825–1890) was a prolific nineteenth-century Portuguese writer comparable in stature to Victor Hugo or Charles Dickens.
2. An inclined plane.
3. Julio Caro Baroja (1914-1995) was a Spanish anthropologist famous for his research into Basque culture and history.
4. The book Ruiz is referring to is most likely Hester Travers Smith (2004), *Oscar Wilde from Purgatory*, London: Kessinger, which is the record of the evocation of the writer's spirit from around this time.
5. Daniel Schacter is a Harvard psychology professor, the author of several groundbreaking studies of memory.
6. In fact the film had an extremely limited cinematic release and went virtually straight to DVD.
7. António Damasio is a Portuguese-born neuroscientist who conducted important research into the relations between brain function and emotions. More recently he has related the findings of contemporary neuroscience to the philosophy of Spinoza. See Damasio 2004, *Looking for Spinoza*.
8. Christopher Fynsk is the director of the Centre for Modern Thought and head of the School of Language and Literature at the University of Aberdeen, as well as being a noted philosophy and literature scholar specialising in the work of Heidegger and Blanchot.
9. Leo Frobenius (1873-1938) was an important German ethnologist and archaeologist, who conducted research into African history and civilisation.
10. Kordofan otherwise known as Kurdufan is a former region of Sudan, traditionally home to the Nuba people.

SELECT FILMOGRAPHY

For a complete annotated filmography (in French) please see *Le Cinéma de Raúl Ruiz*, www.lecinemaderaoulruiz.com/filmographie-et-autres-oeuvres and for an annotated filmography in English up to 2005 see Adrian Martin ed., *Rouge* 2: *An Annotated Filmography of Raúl Ruiz*, www.rouge.com.au/2/index.html.

Abbreviations: *d* – director; *p* – producer; *c* – cinematographer; *sc* – script; *ed* – editor; *m* – music; *s* – sound; *pc* – principal cast.

Tres tristes tigres (*Three Sad Tigers*). Chile, 1968, Los Capitanes. *d, sc* – Raúl Ruiz; *p* – Enrique Reiman, Ernesto Ruiz, Serafin Selanio; *c* – Diego Bonanzina; *ed* – Carlos Piaggio; *m* – Tomás Lefever; *s* – Jorge de Lauro; *pc* – Nelson Villagra, Shenda Román, Luis Alarcón, Jaime Vadell, Delfina Gozman. 105 min., 35mm, b/w.

La Colonia Penal (*The Penal Colony*). Chile, 1970, Alcaman. *d, sc* – Raúl Ruiz; *p* – Darío Pulgar; *c* – Héctor Ríos; *sc* – script; *ed* – Carlos Piaggio; *m* – Mary Franco Lau; *s* – Fernando García; *pc* – Monica Echevarria, Luis Alarcón, Anibal Reyna, Nelson Villagra, Dario Pulgar, Sergio Meza. 75 min., 16mm, b/w.

Nadie Dijo Nada (*Nobody Said Anything*). Chile/Italy, 1971, RAI TV. *d , sc* – Raúl Ruiz; *p* – producer; *c* – Silvio Caiozzi; *ed* – Carlos Piaggio; *m* – Tomás Lefever; *s* – José de la Vega; *pc* – Carlos Solanos, Jaime Vadell, Luis Vilches, Luis Alarcón, Nelson Villagra, Shenda Roman, Pedro Gaete, Humberto Miranda, Carla Cristi, Carmen Lara, Rodrigo Maturana, Aquiles Varas, Ceferino Reyes, Mario Catalan y los Centrinos, Waldo Rojas, Gabriel Pena. 135 min., col.

La Expropiación (*The Expropriation*). Chile, 1971. *d, p, sc* – Raúl Ruiz; *c* – Adrian Cooper, Jorge Müller; *ed* – Valeria Sarmiento; *s* – José de la Vega; *pc* – Jaime Vadell, Nemesio Antúnez, Delfina Guzmán. With the collaboration of the peasants of southern Chile and CORA (Corporación de la reforma agraria). 60 min., 16mm, col.

El Realismo Socialista; Considerádo Commo Una de las Bellas Artes (*Socialist Realism Considered as One of the Fine Arts*). Chile, 1973. d, p, sc – Raúl Ruiz; c – Jorge Müller; ed – Carlos Piaggio; m – Rodrigo Maturano; s – José de la Vega; pc – Marcial Edwards, Javier Maldonado, Juan Carlos Moraga, Jaime Vadell. 270 min., (alt. versions 225 min. and 150 min.), 16mm, b/w and col.

Diálogo de Exilados (*Dialogue of Exiles*). France, 1974, Capital Films. D, sc – Raúl Ruiz; p – Percy Matas, Raúl Ruiz; c – Gilberto Avezedo; ed – Valeria Sarmiento; s – Alix Comte; pc – Françoise Arnoul, Carla Oristi, Daniel Gélin, Sergio Hernandez, Percy Matas, Luis Poirot, Waldo Rojas, Carlos Solanos, Aquiles Varas, Alfonso Varela, Federico de Cardenas, Edgardo Cosarinsky, Valeria Sarmiento. 100 min., 16mm, col.

La vocation suspendue (*The Suspended Vocation*). France, 1977, Institut National de l'Audiovisuel (INA): Caméra Je collection. d, sc – Raúl Ruiz; p – Jean Lefaux; c – Maurice Perrimond, Sacha Vierny; ed – Valeria Sarmiento; m – Jorge Arriagada; s – Xavier Vauthrin, Jean-Claude Brisson; pc – Didier Flamand, Gabriel Gascon, Pascal Bonitzer, Maurice Bénichou, Daniel Gélin, Pascal Kané, Alexandre Tamar, Jean Badin, Françoise Vercruyssen. 90 min., 16mm, b/w and col.

Colloque de chiens (*Dogs' Dialogue*). France, 1977, Filmoblic. d – Raúl Ruiz; p – Hubert Niogret; c – Denis Lenoir; sc – Nicole Muchnik, Raúl Ruiz; ed – Valeria Sarmiento; m – Jorge Arriagada; pc – Hugo Santiago, Eva Simonet, Silke Humel, Robert Darmel (voice-off). 22 min., 35mm, col.

L'Hypothèse du tableau volé (*The Hypothesis of the Stolen Painting*). France, 1978, INA: Caméra Je collection. d – Raúl Ruiz; p – Jean Barronnet; c – Sacha Vierny; sc – Raúl Ruiz, Pierre Klossowski; ed – Patrice Royer; m – Jorge Arriagada; s – Xavier Vauthrin; pc – Jean Rougeul, Gabriel Gascon, Anne Debois, Chantal Palay, Alix Comte, Jean Narboni, Christian Broutin, Jean-Damien Thiollier, Stéphane Shandor, Isidro Romero, Bernard Daillancourt, Alfred Bailloux, Claude Hernin-Hibaut, Nadège Finkelstein. 66 min., 35mm, b/w.

Les Divisions de la nature: Un homme, un château, 'Chambord' (*The Divisions of Nature: A Man, A Palace, 'Chambord'*). France, 1978, INA/Antemme 2. d, sc – Raúl Ruiz; p – Peter Lazko; c – Henri Alekan; ed – Gabriel Zukovik; m – Jorge Arriagada; s – Andrei Siekierski. 29 min., 16mm, col.

Petit manuel d'histoire de France (*Handbook of French History*). France, 1979, INA/FR3: Rue des archives. d, sc – Raúl Ruiz; p – Jean Lefaux; ed – Valeria Sarmiento. 2 x 50 min., video, col.

Des grand événements et des gens ordinaires: Les Élections (*Great Events and Ordinary People: The Elections*). France, 1979, INA/Antenne 2. d – Raúl Ruiz; p – Martine Durand, Dominique Benzadon; c – Jacques Bouquin, Dominique Forgue, Alain Salomon; sc – Raúl Ruiz, François Ede; ed – Valeria Sarminento; m – music; s – Jean-Claude Brisson, N'Guyen Van Tuong. 60 min., 16mm, col.

Zig-Zag-le jeu de l'oie (une fiction didactique à propos de la cartographie) (*Zig-Zag*). Alt. Title, *Snakes and Ladders*. France, 1980, Antemme 2/Centre Georges

Pompidou. *d* – Raúl Ruiz; *p* – producer; *c* – Alain Montrobert; *sc* – Raúl Ruiz, Jean-Loup Rivière; *ed* – Annie Bequet; *m* – Jorge Arriagada; *s* – Roger Vieyra, Jean Hertz; *pc* – Pascal Bonitzer, Jean-Loup Rivière. 30 min., 16mm, col.

Le borgne (*The One-Eyed Man*). France, 1980, Films du Dimanche. *d, p, sc* – Raúl Ruiz; *c* – Jacques Bouquin, Françis Lapeire; *ed* – Valeria Sarmiento; *m* – music; *s* – Jacques Bouquin, Françis Lapeire; *pc* – Jean-Christophe Bouvet, François Ede, Frank Oger, Pascal Bonitzer, Manuelle Lipski, Philippe Collin. 72 min., 16mm, col.

The Territory. Portugal/USA, 1981, V. O. Filmes/New World Pictures. *d* – Raúl Ruiz; *p* – Paulo Branco, Roger Corman, Pierre Cottrell; *c* – Henri Alekan, Alcácio de Almeida; *sc* – Gilbert Adair, Raúl Ruiz; *ed* – Valeria Sarmiento, Caludio Martinez; *m* – Jorge Arriagada; *s* – Vasco Pimental, Joaquim Pinto; *pc* – Isabelle Weingarten, Rebecca Pauly, Geoffrey Carey, Jeffrey Kime, Paul Getty Jr., Shila Turna, Artur Semedo, Camila Mora, Ethan Stone, José Nascimento, João Bénard da Costa, Rita Nascimento. 110 min., 35mm, col.

Het dak van de Walvis (*The Roof of the Whale*). Alt. title, *On Top of the Whale*. Netherlands, 1981, Springtime Films/Film International Rotterdam. *d, sc* – Raúl Ruiz; *p* – Kees Kasander, Monika Tegelaar; *c* – Henri Alekan; *ed* – Valeria Sarmiento; *m* – Jorge Arriagada; *s* – Mildred van Leeuwaarden; *pc* – Fernando Bordeu, Jean Badin, Willeke van Ammelrooy, Herbert Curiel, Amber De Grauw, Luis Mora, Ernie Navarro. 90 min., 35mm, col.

Les trois couronnes du matelot (*Three Crowns of the Sailor*). France, 1982, Films Antenne 2/INA. *d* – Raúl Ruiz; *p* – Paolo Branco, Maya Feueiette, Jean Lefaux, Jose Luis Vasconcelos; *c* – Sacha Vierny; *sc* – Raúl Ruiz, François Ede, Emilio del Solar; *ed* – Janine Verneau, Valeria Sarmiento, Jacqueline Simoni-Adamus, Pascale Sueur; *m* – Jorge Arriagada; *s* – sound; *pc* – Jean-Bernard Guillard, Philippe Deplanche, Jean Badin, Nadège Clair, Lisa Lyon, Claude Dereppe, Franck Oger. 117 min., 16mm, b/w and col.

La Ville des pirates (*City of Pirates*). France/Portugal, 1983, Metro Filmes/Les Films du Passage. *d, sc* – Raúl Ruiz; *p* – Paulo Branco, Hélène Vager; *c* – Acácio de Almeida; *ed* – Valeria Sarmiento; *m* – Jorge Arriagada; *s* – Joaquim Pinto, Vasco Pimentel; *pc* – Hugues Quester, Anne Alvaro, Melvil Poupaud, André Hengel, Duarte de Almeida, Clarisse Dole, André Gomes. 111 min., 35mm, col.

Les Destins de Manoël (*Manoel's Destinies*). Alt. title, *L'Île aux merveilles de Manoël, Aventure au Madeira*. France/Portugal, 1985, INA/Les Films du Passage/Radiotelevisão Portuguesa (RTP)/Rita Filmes. *d* – Raúl Ruiz; *p* – Paulo Branco, Antonio Vaz da Silva; *c* – Acácio de Almeida; *sc* – Raúl Ruiz, João Botelho; *ed* – Rodolfo Wedeles; *m* – Jorge Arriagada; *s* –Joaquim Pinto; *pc* – Ruben de Freitas, Marco Paulo de Freitas, Aurelie Chassel, Fernando Heitor, Diogo Doria, Cecilia Guimaraes, Vasco Pimentel, Jose de Freitas, Miguel Silva. 152 min., 130 min., 16mm, col.

L'éveillé du pont de l'Alma (*Insomniac on the Bridge*). Alt. title, *Sleepwalker on the Alma Bridge*. France, 1985, Les Films du Passage/Maison de la Culture de

Grenoble. *d, sc* – Raúl Ruiz; *p* – Paulo Branco; *c* – François Ede; *ed* – Rodolfo Wedeles; *m* – Jorge Arriagada, Gérard Maimone; *s* – Antoine Bonfanti; *pc* – Michael Lonsdale, Jean Bernard Guillard, Olipia Carlisi, Jean Badin, Melvil Poupaud, Kim Massee, Franck Oger. 75 min., 16mm/35mm, b/w, col.

Voyage d'une main (*Voyage of a Hand*). Alt. title, *Journey Around a Hand*. France, 1984, INA/Ateliers Armand Leibovitch. *d, p, sc* – Raúl Ruiz; *c* – Jacques Bouquin; *ed* – Valeria Sarmiento; *m* – Jorge Arriagada; *s* – Jean-Claude Brisson; *pc* – Franck Oger, Nadège Clair, Camille La Mora, Martine Odile. 25 min., 16mm, col.

Mémoire des apparences (*Memory of Appearances*). Alt. title *Life is a Dream*. France, 1986, INA/ Maison de la Culture du Havre. *d, p, sc* – Raúl Ruiz; *c* – Jacques Bouquin; *ed* – Martine Bouquin, Rodolfo Wedeles; *m* – Jorge Arriagada; *s* – Jean-Claude Brisson; *pc* – Sylvain Thirolle, Roch Leibovici, Bénédicte Sire, Laurence Cortadellas, Jean-Bernard Guillard, Jean-Pierre Agazar, Alain Halle-Halle, Jean-François Lapalus. 100 min., 35mm, colour.

L'Île au trésor (*Treasure Island*). France/UK/USA, 1986/1991, BFI, Cannon, Les Films du Passage. *d, sc* – Raúl Ruiz; *p* – Paulo Branco, Paulo De Sousa, Antonio Vaz da Silva; *c* – Acácio de Almeida; *ed* – Valeria Sarmiento, Rodolfo Wedeles; *m* – Jorge Arriagada; *s* – Alain Garnier, Joaquim Pinto; *pc* – Melvil Poupaud, Martin Landau, Vic Tayback, Lou Castel, Jeffrey Kime, Anna Karina, Sheila, Jean-Pierre-Léaud, Jean-François Stévenin. 115 min., 35mm, col.

A TV Dante (*Cantos IX to XIV*). UK/Netherlands, 1989/1991, Artifax, CAL Videographics Ltd., Channel 4 Television Corporation, Dante B.V., Elsevier-Vendex Film Beheer, K.G.P., RM Associates, VPRO Television. *d* – Raúl Ruiz; *p* – Sophie Balhetchet, Kees Kasander, Denis Wigman; *c* – Edwin Verstegen, Hector Rios; *sc* – Tom Phillips; *ed* – Antony Robinson, Bill Saint; *m* – music; *s* – Nigel Heath, Chris Wyatt; *pc* – John Gielgud, Fernando Bordeu, Bob Peck, Francisco Reyes. 66 min., Video, col.

L' Oeil qui ment (*Dark at Noon*). Alt. title, *Eyes and Lies*. France/Portugal, 1992, Sidéral Productions, Animatografo, Canal +, CNC. *d, sc* – Raúl Ruiz; *p* – Bernard-P. Guiremand, António da Cunha Telles, Leonardo De La Fuente; *c* – Ramón F. Suárez; *ed* – Hélène Muller; *m* – Jorge Arriagada; *s* – Jean-Paul Mugel, Pascal Metge; *pc* – John Hurt, Didier Bourdon, Lorraine Evanoff, David Warner, Daniel Prévost, Myriem Roussel, Felipe Dias, Rui Luís Brás, André Maia. 100 min., 35mm, col.

Trois vies et une seule mort (*Three Lives and Only One Death*). France/Portugal, 1996, Gemini Films, La Sept Cinéma, Madragoa Filmes, CNC. *d* – Raúl Ruiz; *p* – Paulo Branco; *c* – Laurent Machuel; *sc* – Pascal Bonitzer, Raúl Ruiz; *ed* – Rodolfo Wedeles; *m* – Jorge Arriagada; *s* – Laurent Poirier; *pc* – Marcello Mastroianni, Anna Galiena, Marisa Paredes, Melvil Poupaud, Chiara Mastroianni, Féodor Atkine, Jean-Yves Gautier, Pierre Bellemare, Jacques Pieiller, Arielle Dombasle, Lou Castel. 123 min., 35mm, col.

Généalogies d'un crime (*Genealogies of a Crime*). France/Portugal, 1997, Gemini Films, Madragoa Filmes. *d* – Raúl Ruiz; *p* – Paulo Branco; *c* – Stephan Ivanov; *sc* – Pascal Bonitzer, Raúl Ruiz; *ed* – Valeria Sarmiento; *m* – Jorge Arriagada; *s* – Henri Maikoff; *pc* – Catherine Deneuve, Michel Piccoli, Melvil Poupaud, Andrzej Seweryn, Bernadette Lafont, Monique Mélinand, Hubert Saint-Macary, Jean-Yves Gautier, Mathieu Amalric, Camila Mora, Patrick Modiano, Jean Badin. 113 min., 35mm, col.

Le film à venir (*The Film to Come*). Switzerland, 1997, Waka Films AG, TSI Televisione Svizzera, Arte GEIE. *d*, *sc*, *s* – Raúl Ruiz; *p* – Silvia Voser; *c* – Jacques Bouquin; *ed* – Valeria Sarmiento; *m* – Jorge Arriagada; *pc* – Gérard Vincent, Margot Marguerite, Edouard Waintrop, Abdelwaheb Meddeb, Guy Scarpetta, Bernard Pautrat, Waldo Rojas, Féodor Atkine, Jean-Yves Gauthier, Hubert Saint-Macary. 7 min., 35mm, b/w.

Shattered Image. Alt. title, *Jessie*. Canada/UK/US, 1998, The Artists' Colony, Fireworks Entertainment, Schroeder Hoffman Productions, Seven Arts Productions. *d* – Raúl Ruiz; *p* – Barbet Schroeder, Lloyd A. Silverman, Susan Hoffman; *c* – Robbie Müller; *sc* – Duane Poole; *ed* – Michael Duthie; *m* – Jorge Arriagada; *s* – Nelson Ferreira; *pc* – Anne Parillaud, William Baldwin, Lisanne Falk, Graham Greene, Billy Wilmont, O'Neil Peart, Leonie Forbes, Bulle Ogier, Rick Ravenello. 103 min., 35mm, col.

Le temps retrouvé (*Time Regained*). France, Italy, Portugal, 1999, Gemini Films, Les Films du lendemain, France 2 Cinéma, Blu Cinematografica. *d* – Raúl Ruiz; *p* – Paulo Branco; *c* – Ricardo Aronovich; *sc* – Gilles Taurand, Raúl Ruiz; *ed* – Denise de Casabianca; *m* – Jorge Arriagada; *s* – Philippe Morel; *pc* – Catherine Deneuve, Emmanuelle Béart, Vincent Perez, John Malkovich, Pascal Greggory, Marcello Mazzarella, Marie-France Pisier, Chiara Mastroianni, Arielle Dombasle, Edith Scob, Elsa Zylberstein, Christian Vadim, Dominique Labourier, Philippe Morier-Genoud, Melvil Poupaud. 158 min., 35mm, col.

Combat d'amour en songe (*Love Torn in Dream*). France/Portugal, 2000, Gemini films, Madragoa. *d*, *sc* – Raúl Ruiz; *p* – Paulo Branco; *c* – Acácio de Almeida; *ed* – Valeria Sarmiento; *m* – Jorge Arriagada; *s* – Pierre-Yves Lavoué, Georges-Henri Mauchant; *pc* – Melvil Poupaud, Elsa Zylberstein, Lambert Wilson, Christian Vadim, Diogo Doria, Rogerio Samora, Marie-France Pisier, Mathieu Demy. 123 min., 35mm, col.

La comédie de l'innocence (*The Comedy of Innocence*). Alt. title, *Son of Two Mothers*. France, 2000, Mact Productions, Canal +, CNC, TF1, Les Films du Camelia. *d* – Raúl Ruiz; *p* – Antoine de Clermont-Tonnerre, Matine de Clermont-Tonnerre; *c* – Jacuqes Bouquin; *sc* – François Dumas, Raúl Ruiz; *ed* – Mireille Hannon; *m* – Jorge Arriagada; *s* – Jean-Claude Brisson; *pc* – Isabelle Huppert, Jeanne Balibar, Charles Berling, Nils Hugon, Edith Scob, Denis Podalydes, Laure de Clermont-Tonnerre. 100 min., 35mm, col.

Les âmes fortes (*Savage Souls*). France/Belgium/Switzerland, 2001, Les Films du lendemain, MDI Productions, Arte France Cinéma, France 2 Cinéma, Nomad Films. *d* – Raúl Ruiz; *p* – Alain Majani d'Inguimbert, Dimitri de Clerq, Marc Lassus Saint-Geniès; *c* – Eric

Gautier; sc – Alexandre Astruc, Mitchell Hooper, Alain Majani d'Inguimbert, Eric Neuhoff; ed – Valeria Sarmiento, Béatrice Clérico; m – Jorge Arriagada; s – Christian Monheim, Georges-Henri Mauchant; pc – Laetitia Casta, Frédéric Diefenthal, Arielle Dombasle, John Malkovich, Charles Berling, Johan Leysen, Christian Vadim, Carlos Lopez, Monique Mélinand, Édith Scob, Jacqueline Staup, Corine Blue. 120 min., 35mm, col.

Cofralandes, rapsodia chilena (*Cofralandes: Chilean Rhapsody*), 2002. Alt. title, *Impressions of Chile*. Chile/France, Consejo Nacional Cultura y las Artes, RR producciones. d ,sc – Raúl Ruiz; p – Héctor Pino, Cristian Aspée; c – Inti Briones; sc – script; ed – Jean Christophe Hym, Raúl Ruiz; m – Jorge Arriagada, Alfonso Leng; pc – Bernard Pautrat, Malcolm Coad, Rainer Krause, Raúl Ruiz. 311 min., mini-DV, col.

Ce jour-là (*That Day*). France/Switzerland, 2003, Gémini Films, France Light Night , Suisse, France 3 Cinéma, Télévision Suisse Romande. d, sc – Raúl Ruiz; p – Paulo Branco, Particia Plattner; c – Acácio de Almeida; ed – Valeria Sarmiento; m – Jorge Arriagada; s – Henri Maikoff, Georges-Henri Mauchant; pc – Bernard Giraudeau, Elsa Zylberstein, Jean-Luc Bideau, Michel Piccoli, Rufus, Féodor Atkine, Jean-François Balmer, Christian Vadim, Edith Scob. 105 min., 35mm, col. cast.

Klimt. Austria/France/Germany/UK, 2005, Epo-Film, Film-Line, Lunar Films, Gémini Films. d – Raúl Ruiz; p – Paulo Branco, Matthew Justice, Dieter Limbek, Arno Ortmair, Dieter Pochlatko, Andreas Schmid, Ira Zloczower; c – Ricardo Aronovich; sc – Gilbert Adair, Raúl Ruiz; ed – Valéria Sarmiento; m – Jorge Arriagada; s – Simon Gershon, Michael Spencer; pc – John Malkovich, Veronica Ferres, Saffron Burrows, Stephen Dillane, Paul Hilton, Sandra Ceccarelli, Nikolai Kinski, Aglaia Szyszkowitz, Joachim Bissmeier. 127 min., 35mm, col.

La recta provincia. Chile, 2007, RR Producciones, TVN – Chilean Television. d, sc – Raúl Ruiz; p – Christián Aspeé; c – Inti Briones; ed – Valeria Sarmiento; m – Jorge Arriagada et Angel Parra; s – Felipe Zavala; pc – Bélgica Castro, Ignacio Aguero, Ángel Parra, Javiera Parra, Chamila Rodríguez. 170 min., col.

La maison Nucingen (*Nucingen House*). Chile/France/Romania, 2008, Margo Films, Mact Productions, Atlantis Films. d, sc – Raúl Ruiz; p – François Margolin; c – Jacques Bouquin, Inti Briones; ed – Béatrice Clérico; m – Jorge Arriagada; s – Gérard Rousseau, Felipe Zavala; pc – Audrey Marnay, Jean-Marc Barr Elsa Zylberstein, Laurent Malet, Luis Mora, Miriam Heard, Laure de Clermont-Tonnerre, Thomas Durand. 87 min., DV, col.

A Closed Book. UK, 2010, Eyeline Entertainment, Rex Media. d – Raúl Ruiz; p – Tom Kinninmont, Duncan Napier-Bell, Nicholas Napier-Bell, Tom Reeve, Romain Schroeder; c – Ricardo Aronovich; sc – Gilbert Adair; ed – Sean Barton, Adrian Murray, Valeria Sarmiento; m – Stephen Mark Barchan; s – Mike Grimes; pc – Daryl Hannah, Tom Conti, Miriam Margolyes, Simon MacCorkindale, Elaine Paige. 88 min., 35mm, col.

Mistérios de Lisboa (*Mysteries of Lisbon*). France, Portugal, 2010, Clap Filmes, Alfama films production, Arte France. *d* – Raúl Ruiz; *p* – Paulo Branco; *c* – André Szankowski ; *sc* – Carlos Saboga; *ed* – Ruy Diaz, Carlos Madaleno, Valeria Sarmiento; *m* – Jorge Arriagada; *s* – Ricardo Leal; *pc* – Léa Seydoux, Melvil Poupaud, Adriano Luz, Ricardo Pereira, Maria João Bastos, Clotilde Hesme, João Luís Arrais, Afonso Pimentel, São José Correia. 272 min., 35mm, col.

La noche de enfrente (*The Night Across the Street*). Chile, France, 2012, Margo Films, Consejo Nacional de la Cultura y las Artes. *d* – Raúl Ruiz; *p* – Christian Aspee, François Margolin; *c* – Inti Briones; *sc* – Raúl Ruiz; *ed* – Christian Aspee, Raúl Ruiz, Valeria Sarmiento; *m* – Jorge Arriagada; *pc* – Christian Vadim, Sergio Hernández, Valentina Vargas, Chamila Rodríguez. 110 min., 35mm, col.

Linhas de Wellington (*Lines of Wellington*). Chile, France, Portugal, 2012, Alfama Films, Clap Filmes, France 3 Cinéma. d – Valeria Sarmiento (after the shooting script of Raúl Ruiz); p – Paulo Brnaco; c – André Szankowski; sc – Carlos Saboga; ed – Luca Alverdi, Valeria Sarmiento; m – Jorge Arriagada; pc – Nuno Lopes, Soraia Chaves, Marisa Paredes, John Malkovich, José Afonso Pimentel, Melvil Poupaud, Adriano Luz. 151 min., 35mm, col. Dedicated to Raúl Ruiz.

BIBLIOGRAPHY

Acker, Kathy (1996) *Pussy, King of the Pirates*. New York: Grove Press.
Adair, Gilbert (1982) 'The Rubicon and the Rubik Cube: Exile, Paradox and Raúl Ruiz', *Sight and Sound*, 51, 1, 40–4.
____ (1984) 'Raúl: Sheheruizade [sic], or 1001 films', *Sight and Sound*, 53, 3, 162.
Adolfo, Vera (2010) 'Les Spectres de Raúl Ruiz: *La maison Nucingen* (2009)', *Revue Appareil* [Online]. revues.mshparisnord.org/appareil/index.php?id=934. Accessed 21/03/13.
Bandis, Helen, Adrian Martin and Grant McDonald (eds) (2004) *Raúl Ruiz: Images of Passage*. Rotterdam: Rouge Press/Rotterdam International Film Festival.
Bataille, Georges (1991) *The Accursed Share: Volume 1*. Trans. Robert Hurley. New York: Zone Books.
Bax, Dominique, Cyril Béghin, Benoît Peeters and Raoul Ruiz (eds) (2003) *Theâtres au Cinéma 14: Raoul Ruiz*. Paris: Magic Cinéma/Éditions du Collectioneur.
Bégin, Richard (2009) *Baroque cinématographique: Essai sur le cinéma de Raoul Ruiz*. Paris: Presses Universitaires de Vincennes.
Béghine, Cyrile (2004) '*Treasure Island* (*L'île au trésor*)', in Adrian Martin (ed.) *Rouge 2: Raúl Ruiz: An Annotated Filmography*. [Online]. http://www.rouge.com.au/2/treasure.html. Accessed 22/03/13.
Bellour, Raymond (1999) *L'Entre-Images 2: Mots, Images*. Paris: P.O.L.
____ (2012) *Between-the-Images*. Trans. Allyn Hardyck. Zurich/Dijon: JRP/Ringier/Les presses du réel.
Benjamin, Walter (1999 [1936]) 'The Work of Art in the Age of Mechanical Reproduction', in *Illuminations*. Trans. Harry Zorn. London: Pimlico, 211–44.
____ (1999 [1929]) 'The Image of Proust', in *Illuminations*. Trans. Harry Zorn. London: Pimlico, 197–210.
Beugnet, Martine and Marion Schmid (2005) *Proust at the Movies*. Farnham: Ashgate.

Bey, Hakim (2004) *T.A.Z.: The Temporary Autonomous Zone, Ontological Anarchy, Poetic Terrorism*. New York: Autonomedia.
Bickerton, Emilie (2009) *A Short History of Cahiers du Cinéma*. London: Verso.
Bonitzer, Pascal (1999) *Le Champ Aveugle: Essais sur le réalisme au cinéma*. Paris: Cahiers du Cinéma.
Bonitzer, Pascal, Serge Daney, Pascal Kané and Raúl Ruiz (1983) 'D'Une Institution L'Autre: Entretien avec Raúl Ruiz', *Cahiers du Cinéma*, 345, 19–23.
Bordwell, David, Janet Satiger and Kristin Thompson (1988) *The Classical Hollywood Cinema: Film Style and Mode of Production to 1960*. London: Routledge.
Bovier, François (2009) '*Tres Tristes Tigres*, fourchelangues et contes à rebours', *Décadrages: Cinéma, à travers champs*, 15, 57–68.
Boyd-Bowman, Susan (1987) 'Imaginary Cinematheques: The Postmodern Programmes of INA', *Screen*, 28, 103–17.
Brecht, Bertolt (1978) *Brecht on Theatre: The Development of an Aesthetic*. Trans. John Willett. London: Methuen Drama.
Buci-Glucksmann, Christine (1994) *Baroque Reason: The Aesthetics of Modernity*. London: Sage.
____ (2004) 'The Baroque Eye of the Camera (Part 1)' in Helen Bandis, Adrian Martin and Grant McDonald (eds) *Raúl Ruiz: Images of Passage*. Rotterdam: Rouge Press/Rotterdam International Film Festival, 31–44.
Buci-Glucksmann, Christine and Fabrice Revault d'Allones (1987) *Raoul Ruiz*. Paris: Dis Voir.
Editors of *Cahiers du Cinéma* (1983) *Special Issue on Raoul Ruiz*. No. 345.
Chanan, Michael (ed.) (1976) *Chilean Cinema*. London: British Film Institute.
Christie, Ian (1987) 'Raúl Ruiz and the House of Culture', *Sight and Sound*, 56, 2, 96–100.
____ (2004a) '*Los Tres Triste Tigres (Three Sad Tigers)*', in Adrian Martin (ed.) *Rouge 2: Raúl Ruiz: An Annotated Filmography*. [Online]. http://www.rouge.com.au/2/tigers.html. Accessed 22/03/13.
____ (2004b) '*The Penal Colony (La Colonia Penal)*', in Adrian Martin (ed.) *Rouge 2: Raúl Ruiz: An Annotated Filmography*. [Online]. www.rouge.com.au/2/penal.html. Accessed 22/03/13.
Conley, Tom (2007) *Cartographic Cinema*. Minneapolis: University of Minnesota Press.
Corrigan, Timothy (1991) *A Cinema Without Walls: Movies and Culture after Vietnam*. New Brunswick: Rutgers University Press.
Damasio, António (2004) *Looking for Spinoza*. Vintage: London.
Daly, Fergus (2004) '*Manoel dans l'île des merveilles (Manoel on the Island of Marvels*, [3 part French TV series], 1985)', in Adrian Martin (ed.) *Rouge 2* [Online] http://www.rouge.com.au/2/manoel.html. Accessed 18/03/13.
Daney, Serge (1983) 'En Mangeant, En Parlant', *Cahiers du Cinéma*, 345, 23–5.
Deleuze, Gilles (1989a) *Cinema 2: The Time-Image*. Trans. Hugh Tomlinson and Robert Galeta. Minneapolis: University of Minnesota Press.
____ (1989b) 'Coldness and Cruelty', in *Masochism*. New York: Zone Books, 7–138.

____ (1990) *The Logic of Sense*. Trans. Mark Lester and Charles Stivale. New York: Columbia University Press.

____ (1993) *The Fold: Leibniz and the Baroque*. Trans. Tom Conley. Minneapolis: University of Minnesota Press.

____ (2008) *Proust and Signs*. Trans. Richard Howard. London: Continuum.

Dowd, Garin (2009) 'Re-Raúl Ruiz: Returns, Reverberations, Revenants, Remembrance', unpublished conference paper. *Film and Philosophy/Philosophy and Film*. University of Dundee. July 2009.

Dubroux, Danièle (1983) 'Les Explorations du Capitaine Ruiz', *Cahiers du Cinéma*, 345, 31–3.

Dürrenmatt, Friedrich (1985) *The Novels of Friedrich Dürrenmatt*. London: Pan Books.

Ehrenstien, David (1984) *Film: The Front Line 1984*. Denver: Arden Press.

Eisenstein, Sergei (1986) *The Film Sense*. Trans. Jay Leyda. London: Faber and Faber.

Faúndez, Julio (1988) *Marxism and Democracy in Chile*. New Haven: Yale University Press.

Fisher, Mark (2007) 'Lovecraft and the Weird: Part 1.' http://k-punk.abstractdynamics.org/archives/009329.html. Accessed 10/4/10.

Forbes, Jill (1992) *The Cinema in France after the New Wave*. Basingstoke: Macmillan.

Foucault, Michel (1970) *The Order of Things*. London: Tavistock Press.

____ (1995) *Discipline and Punish*. Trans. Alan Sheridan. New York: Vintage Books.

____ (2000) *Aesthetics, Method and Epistemology: Essential Works of Michel Foucault Volume 2*. Ed. James Faubion. Trans. Robert Hurley. London: Penguin.

Freudiger, Alain (2009) 'De Proust à Ruiz, reconaissance dans *Le Temps retrouvé*', *Décadrages: Cinéma, à travers champs*, 15, 69–77.

Godard, Jean-Luc (1986) *Godard on Godard*. Ed. Tom Milne. New York: Da Capo Press.

Goddard, Michael (2002) 'Hypothesis of the Stolen Aesthetics', *Contretemps*, 3. [Online]. http://www.usyd.edu.au/contretemps/3July2002/goddard.pdf. Accessed 30/06/10.

____ (2004) 'Towards a Perverse, Neo-Baroque, Cinematic Aesthetic: Raúl Ruiz's *Poetics of Cinema*', *Senses of Cinema*, 30. [Online].http://archive.sensesofcinema.com/contents/books/04/30/raul_ruiz_poetics_of_cinema.html. Accessed 22/03/13.

Gombrowicz, Witold (2000) 'Preface to "The Child Runs Deep in Filidor"', in *Ferdydurke*. Trans. Danuta Borchardt. New Haven: Yale University Press, 68–86.

Graf, Alexander (2002) *The Cinema of Wim Wenders: The Celluloid Highway*. London: Wallflower Press.

Hammond, Paul (2004) '*City of Pirates* (*La Ville des pirates*, France/Portugal, 1983)', in Adrian Martin (ed.) *Rouge 2: Raúl Ruiz: An Annotated Filmography*.[Online]. http://www.rouge.com.au/2. Accessed 01/4/09.

Hofstadter, Douglas (1979) *Gödel, Escher, Bach: An Eternal Golden Braid*. London: Penguin.

Jayamanne, Laleen (1996) '"Life is a Dream", Raúl Ruiz was a Surrealist in Sydney: A Capillary Memory of a Cultural Event', in Laleen Jayamanne (ed.) *Kiss me Deadly: Feminism and Cinema for the Moment*. Sydney: Power Publications, 221–43.

____ (2002) 'The Ornamentation of Nicole Kidman (*Eyes Wide Shut*) and Mita Vashisht (*Kasba*): A Sketch', *Senses of Cinema 23: Special Women's Issue*. [Online]. http://sensesofcinema.com/2002/23/ornament. Accessed 22/03/13.

Jousse, Thierry (1997) 'Histoire grotesque et sérieuse', *Cahiers du Cinéma*, 512, 55–6.

Kafka, Franz (2007) 'In the Penal Colony', in *Metamorphosis and Other Stories*. Trans. Michael Hoffmann. London: Penguin Classics, 147–80.

King, John (1990) *Magical Reels: A History of Cinema in Latin America*. London: Verso.

Klein, Naomi (2007) *The Shock Doctrine: The Rise of Disaster Capitalism*. London: Allen Lane.

Klossowski, Pierre (1950) *La Vocation Suspendue*. Paris: Gallimard.

____ (1969) *Roberte Ce Soir* and *The Revocation of the Edict of Nantes*. Trans. Austryn Wainhouse. New York: Grove Press.

____ (1985) 'On the Collaboration of Demons in Works of Art', *Art and Text*, 18, 9–10.

____ (1997) *La Monnaie Vivante*. Paris: Rivages Poche.

____ (1998) *The Baphomet*. Trans. Sophie Hawkes and Stephen Sarterelli. New York: Marsilio.

____ (2001) *Tableux vivants: Essais critiques 1936–1983*. Ed. Patrick Mauriès. Paris: Gallimard.

Kristeva, Julia (1993) *Proust and the Sense of Time*. Trans. Stephen Bann. London: Faber and Faber.

Lainer, Grete (1921) *A Young Girl's Diary prefaced with a Letter by Sigmund Freud*. Trans. Eden and Cedar Paul. New York: Thomas Seltzer.

Lardeau, Yann (1983) 'Pas de Faux Raccords sans Accords', *Cahiers du Cinéma*, 345. 29–30.

Le Cinéma de Raoul Ruiz [Website]. http://www.lecinemaderaoulruiz.com. Accessed 22/03/13.

Loewenberg, Peter (2006) 'Freud, Schnitzler and *Eyes Wide Shut*', in *Depth of Field: Stanley Kubrick, Film, and the Uses of History*. Ed. Geoffrey Cocks, James Diedrick and Glenn Perusek. Madison: University of Wisconsin Press, 255–79.

Loveman, Brian (1988) *Chile: The Legacy of Hispanic Capitalism*. New York: Oxford University Press.

Lozachmeur, Erwan (2003) *Ce Jour-Là raconté par Raoul Ruiz/That Day as Recounted by Raúl Ruiz*, France. [DVD extra on *That Day* DVD].

Martin, Adrian (ed.) (2004). *Rouge 2* [Web Journal]. *Raúl Ruiz: An Annotated Filmography*. http://www.rouge.com.au/2. Accessed 01/4/09.

Mazierska, Ewa (2007) *Roman Polanski: The Cinema of a Cultural Traveller*. London: I.B. Tauris.

Naficy, Hamid (2001) *An Accented Cinema: Exilic and Diasporic Fimmaking*. Princeton: Princeton University Press.

Nietzsche, Friedrich (1967) *Thus Spake Zarathustra: A Book for All and None*. Trans. Thomas Common. London: Allen and Unwin.

Pick, Zuzana M. (1987) 'Chilean cinema: ten years of exile (1973–1983)', *Jump Cut*, 32, 66–70.
____ (1993) *The New Latin American Cinema: A Continental Project*. Austin: University of Texas Press.
____ (2004) *'Dialogue of Exiles (Diálogo de exilados*, France 1974)', in Adrian Martin (ed.) *Rouge 2: An Annotated Filmography.* [Online]. http://www.rouge.com.au/2/dialogue.html. Accessed 22/03/13.
Plassard, Didier (1998) 'Récriture et modélisation de l'écran par la scène: les films de théâtre de Raoul Ruiz', in Michel Collomb (ed.) *Figures de l'hétérogène*, Montpellier: Publications de l'Université Paul Valéry. [Version consulted on *Le Cinéma de Raoul Ruiz*].
Prieur, Jérôme (2006) 'From Chile to Klossowski: Interview with Raúl Ruiz', extra feature in 3 *Films by Raúl Ruiz* [DVD]. Paris: Blaq Out.
Proust, Marcel (1992) *In Search of Lost Time: VI Time Regained*. Trans. Andreas Mayor and Terence Kilmartin. London: Chatto and Windus.
Ricciardi, Alessia (2001) 'Cinema Regained: Godard between Proust and Benjamin', *Modernism/Modernity*, 8, 4, 643–61.
Richardson, Michael (2006) *Surrealism and Cinema*. Oxford and New York: Berg.
Robert, Valentine (2009) 'Le tableau vivant chez Raoul Ruiz: l'extension de la perception', *Décadrages: Cinéma, à travers champs*, 15, 38–56.
Rojas, Waldo (2004) 'Images of Passage', in Helen Bandis, Adrian Martin and Grant McDonald (eds) *Raúl Ruiz: Images of Passage*. Rotterdam: Rouge Press/Rotterdam International Film Festival, 7–14.
Rodriguez-Remedi, Alejandra (2009) '*Cofralandes*: A Formative Space for Chilean Identity', in Miriam Haddu and Joanna Page (eds) *Visual Synergies in Fiction and Documentary Film from Latin America*. New York: Palgrave MacMillan, 87–104.
Romney Jonathan (2012) 'Film of the Month: *Mysteries of Lisbon*', *Sight and Sound*, 22, 1, 60–1.
Rosenbaum, Jonathan (1995) 'Mapping the Territory of Raúl Ruiz', *Placing Movies: The Practice of Film Criticism*. Berkeley: California University Press, 222–37.
____ (2004) *Essential Cinema: On the Necessity of Film Canons*. Baltimore: Johns Hopkins University Press.
Ruiz, Raúl (1981) 'Object Relations in the Cinema'. Trans. Jill Forbes. *Afterimage*, 10, 87–94; translation of 'Les Relations d'Objets au Cinéma', *Cahiers du Cinéma*, 287, (1978), 26–32.
____ (1992) 'Two Comments on *Hypothesis of the Stolen Painting*', *Raúl Ruiz Dossier*. Sydney: AFTRS [Translation from 'Camera Je', May, 1979].
____ (1995) *Poetics of Cinema*. Trans. Brian Holmes. Paris: Dis Voir.
____ (1999) *Entretiens*. Paris: Editions Hoëbeke.
____ (2006) 'Une fantaisie "à la manière" de Schnitzler.' *Klimt dossier de presse*. [Available on *Le Cinéma de Raoul Ruiz* Website, http://www.lecinemaderaoulruiz.com/raoul-ruiz-cineaste/klimt]. Accessed 21/03/13.
____ (2008) *In Search of Treasure Island*. Trans. Paul Buck and Catherine Petit. Paris: Dis Voir.

Ruiz, Raúl and Benoît Peeters (2004) 'Annihilating the Script', Helen Bandis, Adrian Martin and Grant McDonald (eds) *Raúl Ruiz: Images of Passage*. Rotterdam: Rouge Press/Rotterdam International Film Festival, 15–30.
Ruiz, Raúl and Frédérique Bonnaud (2001) 'Interview de Raoul Ruiz', *City of Pirates*. [DVD]. Paris: Gemini.
Ruiz, Raúl and Jérôme Prieur (2006) 'Du Chili à Klossowski', *Raoul Ruiz: Ses Trois Premiers Films en France* [DVD]. Paris: Blaq Out.
Ruiz, Raúl and Anon. (1995) 'Entretien avec Raoul Ruiz'. Available on Le Cinéma de Raoul Ruiz [Website]. http://www.lecinemaderaoulruiz.com/raoul-ruiz-cineaste/trois-vies-et-une-seule-mort. Accessed 22/03/13.
Ruiz, Raúl, Pascal Bonitzer, Serge Daney and Pascal Kané (1978) 'D'Une Institution L'Autre', *Cahiers du Cinéma*, 287, 19–23.
Ruiz, Raúl, Thierry Jousse and Jean-Marc Lalanne (1997) 'Entretien avec Raoul Ruiz', *Cahiers du Cinéma*, 512, 57–61.
Scarpetta, Guy (2004) '*Love Torn in Dream* (*Combat d'amour en songe*, France/Portugal/Chile, 2000)', in Adrian Martin (ed.) *Rouge 2: Raúl Ruiz: An Annotated Filmography*. [Online]. http://www.rouge.com.au/2/love.html. Accessed 22/03/13.
Schatz, Thomas (1998) *The Genius of the System: Hollywood Filmmaking in the Studio Era*. London: Faber and Faber.
Skidmore, Thomas E. and Peter H. Smith (1997) *Modern Latin America*. New York: Oxford University Press.
Skorecki, Louis (1983) 'La Traversée du Fleuve-Cinéma Á la Nage', *Cahiers du Cinéma*, 345, 34–5.
Skrine, Peter (1989) *Hauptman, Wedekind and Schnitzler*. Houndmills: Macmillan.
Smith, Hester Travers (2004) *Oscar Wilde from Purgatory*. London: Kessinger.
Solanas, Fernando and Octavio Getino (1997) 'Towards a Third Cinema: Notes and Experiences for the Development of a Cinema of Liberation in the Third World', in Michael T. Martin (ed.) *New Latin American Cinema, Vol. 1*. Detroit: Wayne State University Press, 33–58.
Stam, Robert (1989) *Subversive Pleasures: Bahktin, Cultural Criticism and Film*. Baltimore: Johns Hopkins University Press.
Stern, Lesley (1995) *The Scorsese Connection*. London: British Film Institute.
Sternthal, Barbara (2006) *Gustav Klimt 1862–1918: Myth and Truth*. Trans. Martin Kelsey. Vienna: Christian Barandstätter.
Tesson, Charles (1983) 'Un Cauchemar Didactique (ou la tentative hardie d'établir une bio-filmographie de Raoul Ruiz)', *Cahiers du Cinéma*, 345, 13–18.
Toubiana, Serge (1985) 'Le Havre, ville-studio: Raoul Ruiz (suite)'. *Cahiers du Cinéma*, 377, 'Journal', III.
Wheatley, Catherine (2010) '*A Closed Book*', *Sight and Sound*, 20, 4, 50.
Van Gelder, Lawrence (1973) 'A Chilean Duo: *Que Hacer?* on Bill with *Allende*', *New York Times*, 29/9/73.
Yates, Frances (1966). *The Art of Memory*. London: Routledge and Kegan Paul.

INDEX

Akerman, Chantal 143
Alekan, Henri 1, 50, 54–5, 69
Anger, Kenneth 108
Antonioni, Michelangelo 21
Arragiada, Jorge 121
Astruc, Alexandre 137

Bataille, Georges 40, 78, 107
Battle of Chile, The 25
Battleship Potemkin 73
Baudrillard, Jean 55, 57
Beauty and the Beast 50
Béghine, Cyrile 151
Bellemare, Pierre 109–10, 113, 117–18
Bloody Nitrate 12–13
Borges, Jorge Luis 5–6, 41, 63, 96
Brecht, Bertolt 31, 33
Bruno, Giordarno 126, 131

Captive, The 143
Caro Baroja, Julio 174
Carpentier, Alejo 18
Castaneda, Carlos 114, 116–17
Chabrol, Claude 122
Chambord 50, 54–6, 77
Chanan, Michael 13–14
Chion, Michel 71, 76

Christie, Ian 21, 31, 76, 101
City of Pirates 61, 71, 76–83, 92, 111, 122, 139, 177, 182
Closed Book, A 161–2, 179
Cocteau, Jean 50
Corman, Roger 65–8
Corrigan, Timothy 44–5
Croce, Bernadetto 174–5
Cronenberg, David 86

Damasio, António 183–4
Daney, Serge 38, 76, 84
Dark at Noon 87, 97–8, 131, 151
Days in the Country 158, 160
Deleuze, Gilles 38–40, 63, 142–3
Dialogues of Exiles 7, 31–2, 43, 62, 70

Eclipse, The 21
Einstein, Albert 143
Expulsion of the Moors, The 88
Exterminating Angel, The 67
Eyes Wide Shut 152

Fellini, Federico 6, 50, 63, 110
Femme Nikita, La 119
Foucault, Michel 38, 59, 98, 101, 168
Francia, Aldo 12–13
Frei, Edouardo 11, 14, 21

García Márquez, Gabriel 62
Genealogies of a Crime 119, 131–2, 136–7
Gide, André 42
Giono, Jean 137
Golden Boat, The 83, 87
Gombrowicz, Witold 6, 22
Gorin, Jean-Pierre 24
Gramsci, Antonio 173–5
Greenaway, Peter 43, 50, 87, 93

Haneke, Michael 121–2, 125
Hannah, Darryl 162, 180
Heidegger, Martin 175, 184
Hour of the Furnaces, The 13, 23
Hypothesis of the Stolen Painting 6, 38, 45–52, 54, 71, 86, 90, 112, 131, 151, 178
Huillet, Danièle 52
Huppert, Isabelle 122
Hurt, John 97

Illuminatus trilogy 86
In Search of Lost Time 142
It's Raining on Santiago 33

Jackal of Nahueltoro, The 12–13
Jayamanne, Laleen 63, 75–6, 152
Jean de Florette 137

Kieślowski, Krzysztof 119
King, John 14
Klossowski, Pierre 1, 9, 39–42, 46–7, 59, 101, 155
Kraus, Karl 151–2
Kristeva, Julia 142–3
Kubrick, Stanley 151–3

Lainer, Grete 132
Letters from Marusia 32
Lima, Lezama 100
Lines of Wellington 162, 165
Littín, Miguel 12, 15–16
Littoral: Cuentos del Mar 158

Losey, Joseph 142–3
Lost Highway 120
Love Torn in Dream 103, 118, 126, 131, 182
Lovecraft, H. P. 96–8
Lull, Ramón 126, 151
Lynch, David 120, 172–3
Lyotard, Jean-François 40

Mikhalkov, Nikita 110
Malkovich, John 2, 122, 150, 172
Mammame 87
Manoel's Destinies 82, 143
McKee, Robert 106
Merci pour le chocolat 122
Messiaen, Oliver 177
Miotte, Jean 2, 151
Miotte by Ruiz 151
Morin-Sinclair, Denise 40, 47

Neruda, Pablo 12, 22
Nietzsche, Friedrich 40, 141
Nikita 119
Nixon, Richard 15, 58
Nobody Said Anything 24, 27
Now We are Going to Call you Brother 27

One-Eyed Man, The 71
One Thousand and One Nights 128, 130, 183
Ophuls, Max 151–2, 166
Opinions of Sebastian Melmoth, The 178
Ortega y Gasset, José 175
Ozu, Yasujirō 108

Pagnol, Marcel 137
Pirates of the Caribbean 64
Piccoli, Michel 134, 139
Pick, Zuzana 32, 75
Polanski, Roman 18, 58
Potocki, Count Jan 89, 128
Poupaud, Melvil 85, 115, 129, 133, 150

Price, Vincent   17, 90
Proust, Marcel   142–6, 148–54, 176, 178

Real Presence, The   87
Recta Provincia, La   158, 174
Resnais, Alain   43
Revocation of the Edict of Nantes, The   46–7
Richardson, Michael   62–3, 78, 83, 93
Rimbaud, Arthur   177
Robbe-Grillet, Alain   150
Romney, Jonathan   164
Ronde, La   151–2, 166
Roof of the Whale, The   65, 68
Rosenbaum, Jonathan   18, 54, 69, 75, 92, 96, 99

Sanatorium under the Hour-Glass   97
Saragossa Manuscript, The   97, 128, 131, 169
Savage Souls   132, 137, 180
Schiele, Egon   151, 153, 155–7
Schnitzler, Arthur   151–3, 182
Schroeder, Barbet   110, 119
Scob, Edith   125
Seweryn, Andrzej   134
Straub, Jean-Marie   38, 52
Suitcase, The   18

Tarkovsky, Andrei   66, 108
Territory, The   18, 65–8, 161, 182
That Day   132, 138
Three Crowns of the Sailor   18, 66, 70–8, 131, 161
Three Lives and Only One Death   2, 66, 103, 109–10, 120, 122, 132, 178
Three Sad Tigers   9, 12, 19–24, 27, 30
Time Regained   94, 103, 118, 141–4, 147–51, 153–4, 176
Truffaut, François   85

Ulmer, Edgar   38, 109

Valparaíso my Love   13
Vertigo of the Blank Page   104, 161
Von Schlöndorf, Volker   143

Welles, Orson   63, 72, 84, 174
What is to be Done? (Que Hacer?)   26
Wheatley, Catherine   161
Widower's Tango, The   18
Wilson, Robert Anton   86
Wittgenstein, Ludwig   175

Zig-Zag   2–4, 17, 68, 71, 76–7, 85, 182
Zylberstein, Elsa   138, 150

GPSR Authorized Representative: Easy Access System Europe, Mustamäe tee 50, 10621 Tallinn, Estonia, gpsr.requests@easproject.com